WHERE THE PASSION IS

WHERE THE PASSION IS

A Reading of Kierkegaard's
Philosophical Fragments

by H. A. Nielsen

A FLORIDA STATE UNIVERSITY BOOK

UNIVERSITY PRESSES OF FLORIDA
TALLAHASSEE

University Presses of Florida, the agency of the State of Florida's university system for the publication of scholarly and creative works, operates under the policies adopted by the Board of Regents. Its offices are located at 15 Northwest 15th Street, Gainesville, Florida 32603.

LIBRARY OF CONGRESS CATALOGING IN PUBLICATION DATA
Nielsen, H. A. (Harry A.)
Where the passion is.

"A Florida State University book."
Includes index.
1. Kierkegaard, Søren, 1813–1855. Philosophiske smuler. 2. Religion—Philosophy. I. Title.
BL51.K4873N53   1983   201   83-6923
ISBN 0-8130-0742-9

For Bill, Dorothy, Rose, and Gail

CONTENTS

PREFACE

Kierkegaard's brief work *Philosophical Fragments* first saw the light of day in 1844, some five or six decades after Kant's *Religion Within the Limits of Reason Alone*. It contrasts dramatically with Kant's book at every point, and nothing could be more fundamentally instructive in the philosophy of religion than attending to these collisions between opposing minds of comparable stature. This study began as an attempt to deal with both books, but it quickly became evident that the *Fragments* by itself offers a sufficient challenge. Here Kierkegaard presents the outstanding modern attempt, by a philosopher, to lay out the central teachings of Christianity in a way that preserves the outlines of the ancient doctrine, hard sayings and all. He seeks to do this through fresh wordings, not, like Kant, by means of an interpretation that would soften many of those sayings. Kierkegaard's aim is to help the reader knowledgeable in philosophy to behold the New Testament content as if for the first time, the better to see philosophy itself in brilliant contrast.

The *Fragments* is an algebraic piece. For one thing, its pivotal opening concept, 'the Truth', is taken to signify the same thing for all men, but its content is left unspecified. The correlative concept 'Error' is algebraic but in a way that reflects countless individual differences, so that a reader who aspires to go the whole way with the author's thought-experiment must write his personal Error into the appropriate blank. In reading the *Fragments* with students over the past fifteen years I have seen these and other textual difficulties come up again and again, and it is first of all to shed some light on these problems that I have put together this reading.

A reader of the *Fragments* will be struck by its tightly gathered prose. No one acquainted with Kierkegaard's authorship will doubt that this compressed style is strategic and the farthest thing imaginable from a sign of haste. The *Fragments* is a work in the philosophy of religion; it concerns itself with the problems raised by the broad question "How can human thinking come to terms with the idea of a revelation from outside the human sphere?" The style Kierkegaard chose for the *Fragments* is designed, I believe, so that readers of a later generation can adapt their reading to the philosophical nuances of their own age. Accordingly, my second purpose is to show how his work anticipates many twentieth-century problems in the philosophy of religion.

Page references to *Philosophical Fragments or A Fragment of Philosophy*, used throughout this volume, are to the revised English translation by Howard Hong, published by the Princeton University Press in 1962. The reader will probably want to keep the Hong translation at hand in reading this commentary.

H. A. N.
Windsor, Ontario
Canada

AN IDLER SETS THE TONE

Title page, Motto, and Preface to
Philosophical Fragments

K ierkegaard's authorship, with its medley of pseudonyms, poses a
host of scholarly problems that need not detain us. To understand
the main line of the *Fragments*, however, it is important to remember
that Johannes Climacus, its pseudonymous author, represents himself
as standing outside of Christianity, as explained in the later *Concluding Unscientific Postscript.** Nothing of what is said in the *Fragments*
depends upon the author's being a Christian. In fact, both title and
subtitle refer to philosophy, indicating that the content will consist of
remarks about what man can perceive in his environment or think out
for himself, in contrast to theological and devotional works presented
from a believer's point of view that lean more or less heavily upon
something taken to be a revelation from outside the human sphere.

On the title page occur three questions:

> Is an historical point of departure possible for an eternal consciousness;
> how can such a point of departure have any other than a merely histori-
> cal interest; is it possible to base an eternal happiness upon historical
> knowledge?

To these we must return at the end of our reading; their answers lie
with the entire "hypothesis" of the book. In wording that owes a debt to
the knotty language of G. E. Lessing, they ask: How can I extract any
assurance about eternal matters (for instance, the matter of whether
or not I have to go on being myself forever, and if so in what state?)
from the kind of fact history throws up to me? About such facts, or
purported facts, one can, after all, very easily be mistaken. More than
that, the eternal (whatever that term may embrace) is simply not of my
sphere, where everything either perishes outright or wears away or, if

---

* Trans. David F. Swenson and Walter Lowrie (Princeton: Princeton University Press,
1941), p. 252.

it persists, does so in a relative way. Since everything in my purview is of that sort, nothing here bears any mark of eternality, for even the comparative agelessness or lasting-power of, say, coral as opposed to paper, is not an approximation to eternality. If I cannot say what something eternal would look like, then evidently the word does not function as a label for anything in my field of vision. How, then, can one perishing event more than another advance or enhance what Climacus calls "an eternal consciousness"? For example, just in case I do have to go on being myself forever (and I have no clear idea at all of what that would be like), what could give one fleeting historical moment a sufficiently stronger claim over me than another to make me cleave to it when the gain or loss will be everlasting?

Let us take Motto and Preface in reverse order since the second explains the first. In the Preface, Climacus takes pains to cut his "little piece" loose from the skeins of collaborative thought that create schools, trends, and wholesale excitement. He does not disdain large-scale projects as such, though he pokes fun at some of the more grandiose ones, nor does he envy the acclaim their authors earn. His aim is to single out an intended reader in whom a quite unpublic concern arises. That is, a reader with philosophical leanings may on some occasion wish to rummage through an author's thoughts to see if they contain any ideas he can personally use. According to the Preface, that is the appetite the book is out to serve. This reader, Climacus hopes, will help himself, caring not at all about the author's private opinion, quite willing, in fact, to allow the author a sphere of purely personal concern corresponding to his own.

In the Preface, then, Climacus addresses his piece "To whom it may concern," with no claim that it must or ought to concern anyone. Although more will need to be said about this rummaging kind of reader when we move into Chapter I, a few remarks may be useful here. The reader that Climacus has in mind, as every page shows, is more or less knowledgeable in the ways of philosophy. Even if he is only a beginner, the names of Plato, Socrates, Aristotle, and other figures will mean something definite to him, partly perhaps for their doctrine, partly because the ages honor them as thinkers of the highest calibre. Such a reader will be patient with these men and with their ladders of thoughts; if he is not given to close-grained reflection, the *Fragments* will soon lose him.

Next, such a reader, like Climacus himself, will be standing outside of Christianity, or at any rate both near and far enough to wonder how its teachings relate to philosophy and to what extent they overlap and stand apart. The book is concerned about this matter and will raise two questions besides the three printed on the title-page: what is philosophy? and what is Christianity? Readers who for any reason find these inquiries unprofitable will soon run out of patience with the text. To the reader who feels a need for a clearer understanding of the relation between philosophy and Christianity, so that each may be plainly itself, or so that any accidental verbal resonances between them (if that is what we find) can be discriminated and taken into account, Climacus offers himself as a sort of lens-grinder, a sharpener of perceptions. Through his art the reader may be helped to discern sameness where there is sameness, and where there is not, to discern difference.

The Motto, adapted from a German translation of Shakespeare's line "Better well hung than ill wed," should be read as a foreshortening of the Preface. There Climacus dissociates his piece from all claim to timeliness and fashion, saying that he would sooner have it ignored or overlooked, like a spider hanging in a corner, than absorbed into philosophical table talk about sweepingly large, impersonal topics. Niels Thulstrup's suggestion (in his Commentary on the revised English translation, p. 152 of the 1962 Princeton edition) that "well hung" be understood to mean "crucified with Christ," seems to clash with the intent of the Preface, for it indulges the wrong sort of reader—one who is biographically curious about the author—in a conjecture about Climacus's private opinion.

3

A THOUGHT-EXPERIMENT

Chapter I of *Philosophical Fragments*,
"A Project of Thought"

SUMMARY OF SECTION A

The *propositio* on page 9, declaring that a certain question is to be asked in ignorance, refers to the opening question: "How far does the Truth admit of being learned?" To ask this in ignorance is to suppose a reader who can begin with this question. Section A bids us consider how the Socratic doctrine of Recollection views this question. Socrates assumes that each man has this Truth buried within him from the outset. Thus, with regard to getting hold of the Truth, no man owes thanks to any other man. This is important for understanding the role of any human teacher who might, under the Socratic assumption, help me usher the truth into my consciousness. That teacher plays a midwife's forgettable role, which anyone with similar training might have played.

REMARKS ON SECTION A

A glancing reference to "my eternal happiness" is the only clue Climacus drops to his reader about the *content* of the Truth and about the questions it purports to answer. This is no small clue, however, because the 'my' reveals the questions to be personal ones. Climacus leaves it up to each reader to express them for himself, for it is doubtful that anyone's version of these questions can satisfy another reader or capture the personal tone of his own unknowings. Here is our unpolished version:

A. Is it a great or a little thing to exist as the one I am?
B. Have I a task just in virtue of being born a human being, a task independent of those that might be set for me by my station in life?
C. If so, exactly what is it, and what is my actual present state as regards taking care of it?

The *propositio* at the beginning helps identify the author's intended reader as one who can put to himself questions of this kind without endless preliminaries. This is to say, if a reader can take hold of such questions without first probing into whether they concern every man or just a few, or into Climacus's possibly unhappy relationship with his father, and similar things, then he can figure out for himself what the author means by the Truth, a concept left cryptically blank in the text. The Truth will consist in the answers to his personal unknowings as expressed in those ABC questions, whatever those answers might be, and this fact offers him a perfectly sufficient conception of the Truth for purposes of getting started. On the other hand, a person who finds in himself no patience for the ABC questions, no hollow for their answers to fill, will naturally see no point in going farther into the book. At any rate, the author does not wish to tarry with those readers, even if this leaves him with no reader at all. That was the thrust, we recall, of his Preface.

'Personal' may be too inclusive a category if we are out to identify the kind of question bound up with what Climacus calls the Truth. He is not dealing wholesale with questions we regard as personal in everyday life, for example, 'Do you care for me?', 'Did you mean that as an insult?', or 'What are your politics?' Answers to those can be found in various life-contexts, but the Truth-questions express stubborn unknowings about oneself. Wherever their answers may await me, either in some depth of myself (on the Socratic assumption) or outside me, in any event the sciences do not deal with them. There are also many truths an individual may be anxious to find out over and above those which would answer A, B, and C for him. Those other truths, however, connect at most only tangentially with what Climacus calls *the* Truth.

SUMMARY OF SECTION B

With the phrase "if things are to be otherwise," Climacus breaks with the Socratic assumption and instead assumes that no man has the Truth. Anyone who possesses the Truth does so, on this new assumption, because it has come into existence at some point in time and not because he possessed it implicitly from birth. Call this point of time *the Moment*.

A. THE ANTECEDENT STATE

By our new assumption the individual not only has no claim at all on the Truth, but he is turned away from it, facing the wrong way, absolutely cut off from it. We may call his state Error, emphasizing that he cannot be called a seeker of the Truth since he is already committed to something else. Any relaxation of this stricture that would make it possible for him to acquire the Truth by human effort would throw us back into the Socratic position—that each man possesses the Truth and is parted from it only accidentally.

B. THE TEACHER

This state of Error or alienation from the Truth is one of which the individual can become conscious. Since the Error has to do with a difference, an opposition, between the Truth and what *he* thinks, it becomes Error for *him* only when he can consciously acknowledge it as his own.

By our assumption the Truth must be brought to the individual by some agency functioning as teacher. This much fits in with assuming the Truth to be nowhere in reach of the man. However, just trumpeting the Truth is not enough to put the man in possession of it *as* truth. What is to prevent its looking to him like just another idea among several or many? No, he has to be able to recognize it as true when he sees it. But this is exactly where the controlling assumption of Section B draws a line by supposing him helpless to recognize the Truth. To put the Truth in his possession, then, this Teacher, or whatever we please to call it, must also give the man the ability to recognize the Truth.

If the individual could give himself this ability or get it from other humans, our assumption of Section B would be overturned. Under that assumption, then, only a God could do what is needed to put a man in possession of the Truth.

The ability to recognize the Truth must have belonged to the individual originally as one of his distinctively human powers. Otherwise he would be coming into his essential humanity only at a second stage, for between the time he begins to exist and the time he receives that ability he would lack an essential condition for being human. He must, therefore, have lost that ability, and by his own fault. Not, that is, by an act of God, for the idea of a God omitting some essential in an act of

6

creation, and then supplying it after proofreading the act, would do reckless violence to the concept 'God'.

Being in a state of Error through one's own fault we shall call *Sin*. If we suppose the individual could will himself out of this state, we fall back into the Socratic view of things in which the individual is not destitute of the Truth but only separated from it by a forgetting, or by not yet having thought his way through to it. By our hypothesis, then, I am bound fast to my Error. When I so regard my situation, what name or designation would fit the kind of teacher who gets me out of it? *Savior, Redeemer, Atonement*, and *Judge*. The brief historical Moment of that Teacher's appearance let us call the *Fullness of Time*.

C. THE DISCIPLE

We now turn to the disciple, the individual helped by the Teacher. This man now possesses the Truth, and more immediately the lost ability to recognize the Truth, so he is to that degree a *new man*.

He is a changed man, no longer facing away from the Truth, as we characterized him at the outset. Call this change *Conversion*. His altered consciousness in and after this change we may call *Repentance*. The change itself is enough like coming into existence for the first time to be called a *New Birth*. None of this would be possible without the Teacher, to whom, if we stand by our hypothesis that the Truth is not in man's reach, the disciple owes all thanks.

———

Is that hypothesis thinkable? Is Section B anything more than an unbridled extravagance of words? It speaks, after all, of a second movement from nonbeing to being in an individual like myself, who already quite solidly exists.

———

Once I make the assumption of Section B, it follows that the farthest I can go without that Teacher is to understand that I am in Error. As long as I fall short of understanding that, my place is with Socrates, the full-time thinker on questions of man's true condition, for whom one birth was enough.

* *

The idea that the individual stands in need of a second transition from nonbeing to being, or that he does not yet exist, or has been born one time too few, is an idea that no human, not even the full-time thinker, finds occasion to come up with. Stranger still, therefore, is the fact that there is such an idea in existence. This fact seems to give backing to our hypothesis: the Moment is decisive.

REMARKS ON SECTION B

In asking the reader to break, experimentally, with the assumption that each man has the Truth within him, Climacus sets us no easy task. There is a natural tendency to think along with Socrates on this point, though not to the extent of going all the way with his doctrine of Recollection or the soul's pre-existence. Repeatedly, Climacus warns us that even the mildest sounding compromise with his severe conclusions will tip us back into the Socratic position. "If things are to be otherwise" and the Moment decisive, our break with Socrates must be clean and total. We must set aside in all its forms the idea that an individual by thinking very hard, or by getting help from others who excel him at hard thinking, can arrive at the Truth. Our power to cognize truths without number in everyday life and science, and our unwillingness to admit unknowables, make it doubly difficult to avoid slipping into variants of the Socratic position.

A. THE ANTECEDENT STATE

Especially is this true in Philosophy, where the questions we have called Socratic find classic utterance and where thinkers put themselves forward precisely as seekers of the Truth. Could anything be more wrenching to such a person than the admission that the Truth is the last thing he wants? Under Climacus's hypothesis, what becomes of the great tradition in which philosophers think earnestly about such questions and offer their results to the public? How is it possible for an individual steeped in that tradition to go along with Climacus, even for the sake of experiment, to the extent of supposing *himself* dead set against the Truth? Short of an unthinkable convulsion of thought, how can he charge himself (as the hypothesis demands) with implacable personal enmity toward the Truth? Evidently this will be harder the more ardently he clings to his personal variant of the Socratic view, which is, after all, the normal view, so that a passionate philosopher of the traditional sort is likely to find himself tempted, in the course of this experiment, in either of two ways. Either he will deal playfully with the surface logic of the "Project of Thought," finding a crack here and there that needs retouching, or he will find its opening bid so ruinous a threat to his whole fortune of thought that he will choose to pass.

The alternative to these moves, namely to suppose himself brought under the charge, is much easier said than done. Here one might well pause to ask with Climacus, "Is the hypothesis here expounded thinkable?"

B. THE TEACHER

That the assumption of Error is part of a genuine experiment, not a mere game of deductions from an unexpectedly fertile hypothesis, becomes clearer in Part B, where Climacus gives the reader to understand that the individual's state of Error can be "discovered." It is easy to see that I can claim an Error as *mine* only by finding it in myself, or, as we say, by owning up to it. Still, it is not immediately plain how I am to go about discovering this curious kind of Error that consists in my doing everything I can to distance myself from the Truth. How then am I to perceive this fact, if indeed it is a fact?

Climacus speaks of the Teacher serving as an occasion, reminding me of my state of Error, but it is clear that such a reminder will mean nothing unless I can pick out something in myself corresponding to it. Climacus argues that the individual's Error consists in a hostility not against his fellow man or society but against the Truth, and that it therefore has to be tracked down in the sphere of his thoughts, that is, in the content of *what he really thinks* rather than in his behavior. The charge of Error lays it down that he really thinks the opposite of the Truth.

Discovering my state of Error with the help of a reminder will mean (at least for the reader Climacus has in mind) noticing in myself, and owning up to, a set of *answers* to the questions A, B, and C listed a few pages back. Right or wrong, these answers make up what I really think. Next, it will mean coming to see them as wrong. Thus, my alleged state of Error implies that I am attached to some wrong answers to those questions. This is not to say that everyone has a mature and polished judgment on those questions, but that a non-Christian reader who is at least a strong amateur in philosophy, if he takes the trouble to search himself, can find such a judgment in process of crys-

9

tallizing. For purposes of understanding the *Fragments*, the idea here is not to make the reader put down his book and dredge for joyless, despairing, covert opinions. It is sufficient if he entertains the possibility of discovering, in some culvert of himself, some preformed answers of his own to those questions. The reader who draws a hard line here by insisting that he possesses no such opinions, that he does not really think anything hot or cold, plus or minus on those questions, and that therefore the hypothesis of Error confronts him as a blank wall, must be left to himself. The book does not break stride to contradict or argue with him, but allows in its Preface that many individuals may find nothing useful in it and asks them not to busy themselves further with it or prevent someone else from dipping into it.

Here it may be helpful to pause briefly on the role of the reminder. Normally a person finds no occasion to distinguish between, on the one hand, the things he feels in all honesty constrained to say on questions A, B, and C (for example, that he has no opinion at all concerning their answers), and, on the other hand, *what he really thinks*. Part of the force of the reminder is to disorient the individual who takes his bearings from his own thoughts, by reminding him that they may not be his real thoughts, or his deepest, most hoarded thoughts, so that if the reminder is correct, or is truly a reminder and not a piece of trumped-up nonsense, Error has him flanked on two sides. First, he is in a remediable error in falsely identifying his overt thoughts with his real ones; secondly, Error with a capital E flaws his real thoughts.

The distinction between remediable and irremediable error needs a brief comment. If it happens to strike the individual as improbable that his overt thoughts should differ from what he really thinks, he is of course thrown back on himself to check the matter out. However, let us assume for a moment that what I really think comes to light by one effort or another. At that point I will have cleared up any earlier confusion between my overt and my real thoughts. How am I to detect, though, that the real ones are wrong or false? That they *could* be in error will appear in the fact that they say more than I can rightly be said to know. That they *are* in error is something else, and unless I have the Truth to compare them with (which would go against our hypothesis), how am I to perceive them as false? Even if on first inspection I perceive them to be fishy, full of sour notes, or something of the sort, what is to assure me that the Truth itself is not like that? Nothing, and here I meet the first hint of an uncrossable ditch between myself and the Truth, for I must confess to myself that I could not *recognize* the Truth if it tapped me on the shoulder or otherwise presented itself to my consciousness. What *I* really think has (as far as I can tell) as much chance of being the Truth as any other contender. To use the author's example, the Truth about my eternal happiness (about whether one awaits me, or is worth anything, or what it might hinge on, and so forth), even if the stars rearranged themselves to spell it out, would look to me like just another opinion.

Having satisfied myself as to what I really think, I can now own up to being in a state of Error at least to this extent: my want of power to recognize the Truth cuts me off from the Truth. I cannot distinguish Truth from Error with regard to questions A, B, and C.

The ability to do so—what is it like? The hypothesis excludes the individual from laying hold of the answer. If he is to possess the ability, a source outside himself must bring it. Since by hypothesis all men are equal in the lack, the outside source will not be another man but, as Climacus expresses it, the God. Does the reader then know who or what this God is, so as to be able to follow the developing hypothesis? No. Here is an apparent snag, for if Climacus holds himself free to suppose a living godly power in operation, his hypothesis is something more than first meets the eye. It would seem more appropriate at this point to say that if the individual is to receive the ability to recognize the Truth, it must come to him from a source unknown.

Up to now we have raised no question about how the individual came to lack this ability, whether he once possessed it or not and, if so, who is to blame for its loss. Climacus gives this point a very brief treatment. In a couple of compact *reductio* arguments he lays the fault at the individual's door. First, the idea that one is born a human and then much later given the finishing touch, the ability to recognize the Truth, would be a wholly gratuitous speculation about the manner in which a man receives existence. I do not mean it is any less possible than Climacus's slenderly possible hypothesis, but rather that a learner who has already seen himself to be in Error (cut off from the Truth, unable to recognize it, and above all attached to some questionable answers of his own) will not straightway blame the God or whatever veiled x stands behind his existence. For the time being, at least, the question of whom to blame for his state of Error will remain an open one. Similarly, to imagine oneself originally empowered to recognize the Truth on sight, then later stripped of this power by the God, would be to speak with unbecoming looseness about the God's talents as a maker of men, or the God's revisionist whims in ripping out an essential thread in the human fabric. For Climacus the "contradiction" (p. 18) in this linguistic misdemeanor lies in its clashing with what people conventionally predicate of deity—a point that will concern us in much greater detail when we look into Chapter III of the *Fragments*.

With what justification does Climacus bring in the idea of the learner's having been *created*? Noticing this natural question, Niels Thulstrup comments: "The idea of creation is here advanced as self-evident" (p. 191), but here our difficulty begins. To whom is it self-evident and in what sense? Climacus's argument seems directed against the pointlessness of blaming one's essential lack upon whatever unknown x brought one into existence as a human. It is pointless not because it would clash with a *biblical* doctrine of creation, for the x need not be specified here in a Jahwist direction or with connotations of a lordly and personal Creator. Rather, to attribute oversight or absent-mindedness to the x, which after all is unknown, would smack more of unquiet *ressentiment* than careful reflection. Climacus employs a philosophical catchall, "contradiction," to condense the point.

Still, why should Climacus think of the ability to recognize the Truth as an *essential* feature of humans, one which must have belonged to each man primitively? Does the hypothesis of the Moment force him to this view, or is a new hypothesis announced here for the first time? For it would be no small make-believe to assume we have a full picture of man's essence that lets us perceive the missing ability as an original component. Why not instead suppose the lack of this ability to be a matter of accident and nobody's fault? Climacus dismisses that possibility in a few words. The individual's being in (or out of) the Truth is an essential matter because the Truth in question is about himself personally; it is the Truth about whether or not he is in fact expressing the 'essence' or 'nature' that properly belongs to him, or in short whether he is in fact himself or something less. Our terminology here is somewhat frigid and scholastic, but the issue is one which the individual can reformulate to his own taste, for instance in the idiom of our questions A, B, and C.*

Let us make an attempt at this. To begin with, questions of the ABC type bear on the entire character of my personal existence. They raise the matter of whether or not I am doing what I ought to be doing and becoming what it befits my kind to become. This is not to presuppose a primordial divine planner of men whose design I am either conforming to or in my forwardness defying. That is, I can generate the ABC questions strictly within my capacity as language-user, whether I happen to regard myself as the creation of a deity or not. Next, while unknowings about the exact time of day or the number of coins in my pocket are accidental and inevitable, A, B, and C represent unknowings of a strikingly different order. They concern whether, in the definitively human capacity which enables me to form an opinion of myself and assign a measure of worth to myself, I am assigning a correct one or not. In brief, they concern whether or not what I really think of myself is true. The power to make out whether it is true or false is the power Climacus takes to be an original component in every human package.

Now the fact that a particular learner does not presently possess this power, or at any rate cannot presently exercise it, is something he can discover on his own, with or without a reminder from the Project of Thought. Secondly, to go all the way and declare that he originally possessed it but somehow lost it would hardly do him credit as a thinker since he would be professing to recall what he cannot recall, although his assertion would be formally compatible with the Moment-hypothesis. On the other hand, Climacus proposes more moderately that the ability to recognize the Truth is a key component of my original humanness. This amounts to saying that my personal lack of that power leaves questions such as A, B, and C *open* and thereby undermines my confidence concerning the way I live, even if my life conforms to the national ideal of what it means to be a splendid man or woman. This creates a gap between public performance and self-assurance that can trouble even the best-ordered life with uncer-

---

*This possibility of cutting free from older terminologies can help me get my breath back if I should hear of a late-breaking discovery that humans have no 'essence' or 'nature'. On the other hand, I should not want to lose the small share of credit due me from the fact that the discoverer was of my own kind: a language-user.

tainty: Have I been living a fully human life or just going through the motions?

Where does the fault lie?

According to Climacus, the God is not to blame for my lack of that power, nor is chance. That leaves only myself, the individual. However, laying the blame on myself is complicated by the fact that I cannot recall first possessing the ability to recognize the Truth and subsequently letting go of it or throwing it away. (If I could remember such an event, then I could remember the Truth as well and shatter any hypothesis that would suppose me to be in Error.) Thus memory affords me no direct basis for blaming myself, although this fact need not represent memory's final word on the subject. That is, if I remain for the moment pretty much in the dark concerning how my situation came about, then at least (assuming I have followed the author in his Project thus far) I am not in the dark as regards knowing what I really think. On the contrary, I have found myself attached firmly to that, and I know also that it was no one but myself who *consented* to think what I really think. Suppose, for example, I think it a matter of no great account to form any definite views at all, either polemical or irenical, on questions A, B, and C, and merely leave them up in the air with a shrewd 'I'll wait and see'. I hold tightly to this and express my grip on it in daily life by turning up my nose at definite ideas. This means, however, that on the question 'Is it a great or little thing to exist as myself?' I really think my existence is not worth the effort of framing a definite evaluation. Now if this last is a bit of what I really think, it is far from indefinite, and by reflecting one level further I can uncover the consent that fastens me to it and makes it mine, along with the more or less fervent conviction that if the Truth is anything different from what I really think, I want no part of it; it is to be ignored, forgotten, or railed against.

At this point Climacus brings in the word *Sin* as a name for the individual's state under the hypothesis of Section B and forges the first explicit link between his Project and the New Testament. The descriptive names now proposed for the Teacher come from the same source. As Savior and Redeemer this Teacher saves the individual from bondage, bringing him the Truth and restoring his power to recognize it. Cut off from the Truth and shackled to what he really thinks, the individual has been reminded also that his consent to untruth is binding.

14

This can seem an overstatement even to a reader who has gone along with Climacus as far as discovering himself to be in a self-imposed state of Error, but it is the only possible continuation if he is to stay within the author's hypothesis: the Moment is indispensable if he is ever to learn the Truth. In practical terms, the difficulty is this: *How by willing can I come to think the opposite of what I really think?* Brainwashing might get me to gainsay it and (where public behavior plays a part) to playact the opposite, but my will is checked when it comes to unthinking what I really think, and doubly checked when I do not know and cannot recognize the Truth that is to be thought in place of it.

The Moment-hypothesis thus posits a Teacher with the power to effect a humanly impossible change in the learner's relationship to the Truth. Here a problem comes to mind. Why should there be only two possible positions concerning that relationship, the Socratic position and the Moment? A quick reply is easy enough to come by: either the Truth is latently within the learner (the Socratic position) or it is not. On the other hand such a compressed either/or is hardly enough to do away with our problem.

To start with, if for any reason someone wholly despairs of learning the Truth, this will in no way count as a clear third possibility over against the Socratic and Momentist possibilities. Those are meant to exclude any third possibility by leaning on the logical principle of Excluded Middle: the individual either possesses a handle on the Truth or he does not. To express despair of learning the Truth plainly takes sides against the Socratic position, and from this a conditional follows: *If* he is to learn the Truth, an unknown source must bring it to him. The despairing gesture, which appears to dismiss the Moment-possibility along with the Socratic, suffers from a touch of obscurity. That is, it expresses a firm opinion concerning what the unknown has in store for the individual. Let us honor the person who expresses this opinion (that is, that the unknown has nothing new to teach him) by supposing that he is not merely relieving himself of a frivolous sigh but truly thinks this. If that is so, and if we may therefore assume that he has at least heard of the Moment-idea as a preliminary to rejecting it, then he will hardly have missed hearing the concomitant charge of Error it lays against what he really thinks, including the aforesaid opinion. But to accuse of Error his thought that the unknown has no news—this sounds a little like a piece of news from the unknown, so that his thought comes forth with a lien attached to it and cannot be hailed as a thought independent of the Moment-possibility.

What appears to be a clear third possibility can arise where someone sets his face against questions such as A, B, and C. Let us consider two variations. First, someone could remark, "Both the Socratic and the Momentist differ from me in assuming that A, B, and C are meaningful questions. I do not find them so. I do not understand them." Whether these remarks represent a fully formed point of view or something less we must leave undecided, but at any rate such a person must for the time being be classed with readers who would find nothing useful in the *Fragments*.

We turn next to an objection which, like the last, seeks a clean break between the individual and the personal questions that embroil him in the Project of Thought. This objector might say, "Your Socratic and Momentist positions are not exactly meaningless; no, that is the wrong word. They are *unhealthy*. Isn't it quite plain that the personal questions on which both are based represent a twisting and wrenching of human consciousness to make it face *inward*? We could even call this a *crippling* of human consciousness. The more you let it set in its twisted posture, the more brittle-boned, club-footed, and generally unfit you become for open-air doings that result in triumphs, and the more weepingly allergic to sunshine and oxygen."*

To a learner who has found himself to be in Error, this objection will perhaps not seem as startling as the fact that he is in Error, yet it offers a challenging dialectical workout. It seems by a sideslip to place the objector clearly outside the two basic positions. By his standard of human healthy-mindedness, the very asking of questions A, B, and C exhibits a turn toward the sickly-minded. At the same time, however, adopting that standard seems to mean accepting certain answers to those questions, for it indicates that I do after all confront a primary task, namely to bring myself as near as possible to that standard of health and to keep myself there. But where did the standard come from? If from nature or imagination, then from man, and our objector belongs to the Socratic camp. The possibility that it may have come

*This view finds dramatic and powerful expression in Friedrich Nietzsche's *The Joyful Wisdom*, trans. Thomas Common, in Oscar Levy, ed., *The Complete Works of Friedrich Nietzsche* (New York: Russell & Russell, 1964), vol. 10, sec. 354, pp. 296–300.

from a mortal who has shot pretty far out of sight of the rest, geniuses and all included, far enough even to constitute a new type, would release a jet of paradox blacker than squid-ink into the waters of reflection. The philosopher's appearance on the scene would then constitute something like the Moment, yet if he is in fact a human like the rest of us, his thoughts will amount to nothing more than a modified version of the Socratic position that the Truth is within man.

The outlook of the last objector has depths it would be injudicious to pass over. For one thing, it proves beyond doubt that one can first of all refuse to countenance questions from that side of human consciousness which directs itself inward, yet at the same time continue to be a thinker, even an eminent one. For such a thinker questions A, B, and C lose their pertinacity. *Mens sana* becomes the new priority, yet such a thinker will be consistent and self-critical enough to see that he cannot keep the walls of this structure from swaying unless he flings out two buttresses: first, a theory of what human health consists in, and, secondly, a schema for the concept 'eternal'. Together these offer at least seeming assurance against premature collapse of the subject, who can thus keep up his spirits right to the end. In briefest form, such a theory and schema might read:

1. The highest badge of manhood is the badge of the undeceived.
2. The schema for the concept of eternity is the cycle, the recurrence atom-for-atom of everything one has witnessed or gone through.

It is not hard to see in such a position, side by side with its undisputed possibilities for personal daring, a built-in defensiveness against the very idea of the Moment and its correlative idea that the individual is in Error. Both of those ideas acquire impact from their whisper to the individual that the historical heat is on him, that is, that even if he looks pretty much like countless others in the long genealogy of the Joneses, in the privacy of himself and in the eye of the Moment he is unrepeatable. In short, the schema of a cycle does not apply to him, and in this fact we can make out the reason why a learner who has come to see his own Error will have to smile at the suggestion that his inward-looking shows a more or less profound crookedness. Would he not be the first to admit that an overture had been made to a side of him that he did not consider his best side, namely the inside?

C. THE DISCIPLE

The newness in the changed or converted "new creature" of whom Climacus speaks, if we keep within the langauge we have used thus far, consists in the man's turning his back on what he really thinks and letting himself be assisted in un-thinking it or in coming to think the opposite of what he has for some time really thought.

· More about the disciple and what awaits him will appear in the next chapter. However, this is a suitable place to gloss Climacus's treatment of Sin. As Niels Thulstrup points out (p. 191), some Kierkegaard scholars find it an overintellectualized account. Expounded in terms of the concepts 'Truth' and 'Error' (and in our remarks in terms of 'what I really think'), Climacus's account easily gives the impression that Sin has its locus in the brain and that its expressions in the sphere of conduct (particular misdeeds) enter very palely, if at all, into the picture. The essential fact, it seems to me, is again that Climacus is cloaking the concept of Sin for the eye of that reader who feels at home in the world of ideas. Accordingly, Christianity is being presented under the species of a thought-structure or hypothesis, an idea someone wishes to try out on paper. The notion of trying out Christianity on paper, a medium alien to it, is for more than one reason a curious one, but this only limits the number of readers who might find something useful in seeing it done. At any rate, the fact that the concept 'Sin' is introduced in tandem with the concept 'Error' means that any individual's *thoughts* can count as an instance of Sin. As regards intellectualizing Sin, we may again recall that a philosopher who typically puts his thoughts into words might also put them into deeds, nor is it questioned that many individuals scarcely ever put their thoughts into words. The reader who has no time for excursions into dogmatics should keep in mind that Climacus is not *defining* the concept of Sin here, as he does in other works Thulstrup mentions, but putting a handle on it that fits the palm of one sort of reader. In short, if Sin is an "existence-determinant"* that saturates the total life of an individual, then it holds in the domain of thoughts as well as of conduct and feel-

---

* Søren Kierkegaard, *Concluding Unscientific Postscript*, trans. David F. Swenson and Walter Lowrie (Princeton: Princeton University Press, 1941), p. 518.

ing, and certain readers more than others will meet it there on familiar ground.

Is the hypothesis thinkable? This is an insistent question and one that calls the Project to task for possibly thinking beyond the limits of thought, or for pushing language beyond its limits. To start with, it was a tricky enough hypothesis we were asked to consider, calling on the reader to suppose *himself* in Error and to weave that supposition energetically into his personal reduplication of the Project. Then, as it develops, the Project gives rise to deductions that throw its own thinkableness into doubt by concluding that the individual cannot get the Truth except by the unimaginable device of a new creation, a fresh transition from nonbeing to being. Here, it would seem, artful invention has outraced imagination and created expressions with nothing to express, which is pretty nearly the formula for nonsense. This hypothesis that steers one to the edge of nonsense—is it thinkable? The reader could easily sum things up by saying, "Looking back over the mental calisthenics this Project has put me through, it seems that a forfeiture I cannot remember put me into an invisible bondage, and now I'm called to enter into a new state I cannot even imagine!" Climacus can hardly be charged with making the hues of his Project blend softly into the common landscape. If anything he seems overzealous in stressing how normal and accommodating the Socratic way is, how off-the-path and full of briers his own Project. How could it occur to me that a personal but immemorial event placed me in chains I cannot see and whose removal amounts to an incomprehensible 'second birth'? So Climacus's hypothesis has quietly sabotaged those mental faculties by whose aid humans figure things out—memory, sense-perception, imagination. Without these we could not even compose fairytales.

The queerness of his hypothesis is not lost on Climacus. At this point (pp. 24–25), turning it over once more, he merely warns against haste in pronouncing it either thinkable or unthinkable and pauses before coming back to it.

What does it mean to be able to recognize the Truth?

In the paragraph on pages 25–26, Climacus gives a hint of content to the very blank conception of a human originally in possession of the power to recognize the Truth. Such a human, he says, "thinks that

God exists in and with his own existence." However, it is far from clear what that piece of thinking comes to, or how Climacus himself comes to perceive in it anything beyond the tissue of its words. If we presume both author and reader cut off from memory of the transition to their hypothetical state of Error, it is a mystery if not a slip in the text to go on as if the pre-Error state were describable. Slip or not, the paragraph as a whole fits in with the Moment-hypothesis. That is, the power to bring the learner *beyond* the point of awareness that he is in Error lies entirely with the Teacher, who may (but need not) endow him with the Truth and the *sine qua non* for recognizing it. Without further help from the Teacher, the learner's awareness of his Error gives him a clearer estimate of his situation than before, but his drift is still away from the Truth, and he cannot recover his original condition by recollecting his pre-Error situation.

Although the logic of the Moment-hypothesis rules out descriptions of the pre-Error state, it is possible to give some content to the expression quoted above. Most of us have known some religious person (on this point it scarcely matters which religion) who leans from day to day on the principle that God will come through when the cupboard goes bare, who when things are bleakest finds help in windfalls which to someone else would seem contemptibly small and mean. The person puts up with a great deal on this principle, but breaks out in exasperation just often enough to show that for him this leaning on Providence takes effort. Moved to explain himself he might say that when you are clinging to God's coattails and being whisked this way and that, it is hard to keep thinking yourself safely in His pocket. This person's effort shows him *straining* to "think that God exists in and with his own existence." His lapses show that he does not really think it, or does not think it all the way, but keeps a room swept for the opposite thought.

Nowhere in the *Fragments* do we find reference to how Error came into the world, and reference to how it takes hold of the individual is very scant. The point of sidestepping those questions is partly to prevent discussion from straying into the cavernous specialism of dogmatics. The stronger reason by far, however, is that the learner's present bondage to Error is the matter of primary concern, regardless of how it originated in himself or the race. That is to say, since the author's purpose is to bring out a contrast between philosophy and Christianity in terms of the individual's relationship to the Truth in each, a reference to Error is indispensable, but the question of origins may be left to inquiries employing higher magnification.

Can Hypothesis B be proved?

The closing passage of Chapter I, which offers a "test" that "proves" the Moment-hypothesis, calls for a detailed look. It purports to prove that, as between the two incompatible and fundamental positions, the Socratic position and the Moment, the second one is correct. That is, the individual has not got the Truth, and if he is to possess it, it must be brought to him in the Moment. This is, of course, a central claim of the New Testament, though Climacus does not yet go so far as to iden-tify the bringer of the Truth with a specific personage in Roman times. However, the mere idea of *proving* any New Testament claim at all is audacious enough to call for a close watch over Climacus's moves, es-pecially since in his third chapter he will treat as "folly" the attempt to construct proofs of the God's existence.

The nerve of the proof is that the Moment-hypothesis is not the kind of thought-composition men put together. Yet such a thought-composition is to be found in the world (in Christianity, in the New Testament from which Climacus "plagiarized" his Project). Therefore a thought-composition exists which bears the imprint of Not-man.

The negative premise aims to show that nothing having the internal thought-structure of his Project could be an end-product of *human* effort. But what does it mean to say this? It sounds dictatorial to claim that there is any ensemble of sentences which men are incapable of putting together. How then is the negative premise to be established?

As Climacus draws up the argument, his reasoning goes like this: "I (or any human being like myself) can gaze about me all I please, but I will find nothing in common experience to suggest to me that I have in some unrememberable episode cast aside the power to recognize the Truth, and nothing to suggest that this power, once lost, is irrecover-able, or that I will possess the Truth only if something higher than man gives me back that power and also shows me the Truth. No mat-ter how diligently I ponder my existence, letting every other piece of business slide for the sake of pondering, I cannot conceive of anything that would lead me to take the measure of my situation by saying I have yet to come into existence, I have been born one time too few. Even if inexplicably my mouth formed those syllables, I could do nothing with them for I have no conception of the remedy.

"Yet such a cluster of thoughts exists. This tells me very little, to be sure, merely that there exists a set of thoughts which are in no way my own and which I cannot imagine anyone who sees the world as I do finding reason to utter. If they were ever to be uttered in an *occasioned* way, it would be by a being so manifestly unlike my kind that I should have no name for it except Not-man.

"But here I have plainly blundered out of my depths, for why should something that is not man and would presumably be unvexed by human troubles, so far concern itself with my situation as to call it to my attention?

"Yet the *existence* of those thoughts—what can it mean if not that this has happened?"

Here we have the curious piece of reasoning that concludes Chapter I, doubly curious because it pronounces on the *truth* of the Moment-hypothesis, not merely upon the consequences that would follow *if* it were true. It is striking that Climacus should find it possible for someone standing wholly outside of Christianity, namely himself, to accept it as a proof and continue to stand outside of Christianity. As far as Climacus is concerned, perceiving the Project as a thought-structure alien to the kinds humans produce does not constitute *believing* the New Testament prototype of this Project in the sense of becoming a Christian. The proof merely bids the reader to take notice of a thought in the world that cannot be laid to a human thinker and expresses the author's astonishment at the strangeness of this fact.

To make this distinction clearer, the existence on earth of a thought which (a) deals with the very questions the Truth is about and (b) is not of human making testifies (for Climacus) that there *has been* a Moment. Nothing coercive of belief in the New Testament can follow from this, however, for two reasons. First, neither Climacus nor anyone else is in a position to say that there have not been two or a dozen or a thousand such Moments. At best, the proof proves that there has been at least one Moment. To prove that *the* Moment which the Project describes, modeling itself on the New Testament, is decisive for every learner, would be a quite different accomplishment. This point will loom larger when we discuss the title page questions in our closing chapter. The second reason concerns another point to be discussed at greater length later, the special meaning of 'faith' spelled out in Chapter IV and the Interlude. To express the reason briefly for our immediate purpose, accepting the Climacian proof in no way makes one a believer; concluding that the thoughts in the Project arise from a nonhuman source falls measurelessly far short of having dealings with that source, that is, of becoming a disciple in the New Testament sense. With the proof in hand (assuming it can weather criticism), one will perhaps profess no doubts that those thoughts are not of man's devising, but 'faith' belongs in another category altogether.

Meanwhile the proof itself, at one instant seeming to prove so much, at the next so little, appears internally vulnerable in several ways. Let us consider these.

Someone might say, "It would take linguistic sensitivity in an unheard-of degree to be able to look at some sentences, for instance in the Project of Thought, and detect with confidence that the thoughts they express did not come from humans. If the Climacian proof stands or falls with that bit of sleuthing, I am afraid his only sympathetic readers will be enthusiasts. We have no clear criterion for picking out nonhuman thoughts from all the thoughts there are, and I should think it would be all but impossible to set limits to the kinds of thought-combinations an overstimulated mind could come up with."

A second line: "The proof in question is a mere simulacrum of ordinary inference. The norms of logic lay down conditions for inferring one proposition from others, and Climacus follows those. But logic also supposes that the premises make sense. In our example, however, we have a premise that says: 'Only Not-man could find occasion for formulating such-and-such a thought', or something similar. Now if, from the added premise that such a thought is in circulation, you infer it came from Not-man, formal logic lodges no complaint, for it does not investigate whether the premise is a good sentence but, rather, presupposes it and merely inspects the 'If . . . then . . .' form of the inference. Now when I step back and ask myself, 'How on earth could anyone *establish* that only Not-man could find occasion, and so forth', I find the answer mischievously elusive. In my view, therefore, we have here something that *looks* very much like a piece of valid reasoning but is in certain respects too anomalous for me to say it *proves* something."

A third: "The premise speaks of a thought no man could think, and this is where we ought to direct attention. However you express it, the idea that the individual can only be set right by an *unimaginable* transition (New Birth, nonbeing into being, or what you will) is unintelligible. The words are scrambled beyond hope of clarification. The proof rests then on an irremediable obscurity."

The proof, so lightly and almost gaily tossed into the stream of Climacus's thought as not to have won much notice from commentators, seems hardly worth the effort of firing such heavy guns. However, it repays a closer look in the light of its author's basic intention to let the essential notes of the New Testament come forth over the drone of usage.

The proof offers to loosen the grip of the idea that the Project must be some human's thoughts, perhaps those of the Apostles or some other ensemble of men. It invites the philosopher to put aside the distance-lending lens-system that goes with that idea and determines the sort of critical stance we take toward people's thoughts. That is, the Socratic assumption back in Section A is the *normal* one, and, as a result of taking it for granted from day to day, philosophers can find it hardening into a sort of apriorism: any thoughts we actually encounter must be presumed to be human thoughts. Indeed, it would be hard to imagine proceeding from day to day on any other assumption. It is just here, however, that the Project asks the reader to suspend his normal or working pattern of suppositions, and Climacus in his repeated warning against lapses testifies to the difficulty of doing this steadfastly.

Part of the proof's role, then, is to prevent the normal assumption from stiffening into a fixed apriorism when the going gets hard. In effect, the proof is a device designed to free us from that apriorism so that a reader can frame this question: "How could a human like myself say to me, in all seriousness, that my state of wrongness is such that I no more exist now than before I was born, or than if I have never been born, and that I must come into existence all over again if I am to have a share in the Truth? If the speaker is a human like myself, he is hardly in a position to discover such a state in me, and furthermore the violence he commits against grammar is alone enough to cut me off from understanding him. With fairytale, poetic rapture, legend, venerable myth, fantasy—with these I can make my way, but not with this!"

Going further in trying to grasp the role of the proof, it is helpful to ask what questions would be settled if a reader found himself able to say, with Climacus, "Yes, there is no question about it, the thoughts in this Project emphatically do not issue from my kind of being." To bring this out, it is useful to remember that Climacus's proof comes on the wings of a rhapsodic flight. He calls it a "spell," but can hardly intend it as a strict requirement that the reader share his enchantment. Besides, the proof is a dead end religiously. That is, the idea of proving, for pastoral and apologetic purposes, that such-and-such a thought did not come from a human source would open up endless byways such as the objections cited a few paragraphs back, not to mention the scholarly labors needed to show that the Project is a faithful mirror of the New Testament.

Where the scriptural prototype of this Project is constantly audible, at least in hackneyed, washed out, or profane versions, in everything from holiday carols to cursing, custom can blur its pristine contours. To counteract this, Climacus practices the art of noticing, of being struck by, the all-too-familiar. When he lets himself be struck, the result is not instant religiousness but a freshening of wonder at seeing something familiar for the first time, and the proof here is an expression of that wonder. The reader's small "Eureka!" in sharing it falls infinitely short of professing personal faith in the Moment. It is, however, a profession of freedom from the grip of an assumption that generally goes without saying: Any thoughts that cross my desk are surely and without question *someone's* thoughts, the thoughts of someone like myself.

So important is this deep-running assumption that one would not go far wrong in saying it underlies the whole problem-complex of Philosophy of Religion, at least in its twentieth century linguistic turn. The primary office of Climacus's proof, I believe, is to weaken its hold. To suppose that any thoughts we run into are surely some human's thoughts is in one sense truistic. Experience so tirelessly reinforces it that it goes without saying. However, a subtle chemical change takes place in the transition from supposing that truism to supposing instead, "There *cannot* be a thought except it be the thought of some human, or of something quite like a human." This transition from truism to apriorism is packed with freight, for the unconditional "cannot" expresses a staunchly Socratic position concerning the Truth. A reader cannot hold on to it and at the same time jump with both feet into the Project.

Letting the apriorism go can be especially hard for someone schooled in philosophy, which trains a person by exposing him to people's thoughts, and trains him more particularly in *how to handle them*. For example, to be able without a second look to categorize any thought as *someone's* thought immediately sets that thought at a suitable distance and angle for cool viewing. What does a philosopher do when a thought comes before him? Various things: perhaps he applies a criterion of meaningfulness to it, isolates the assertion it makes, scours it for influences from earlier thinkers, looks for accompanying evidence, inspects its logical linkages, translates it into a more accustomed terminology, ventures interpretations of it, and similar things. To do them well demands great pains, along with skill in the use of special optics.

Suppose on the other hand that the thought he is dealing with is not someone's thought. Then the normally harmless apriorism, that it must be so, becomes Procrustean. Suppose the thought prefaces itself by saying, "Read me with your naked eye." Then the special optics, the most up-to-date zoomar lenses, can become devices for misreading, or missing the point, or at any rate controlling the shock and burn-power of any light the thought might give off. In short, the optics can function as a kind of shielding like the goggles a welder puts on to cut down glare. In this way the original thought appears only in featureless silhouette. Suppose the thought concerns the Truth about A, B, and C and wishes to announce itself as the overthrow of the Socratic position. Then, since by the apriorism it *cannot* be anything but some human's thought, the "cannot" keeps it harmlessly within Socratic bounds.

This puts us in a surer position for understanding how Climacus implicates the reader himself in the judgment that this Project is no human production. If, indeed, the Project falls outside that category, this fact will present itself only to someone who sets aside any special viewing equipment. This is precisely the sense in which an educated reader's task can be extraordinarily hard, and in which the uneducated enjoys a certain advantage over him. But why in the first place should anyone wish to remove an apparatus he has spent years assembling at great cost? Even if he should wish to, how is this to be done, and what assurance can he count on of seeing anything worth seeing once his optics are laid aside? Finally, this dismantling of one's special optics— how can it signify anything but throwing away all of one's critical and evaluative faculties and leaving oneself open to every kind of sophistical hocus-pocus?

To start with the first of these questions, the essential purpose of setting aside special lens-systems is simply to permit us to read the Project as unadorned human beings. This is not a whimsically imposed requirement but arises from the fact that the Project refers itself directly to that unbespectacled and originally naked eye of its reader. That is, it introduces to begin with the possibility of *his* existing in a state of Error. Special optics interposed here can screen out the blistering rays that might touch him personally. By habituating his reader to treat the Project as 'somebody's ideas', his special viewing-lenses can filter out the dangerous end of the spectrum and censor the possibility that the Project is something quite different from that, something pointed straight at his personal existence. To approach it with the naked eye is therefore to be free to discover what category, if any, it fits *itself* into, rather than to foreclose *a priori* the (slim) chance that it is not some human's thoughts after all.

The essential purpose of removing one's special optics, then, is freedom. It is the freedom to pick up, and to read as they were meant to be read, any and all communications addressed to the individual personally and intended to be read with the unshielded eye. Whether he happens to react hot or cold to their content is another matter entirely. As the appendix to Chapter III of the *Fragments* will remind us, the choice between those two courses always remains open.

Our second question concerns how those optics are to be removed. On this point we can only return to the example in which a reader becomes alerted—for instance through Climacus's jarring suggestion that the Project is not a human artifice—to one or more of his assumptions before they harden into dogmas. What this reader will see when he puts in abeyance the assumption that the Project is "somebody's ideas," will come into focus in the next chapter.

Finally, laying aside one's philosophical apriorisms in order to approach the Project as a human being implies no dulling of a person's critical eyesight but, if anything, a quickening of it, the removal of a veiling or censoring assumption. It remains true in an obvious sense that to take away my dark glasses is an impoverishment, for it means stripping myself of the power to *handle* thoughts in the sense of retaining firm control over their power to affect me, a control that belongs among my fairest possessions in the sphere of consciousness or, loosely speaking, of spirit. Take it away and I become measurably poorer in spirit, immeasurably more sensitive to the burns that certain thoughts can inflict on my kind of being.

In sum, the aim of Climacus's proof, it seems to me, is to break down the apriorism that would heedlessly assimilate his Project into that class of thoughts which trained minds know well enough how to handle. His target is the assumption that the Project, *qua* thought, *has* to be "someone's thought," but he is not proposing that the reader adopt some fantastic alternative squint that would reveal it in a damascene light to be the Word of God. Far from it. The aim is to behold the Project with *no* category pre-set to receive it, so that no pre-set category will get in the way of seeing it. The naked eye risks dazzle and permanent scars on the retina, but one thing is certain: no reader can share Climacus's judgement that the Project is not of human devising unless he first sees the Project.

Climacus's concern to shake the hold of this apriorism stands behind his warning that we should take our time deciding whether his Moment-hypothesis is thinkable or not. That hypothesis includes, among other things, the idea that there *could* be nonhuman thoughts in circulation. If I, the reader, find myself very short-fused and ready to bang out a "No!" or "Preposterous!," the warning gives me pause. How much of my reaction springs from habits of reflection that would screen out *a priori* all thought but human ones? If, on the other hand, I should be very quick to cry "Yes!," have I perhaps passed too swiftly over the dark features this possibility must present to any learner presumed to be in Error?

In his second chapter, Climacus puts further touches on the Project of Thought and also repeats the proof we have just looked at, though in a new key.

IN SEARCH OF AN UNDERSTANDING

Chapter II of *Philosophical Fragments*,
"The God as Teacher and Saviour:
An Essay of the Imagination"

SUMMARY OF THE TEXT UP TO SECTION A

Climacus returns to the human teacher-student relationship. When the topic of instruction is the Truth about the individual himself, each party has that Truth latently to begin with, so there can be no unforgettable debt to the other for bringing it out. This is the Socratic view. But when we abandon it and move into the Moment-hypothesis, where the bearer of the Truth is the God, this two-way street becomes one-way. The God is not moved by need, as the human teacher is. His motive for becoming a Teacher can therefore be nothing but love. "His love is a love of the Learner, and his aim is to win him" (p. 30). The learner may, of course, refuse to be won.

The God's love is an unhappy one. A Socrates may be superior to his student in self-knowledge and dialectical skill, but the student can at least come to an understanding with Socrates and make himself comfortable with the idea that Socrates wishes him to become his equal in those accomplishments as he is equal already in the matter of being a fellow human. However, when the God out of love moves for a similar understanding, we depart from the range of ordinary human differences.

Climacus chooses the "earthly figure" of lovers to illustrate, since it is the God's love that makes possible the union. In the king's love for a poor girl we may read some hint of the depth of the breach between God and learner, even though between king and maiden there is only a difference of life station.

Climacus hands over to the poet, the man most accomplished in delicacy of expression, the problem of how to effect an understanding between the God and the learner. What comes next is to be read, then, as

a poet's attempt at imagining how the God could establish a footing
with a learner who is without the Truth and in Error by his own guilt.

REMARKS ON THE TEXT UP TO SECTION A

Chapter I is a philosopher's effort, Chapter II a poet's. In this contrast Climacus's style is true to the title of his book, for the resulting
'fragments' do not go together as parts of a homogenous synthesis but
rather as mosaic chips in the reflective life of a single human being, an
author who spends one hour thinking mostly like a logician and the
next like a lyricist. The god as Teacher and Saviour is his constant and
unifying theme.

In the prelude to his lyric, Climacus makes references to the Unmoved Mover of Aristotle's *Physics*, situated altogether apart from
earthly occasions, and makes contrasting references to a clearly personal God "eternally resolved to reveal himself." Jumping from one
conception to another as it pleases him, Climacus moves very nimbly
within this unstable array, concluding that love alone could move the
God to make his appearance in the historical Moment. These moves
take place under the 'if' of the original hypothesis: *If* we assume the
learner to be so totally in Error's thrall that only from Not-man could
the Truth and freedom be brought to him, then the one who brings it
could be moved only by love.

A passage such as this puts heavy strain on the philosophical reader
who puts a premium on lucidity. Suppose, for example, I assert a
failure of comprehension here and protest that I simply do not see
what 'love' could mean when the word is cut loose from its familiar
human contexts? When this door is opened a crack, hosts of problems
arise about predicating human or earthly attributes of the transcendent. These are serious questions, and they protect us against the type
of loose discourse in which anything goes when we are speaking of the
Jenseits. In generalized form these questions might reduce to this:
'Before we continue, please explain to me how it is possible to employ
expressions like "love," "grief," "unhappy," and so forth, detached from
their earthly surroundings.'

Climacus wishes to excuse himself from such questions at this
point, not because they are irrelevant or without force, or because he
holds metaphysics in high evangelical disdain (for he will shortly ex-

pose his reader to a potent dose of it), but because they are untimely. He puts his poet-side forward at this point, as if to say, 'Save those until another mood is on me. Just now the mood is lyrical. As a human being I can wish to be that for an hour, after which the analytical mood may if it pleases scratch out every line. But something would be fishy if I choked off the lyrical because the analytical waits in ambush for it. Having an hour ago produced a thought, the spirit comes over me now to produce a poem, and I must be careful not to abort the poem, doubly careful since I am the kind of being that has been known to practice lyricide because I became "angry with the thought".'

Climacus has said the God as Teacher could be moved only by love. But suppose I felt the impulse to take another direction and said, 'Why necessarily love? Why couldn't the God be moved by wrath to reveal himself to his errant creature, or to reveal just enough of himself to make him scream and shrivel?' On the face of it this would seem to challenge the author's quick, one-two-three inference, based on classical premises, that the God is not moved by anything outside himself or by sudden impulses. This challenge, however, would renew the metaphysical one we just spoke of, asking in effect, though in a shriller octave, why one predicate ('love' or 'hate') won't do just as well as the other when we are speaking of the inaccessible God. The challenge must be put off until Chapter III for the same reason. An author must begin somewhere, and Climacus has not yet set up equipment for meeting all possible shades of response.

There is also, however, a sense in which the challenge is timely since it recalls the reader's hour-by-hour dialectical task in working through the *Fragments*: the task of weaving into his reasonings the dark reminding thread of his Error. That is, when I have traveled this much of the way with Climacus, and now wish to come up with the challenge notion that the God's motive might as plausibly be hate as love, I can remind myself that my notion is itself subject to review. If it is merely a passing thought, I can jot it in the margin for future consideration. If, on the other hand, it belongs with what I really think, its dark thread ought to show.

If we ask, then, by what right Climacus plucks out of the air these allusions to the biblical God, the God of the Moment-hypothesis, and Aristotle's metaphysical deity and weaves them with swift fingers into his carpet, the answer seems to be: by a poet's right. This license to help himself to what is in the common air, or may be poetically posited, is part of what gives the *Fragments* its name and the look of a patchwork rather than a continuous bolt of fabric. It fits in also with the whole Climacus-norm, powerfully reinforced by example in the *Concluding Unscientific Postscript*, of what philosophizing *ought* to be like. Besides leaving room for the passional and poetical elements in human reflection, this norm will on occasion applaud the order, elegance, and unity found in the great systematic philosophers.

It is appropriate, then, for Climacus in his lyrical hour to move out of the sphere of immanence by simply employing words like 'God' in conventionally respectful ways, anthropomorphic ways if you prefer, instead of first constructing a system of metaphysical cantilevers to prove he is not doing the impossible. We might say that Climacus is not doing what many philosophers would call 'theism' but, rather, producing poetry. If the poet is to lean upon those timeless conventions and abide by them, then love will be what moves the God to reveal himself, for convention hangs back from hooking raffish predicates such as 'hate' to the word 'God'.

In this chapter it is not the God of abstract transcendence that concerns us, but (in keeping with the Project) the God come to earth as Teacher, who faces the task of making Himself understood as a basis for winning the learner. The learner is not to be won by a finesse, but must understand in some way what the Teacher is about. The equality or common ground for such an understanding (on the human level) consists in the fact that Socrates and his student are both men, with language and upbringing in common. Even with that common ground an understanding may be hard to reach and the teacher hated and resisted, for the student may realize how painful it can be to separate what he knows from what he does not know. If there is such a thing as resenting the fact that I stand in the relation 'student of' to another, the understanding has to overcome this. When we shift over to a love situation, to the king and the poor girl he loves, the inequality deepens to a point where words falter. The long and short of it is that the king must watch his every step and word, because the maiden can so easily be made unhappy. The starchy formalities that protect commoner as much as sovereign hardly exist between lovers. In lighthearted moments, a king can quip about his bloodline, his crest, his rank, but can he quip about hers? If she came from a hovel or ghetto, can he lightly

use those words in her presence? A king ought to be free to say whatever he wants, but when his heart would welcome a lowly subject into
equality with him, the picture changes, for his spontaneity can set off a
joyless sense of owing in her.

In place of the king we read the God, and of the girl, the learner; and
here Climacus turns to the poet, for imagination must now cut itself
loose from the novelist's probabilities and any actual case-histories of
anxious kings. Two great stones block the way to an understanding
and must be rolled back before the poet's problem is solved. First, the
Teacher is the God; second, the learner is in Error.

The first means that the gulf which love seeks to bridge is not of the
sort caused by fortunes of high or low birth or other human circumstances. There is a creator-creature inequality to begin with that sig-
nals a block from the learner's side, that is, the possibility of a wounded
creature-shyness. Insofar as awe is natural to us, the idea (however
dim and poor) of *equality* with the God goes against something natural. Within the human order, equality-expressions such as 'sharing
each other's lives' carry no awful hint of one party absorbing the other,
or of the other owing the first one everything. Here, however, descriptions of *what it is like* to be won by the God, to approach 'light unap-
proachable', elude even the muse of fire, not to speak of the hardest
ratiocination.

When we add the second factor, that the learner is in Error, the
poet's difficulty increases exponentially. That is, what the learner really
thinks is not only different from the Truth but straightway opposed to
it, so that creature-enmity must be reckoned in with the creaturely
awe we spoke of. What he really thinks on questions A, B, and C has
very much to do with himself and the God and ranks among his great
possessions, not only as what he *does* think but also as what he *wants*
to think and makes himself responsible for thinking, so that the heavy
mineral vein of this guilt must be added to the weight of the stone that
is to be rolled away. If we let this factor, the learner's Error, lapse from
memory, the final sum comes out wrong. In cleaving to what he really
thinks, the learner has already anticipated, so to speak, the God's overture and turned it down, and this fact sends shockwaves backwards
and forwards in the book, wherever it seeks to intimate what the God
as Teacher is up against.

The *prima facie* equality enjoyed by the learner and the God in that they share a language (since, again, reverent convention does not permit the slapdash judgment that the God is at home only in his own dialect) is not enough to ensure the needed understanding, for it may happen that one of the parties does not desire an understanding. On top of this, the learner who has discovered his Error is aware that he has already made a choice in attaching himself to what he really thinks, so that any conciliatory overture from the other side can very easily turn surprise into downright embarrassment since the matter is after all so very personal.

If this equality cannot be established, Climacus writes, the God's teaching becomes "meaningless, since they cannot understand each other" (p. 34). This sense of 'meaningless' should not be confused with any cool and official sense of the term, as, for example, when a philosopher lays it down that certain sentences which do not admit of experimental verification are to be counted meaningless. We may remind ourselves of the distinction in this manner. Suppose a learner to be actually called or invited (say by someone's preaching) into a new situation of equality with the God, for instance, sonship. Since the learner is in Error, the new situation will be one in which he owes everything to the God, and immediately the whole notion of equality is undermined, for what sort of equality is it which calls for one party to exhaust himself in unilateral thanksgiving? Surely it is an unthinkable species of equality, and if the preacher tries to save it by proclaiming that the Error of the past will be forgiven clean out of memory, to the learner this idea of the God's forgetting can be a very hard knot. On his own side of it, the business of owing another everything is not such a weekday experience that he can safely promise *himself* to forget it, and the God's having a rusty memory is a matter he is perhaps too respectful to care to go into.

This is a sample of the kind of unintelligibility that can confront the learner, and here the cry 'Meaningless!' can quite understandably come forth as a protest torn from a human throat. On the other hand, the philosopher's use of the term as described earlier is not a wounded outcry against something preached to him personally, but a cool judgment that says: 'Such and such a sentence S does not satisfy such and such a criterion C', and his use of the word 'meaningless' is an abbreviation for this cool judgment. While it would be overweening to declare that an objective criterion of meaningfulness is of no use in any

34

discipline, it seems conspicuously out of place applied to communications that call for a personal decision. That is, the person would be permitting a gadget to make the decision for him—a little like flipping a coin.

When the Teacher is the God, then, and the learner in Error, what will make it possible for them to reason together and arrive at the needed understanding? The distance between them is great, so great that the learner cannot imagine ahead of time, as in a human love-situation, what he will be letting himself in for if the God succeeds in winning him. At the same time, if the God is to do this not by command or coercion but from Love, the learner must be given to understand something of what the God is out to do. To this end, the poet imagines, the God will choose among certain possibilities.

SUMMARY OF SECTION A

The union might be brought about by an elevation of the learner. This would be as if the king saw to it that the poor girl were transported into the whirl of court life, where a fresh orchestra starts up as soon as the last one stops. But this would be a deception, like a dose of some ecstasy-drug that turns a squalid setting into splendor. What would it be but a power-play that preserves the inequality and obscures that fact in showers of joy?

What the learner would call happiness is not what the God knows is happiness for him. This fact constitutes a terrible bar to any understanding, a bar that can be only hinted at in the human sphere, where one person's knowledge is not very much greater than another's, and where two people can understand each other more or less on the subject of happiness.

REMARKS ON SECTION A

The God is resolved to reveal himself and to seek an understanding with the learner in order to bring him into love's equality. Here the poet's make-believe consists in going on as if he could don the godly mantle, survey the God's possibilities, and narrow those down in a summary manner to a matter of either elevation or descent.

The first possibility, elevation of the learner, Climacus presents in two forms, both involving deceptions. First, the God might pitch the learner into a state of ecstatic rapture, eclipsing the everyday consciousness that is the human creature's benchmark. How would this constitute a deception? Well, the learner is in Error. An infinite inequality yawns between himself and the God. Without the permission that would issue from an understanding, the God's raising him up could impart only an untrue picture of the learner's present earthly state. In short, it would make him forget who and what he really is. Secondly, the God might transform not the learner but himself, in this instance into the Most Dazzling, the Most Eyecatching Thing, but in truth the God is not a sensational apparition.

These possibilities are denied him, then, but the God remains intent on revealing himself, not bypassing the learner's understanding but by means of it leading the learner into the equality of love. Here, after making every allowance for poets, the reader might protest that language has been stretched to where the pathos becomes all-too-human, for we now speak of the God's *anxiety*. One can halfway understand a sublimity of love, but anxiety is hardly a state that can be ennobled by imagining a more and more "unspeakable" intensification of it, since in human life this approaches the clinical rather than the ideal. In short we have no working concept of a *divine* anxiety, though we may stand at ease with many different models of divine love, peace, harmony, and the like.

When we step back from the poem, then, it can easily appear that the ligaments of correct discourse have been torn. In its cantos, anxiety, dilemma, sorrow, solicitude, and grief take their places alongside love and blessedness in the orchestration of heaven, and what queer, earsplitting strains they make when the poem is done and the critical mood returns!

SUMMARY OF SECTION B

The understanding must come about in some other way, if at all, so as to incorporate the learner's awareness that (a) there is an inequality and (b) because of his Error he owes the Teacher-God everything.

If we rule out an elevation, we are left with a descent. The God, under this 'if', must become the equal of the lowliest man, a *servant*. The God's 'becoming' at this level expresses the seriousness of his desire for equality with the learner. At the same time it positions the God dangerously, with a risk to the desired understanding, because he remains the God in all this, and learners may choke on the thought that this is the *God*, or on the thought that *this* is the God.

The God will appear incognito, but his servant-form is real, and accordingly he goes through the worst of what the poorest go through, death included. His aim is the equality of love with the humblest beloved, and the cost to himself is suffering.

*   *

The poem done, its familiar ring opens the poet up to charges of plagiarism. But this poem so far outreaches human invention, is so far removed from what men call poems, that its presence among us constitutes 'the Miracle'.

REMARKS ON SECTION B

Once the wells of possibility scouted in Section A prove dry, and the poet's logic leaves the God's descent as the only possibility, the momentum of Chapter II picks up. 'Descent' here signifies 'in the direction of the learner', that is, the learner is to be *approached*, and by the God who is eternal and changeless, who is not in the sphere of becoming where one thing lies at a little distance from another and can swing closer or veer away. To approach this learner in a way he can notice amounts to coming into the learner's sphere, into time or history. Further, the approach will not be like one mindless mass brushing close enough to cause Newtonian shudders in a smaller one, but will be aimed at an understanding. For my kind of learner, the business of coming to an understanding is typically a matter of using words. Thus, in whatever unsearchable manner the God of the Project might engineer his descent, if an *understanding* with me is what he bids for, then the tokens of his overture will be words, and by words he will set about revealing himself. If this conclusion seems too quick and cramping, we may think back to Section A of this chapter, where more direct approaches to *this* kind of learner were exposed as potential deceptions, fatal to any understanding.

Returning to the poem, the God's love is for the learner, and his desire is for the learner's real happiness, not a pinchbeck substitute, howevermuch that might please the learner. The purpose of the God's descent is to make this happiness available in truth. In the poem of Chapter II, the need for an understanding blocks their union, for the learner may *refuse* to understand, and the God's unhappy love is now characterized as "unspeakable anxiety." For the God is in a sense really disarmed in his approach to the learner, and the learner, as we recall from Chapter I, is in Error, his posture toward the Truth combative. If the Moment is to be decisive for *this* learner, the God must not use his power to stun him out of his freedom. His power sheathed, the God must step into a situation in which the learner can react in more than one way and is not only free to refuse an understanding but is actually so inclined. Here all the makings of anxiety are present. "If the Moment is to be decisive," then, the God must seek an understanding with each learner by becoming the equal of the lowliest, must suffer anxiously over how his overtures will be received, and must watch his every step.

As the author's hypothesis develops under its governing 'if', we are asked to see the God caught in something like forced moves. To relieve any cramp that might trouble us at this thought, we need to recall a pair of factors introduced earlier:

1. the God's love for the learner; and
2. the kind of creature this learner is.

The God's moves are forced (under the governing 'if', of course) by the God's disarming himself for the learner's *protection*—against having his creatural integrity crushed, against being dazzled out of his mind. The God's love for his man-creature includes respect for man's created powers of thought and discourse and for his capability of using language carefully in order to arrive at an understanding. Any power-play revelation by the God that would elbow human rationality out of the picture, bypassing man's discursive kind of consciousness, would be tantamount to reversing our earlier assumption that the God is moved by love of each learner *as is*, or as we know ourselves to be in our ordinary self-knowledge. This includes knowing myself to be a creature of the word, a language-user, and moreover, or as a corollary to that, knowing myself to be a free creature in a sense that has nothing to do with the "bondage" discussed in Chapter I, a state which, as Climacus represents it, is itself freely chosen. Respect for this side of human nature is part of the God's constraint.

Here we might note that in recent years, thanks largely to Jean-Paul Sartre, some thinkers have become very hesitant or negative about whether man has a 'nature' at all, much less a created one. They propose that a human being is as malleable as dough to begin with, and acquires, through a series of choices, whatever group of features it pleases us to call his 'nature'. Without speaking for or against this position, we observe that Climacus does not bother his head with any difficulties it might present. A strong conviction along Sartrean lines would, of course, be open to second thoughts insofar as it reveals something of 'what I really think'. Aside from that, speculation as to whether men have a nature or not is away from Climacus's point since his references to the way men are, for example, that we are conscious creatures who make choices and use language, are doctrinally too bland to attract the attention of skeptics.

It is man's being the kind of creature he is, then, and the God's loving him as he is, that moves the God (under Climacus's 'if') to disarm himself, descend, and approach the learner who is in Error. For the individual's sake he lets himself be reduced to that most awkward extremity of anxious helplessness. If I recoil at the thought of a God thus constrained, then I can .catch myself recoiling at the thought that he loves precisely the one I know myself to be, or at the thought that his love is all that tender or, to put it differently, so personal that it foregoes anything like coercion and instead approaches in quest of an understanding.

This understanding—what is it supposed to accomplish? The king-and-maiden analogy, meant to "quicken the mind," offers an earthly illustration of what can happen when the manifestly unequal is invited to become an equal. How easy for an offhand word from the king to wound that girl! The closer she is to having nothing to give, the more that invitation is fraught with power to hurt her. For the girl to arrive at an understanding here means adjusting herself to the thought that she is singled out to share the throne as she is, not as a princess of the blood dowried with gems and lands, cushioned by years of coaching to anticipate the king's proposal. It is just the opposite, with herself alone to offer and not even a festal gown.

The learner's understanding must adjust itself to the idea of living in a far more searing limelight than bathes any human throne, and if the maiden in desperate discomfort contrived to make herself uncomely, or to hide, the learner has no such chance because the God has become as unbeautiful as the lowliest and knows every squalid hiding place. Moreover, although the God does not coerce, he will wait. And for the learner still another factor weighs: he is guilty before the God. There is all this for an understanding to take into account.

At this point questions can arise once more about putting together the concept of God with words like 'grief', 'sorrow', and 'anxiety', questions of this form: 'All this throbbing and feeling sorry for the God, this indirect pressure on the learner to let up, to have a heart, and so forth, may be integral to the prose-poem. However, in order to be quite clear about how the language of anxiety applies, are we to assume that the God as Teacher has emptied himself of his godly foreknowledge? Does he not know ahead of time (or outside of time, whatever that may mean) how this or that learner will receive him? Anxiety over an outcome, after all, sits very uneasily with omniscience!'

As soon as the Moment-hypothesis gets on paper, questions like this one reveal zones of obscurity and turbulence bordering its central idea: the Deity in time. They press us to explain how we are to *think through* the idea of the God's making himself into the likeness of man in order personally to come to the learner. Reason can discover any number of logical jams, such as the clash between omniscience and anxiety, just beneath the smooth surface of the original anti-Socratic hypothesis. The specific clash in question is historically important, however, and well worth pausing over, having been raised to prominence by no less a figure than Kant.* For one thing, it reminds us of the normalcy of the Socratic alternative. It shows also that the immanent logical contradictions in the Moment-hypothesis make it a very unlikely one for thinkers to formulate on their own and take seriously.

Under the 'if' of his hypothesis, Climacus has been poetizing from the divine point of view and barricading the God's possible avenues until only one is left: If the Moment is to be decisive, the God will descend in the form of a Teacher and Servant to seek an understanding with the learner. The factors all told lead Climacus to picture an anxious God-man stepping fearfully among eggshells. Still, all-knowing, the

*Immanuel Kant, *Religion Within the Limits of Reason Alone*, trans. T. M. Greene and H. H. Hudson (New York: Harper & Bros., 1960), pp. 54–72.

Teacher must know (it would seem) exactly where to place his foot. How then will he suffer anxiety who has instantly to hand, in two columns if he wishes, the names of those who will reach a happy understanding with him and those who will turn away? If the all-knowing himself appears in the Moment, how can the tension in his confrontation with the learner be anything but theatrics, the most patent sort of make-believe?

Here the poem snags on the concept of *omniscience*, which certainly belongs among those attributes reverent convention ascribes to deity. The briefest reply would be a review of things already said, for instance that the learner is in Error, that other modes of bringing him around have been x'd out, and that the human servant-form is an earnest of the God's desire for equality with the learner. To get this answer into finer focus, however, the reader who has come this far has to put *himself* into the question somewhat in this way: 'How could the God's anxiety in his confrontation with *me* be anything but playacting? My name, too (since I come under the hypothesis), he can look up in his columns!' If, as a learner myself, I dwell on this modified form of the question, something begins to come out concerning the depths of both my Error and my talent for compounding it. In the first place, the learner's own self, here brought into our new form of the question, is where the passion is. The new form of question merely acknowledges the quality-gap that divides a logical clash *per se*, between two propositions or predicates such as 'omniscient' and 'anxious', from a similar clash occurring in the context of the God's seeking an understanding with *me*. The second clash is what the whole Poem is about.

The godly anxiety we are discussing, in other words, contains as one factor the power which I, the learner, personally possess to make matters awkward for the God, to make the God suffer, and for this reason passion is inextricably bound up with the issue of whether I should want to do so or not. In this way the original logical problem of reconciling two repugnant predicates, which has taxed the greatest theologians, becomes *their* problem, while my own becomes a rather different one, and maybe less taxing. That is, if it occurs to me to wonder whether the God of the Project and Poem would in actuality be anxious in his quest of an understanding with me, or whether I could in actuality turn myself into a locked door—well, considering all the restrictions Climacus has wrapped him in, his dread of bruising me, his respect for my creatural liberty and all the rest, no doubt I could come up with something. Suppose, for example, it were important (for whatever reasons) that I, the learner, a temporal, historical creature, *lose no time* in coming to this understanding with the God. My small stone would not be much of a block to omnipotence on the march, so good at rolling back stones, but as long as omnipotence held itself in check I would be good for a little shilly-shallying and frequent coffee-breaks.

In this way the notion of the God's playacting at suffering (pivotal in Kant's interpretation of the New Testament), and with it the whole riddle of his foreknowledge, transforms itself into a manageable question once I place myself, as learner, body and soul into the question. Apart from its reference to myself the difficulty is a hard logical knot. Speaking of that logical or linguistic problem, it is important not to let the smoothness of Climacus's poem mislead us into assuming that we know what an omniscient being is like, whether sorrow and anxiety, for example, would be entirely out of the question for it, or what it might cost such a one to love and not be wanted. 'Still, omniscience is omniscience,' we might feel like saying, 'and the concept is answerable to its definition'. Perfectly true, but it goes beyond this to suppose the predicate 'omniscient' is *used* to tell us what its subject is like, the way '8X' on a binocular tells us what order of magnification to expect when we look through the glass. 'Omniscient' need not be used as a description in that sense but might function as a formal abbreviation for certain of those reverent conventions of normal speech we noted before. In that sense it can work as a grammatical predicate, signalling the impropriety of using such expressions as 'shortsighted', 'gullible', and 'absent-minded' when speaking of deity. This point will be dealt with in greater detail in the next chapter.

Is this Poem thinkable?

The Poem stops here, and a full chapter intervenes before Climacus takes up his story once more. He steps back now for a look at his Poem, owns up once again to an act of plagiarism, and calls it no poem at all "but the *Miracle*." Just as Chapter I ended with the Moment-hypothesis revealed as something more than a hypothesis, this one ends with the Poem revealed as a nonpoem, that is, not a human composition. The authorship of the Poem, Climacus says, presents "a difficult case," all the more so because the poet has made believe he could vault up to the God's altitude, appropriate the God's faculties, and take survey from there. This kind of make-believe is by no means unheard-of. Poets, philosophers, and mythmakers often indulge in it, but the Poem of Chapter II, Climacus tells us, is not within the range of human invention, for it contains a factor that could not possibly occur to humans. This claim seems to fling out a feisty challenge to the reader's powers of imagination. Surely, one would like to reply, the poet's free-wheeling genius is as unbounded as the sphere of possibility itself, or at any rate the sphere of sentence-constructability.

The specific possibility which Climacus says is *impossible* for humans to have dreamed up is that "the God would make himself into the likeness of man" (p. 44). When we take this phrase by itself, immediately instances flash to mind, variations on the incarnation theme. Hindu lore, where some notion of a Creator-God can also be found, is loaded with them. Elsewhere, too, one finds myths in which gods assume human form and even enter into love or combat with mortals. Gnostic sources present dim analogues. In short, it is just as easy to make up sentences of the form, 'The God took the form of so-and-so' as for some of the late Mahatma Gandhi's admirers to proclaim him a god and put up statues of him in temples. If the '*Miracle*' peroration in Chapter II is to weigh more than a mere vapor, then, readers will have to go outside its few pages to make out the staggering possibility presented in the Poem.

The peroration rests also on the related claim that, without a sign from the God, it could not enter into man's mind "that the blessed God should need him" (p. 44), hence the presence of that thought in the world is itself a sign from the God, or at any rate from Not-man. A poem in existence but beyond human devising would indeed imply a poet not of this world, but how does the Poem in question so identify itself to Climacus? That is the reader's problem here, and in a curious way, though consistently with all the rest of his book, Climacus summons the reader to take part in proving that the Poem is no human composition. In one sense this is quite easy to do; in another it is extraordinarily difficult. The more educated the reader, the more richly any linguistic construct such as a poem will resonate with allusions to other constructs in the same medium. Despite these inevitable resonances, Climacus demands that his reader wrest himself from the grasp of the idea that any poem as such *must* be of human devising. This exactly parallels the task of freeing oneself from the apriorism discussed in our chapter on the Project of Thought.

The supposition that any given poem is the work of some poet or other is a truism, as safe as anything can be. However, to appreciate Climacus's design it helps to bear in mind how very closely this truism is bound up with norms of reaction to poetical works. If I am a poet, let us say, chances are that my education has prepared me to meet just about anything in that domain. The more disciplined and drilled I am in linguistic arts, the more practiced I am, for instance, at picking out resonances between one such thought or poem and earlier or later ones. When a piece of fancy crosses my well-used desk, training has taught me to set about mastering or analyzing or penetrating it and above all has shown me how to keep a proper distance. Thus, for instance, when I read *Don Quixote*, I can keep enough distance to prevent my confusing my own existence quixotically with the hero's under the truistic assumption that *Don Quixote* was put together by a person or persons essentially like myself—an assumption that is practically certain never to trick me and which, in fact, constitutes my initial bond of genial affinity with the text. So perfectly second-nature is this truism, especially to an educated person, that it would be remarkable if he could even begin to specify what an exception would look like.

'Very well,' someone might interrupt, 'let us break off with any "must" that might cling to this truism, and lay it down as a principle that a poem *need* not have been put together by a human artificer. But in order for this sliver of a possibility to take on any substance, you have to clarify the *alternative* to regarding the Poem as some human's Poem. Since it can hardly prejudge anything to say it is made up of cantos, let us begin with that. Now what category am I supposed to assume the piece belongs in? I cannot *assume* it is "the Miracle" (whatever that may mean), for that is to be the author's *conclusion*. And you are not allowing me to assume either that the scriptural source Climacus is reclothing for us is "the record of some early people's religious experiences" or "some moral precepts couched in parabolical forms of expression," since these would only be rather stuck-up versions of the original truism. But what is the alternative?'

Again, Climacus's alternative is to approach the Poem as nearly as possible with no categorial bed made up to receive it, or at any rate with no category more concessive and preformed than 'Poem' itself. The category 'someone's poem' is not quite so neutral as one might first suppose. As observed in relation to the Project of Thought, it can trap the reader in a covert and unbending commitment to Socrates' position on the Truth. Aside from that, Climacus finds in the Poem a thought too stupid ever to enter anyone's mind, so that in an odd way the Poem is an insult to the poet's craft or belongs in another category altogether. The all-sufficient God casts himself out of heaven, turns himself into the squalid likeness of an outcast, and makes himself the unwanted, having in mind in all this to remake the outcast into a likeness of himself. Whether this theme could possibly suggest itself to a human being is perhaps unanswerable if taken as one of those moot symposium questions that arise in the heady table-talk of a Goethe or a Yeats. Climacus seems to have a different emphasis in mind: how would an outcast answer it?

That is, the learner in Climacus's *dramatis personae* is by hypothesis in the grip of a discoverable Error that places him outside the pale of Truth. How will he answer in his own name? The reader needs no special intuition to perceive that men like himself have no interest at all in bringing that obscure side of themselves to light, much less doing something about it, but rather treat the matter after the fashion of Legionnaires, honoring each man's alias and secret. In Climacus's hypothesis, however, the God descends out of boundless concern over just that, precisely in order to help the learner unthink what he really thinks and bring him to birth anew, cleansed of it.

As we conclude our remarks on the Project and Poem several points are worth making. First, the more we probe, the less surprising it is to be asked whether the Project of Thought is *thinkable*. Climacus develops a hypothesis of almost bottomless dialectical complexity, in which the sand and grit of existence keep getting into the gears. From the opening denial of the Socratic assumption through all the forced moves thereafter, the deductions are interwoven with very prickly considerations of what the individual really and privately thinks of himself. These make it possible for him to *put on* the hypothesis, or to place himself in its leading-strings to the extent of discovering that 'what he really thinks' is poisoned. Internalizing the hypothesis in this way is far too athletic a task for an author to demand of his reader as a

45

prerequisite for understanding his primary point, namely, that a bottomless chasm exists between philosophy and Christianity. Yet is it not just as difficult to *imagine* oneself outside the pale of Truth as it is strenuous to *discover* oneself there? This is especially true if one is a philosopher for whom the gravitational pull of the old and natural Socratic assumption never lets up. Thus there seems no quick answer to the question: Is this hypothesis thinkable?

Four brief comments need to be made here. First, why does Climacus tie this discovery of one's personal Error to the Moment-hypothesis? If it is genuinely possible for the learner, any learner, to discover this Error, why couldn't Socrates, the venerated digger after self-knowledge, have come up with it independently and let the Greek world in on it? The answer, judging from Climacus's spare references to Sin, seems to be that Socrates found no occasion to suppose there might be a difference between his frank-hearted 'I do not know' and what he really thought. He had no prompter (and what man could find reason to prompt him?) who could lead him to a hidden but discoverable chamber of thoughts below the level of his perfectly honest confession of ignorance. The only intimation of this appears in his faintly paradoxical admission that after a lifetime of sounding himself he had not touched bottom.*

Secondly, as the reader will have noticed before now, it would be next to impossible to work with expressions like 'knowing myself' and 'what I really think' without creating unwanted resonances with psychoanalytic concepts such as 'the Unconscious' and 'preconscious'. Distinctions are easy enough to make if we bear in mind that 'what I really think' has to do specifically with questions such as A, B, and C, not with infantile sexuality or filial relationships. The only threat to clear thinking from this quarter would arise if a reader *interposed* psychoanalytic concepts between himself and those, if he said, for example, 'Surely theorists and clinicians from Freud until now have seen all there is to see of the thoughts, happy and unhappy, that people really think, or think without realizing it. It would therefore be a waste of time to roll up my sleeves in search of what *I* really think, for those pundits will have seen it all before, especially anything shocking'. In

*Plato, *Phaedrus*, in *The Dialogues of Plato*, trans. Benjamin Jowett (New York: Random House, 1937), p. 235.

46

this way a person can of course protect himself from any interior sur-
prises the Project might hold in store for him on the most intimate
matters of all.

The third brief comment is this. In an oblique way the Project as a
whole seems to anticipate recent clamor over the disturbing unverifi-
ability of religious statements. Even if we assume that verifiability or
falsifiability is a minimal condition for meaningfulness (an assumption
which raises many awkward questions beyond the scope of these remarks), that condition is squarely met in the Project, which hypothe-
cates that the learner is in Error by his own guilt. As a particular
learner, his point of entry *into* the Project (in case he wishes to do
more than look it over) is by way of a proposition that he can set about
verifying for himself. This may require more than five minutes, but the
length of time is not at issue. At any rate, it means he can enter into
the Project with the relaxed understanding that it contains (in so far as
it applies to himself) at least one eminently verifiable proposition and
is thus something different from a curious little calculus. A learner
who has verified it for his own case will understandably take a sus-
picious view of any wider public demand for verification in the sphere
of religious language since that demand (in so far as *he* finds it importunate) can now be inspected for any relationship it might bear to *his*
Error.

The learner who has discovered his Error will not be put off by
someone's remarking, 'But this is a verification only for your own subjectivity, so it is not strictly a verification at all. A fact that is a fact only
for a single individual subject surely belongs to the poorest grade of
facts, since it is only subjectively a fact'. Whatever its merits otherwise, this is an important objection because of the weight Climacus
places on subjectivity in the *Fragments* and *Postscript*. Regrettably,
the division 'subjective/objective' pays dearly for its compendiousness
by concealing some internal distinctions. For example, my discovery
that I really harbor such and such an opinion about myself turns up
within the consciousness of a single subject and may for various reasons remain perfectly unknown to the rest of the world, at least until I
confess it. However, the fact that I discover it in myself is not subjective in the same sense as is the content of my discovery, which is ad-
mittedly not only a subjective opinion but, according to the Moment-
hypothesis, quite wrong (which, indeed, locates it about as far as can

47

be from objective fact). In other words, I may be coldly objective in the matter of discovering something in myself, even if *what* I discover there turns out to be a thought which is subjective in the worst possible sense. The confession that I discover it in myself weighs as much as any other confession I might make of love, hate, and the like. Similarly, if on reflection I should come to blame myself alone for cementing myself to my opinion, this assignment of personal blame will be subjective in still another sense. As distinctions of this sort present themselves, it becomes clear that 'subjective/objective' is far too macroscopic a divider to be very useful for close work, particularly for classifying the types of judgment that may arise in the course of someone's self-scrutiny.

Finally, although Christianity is not mentioned by name until the last few pages of the book, our closing word about the first two chapters ought to take note of a real danger. A reader racking his brains over the Project and Poem might easily come to imagine that the dialectical equipment they call for is indispensable for understanding what Christianity is all about, and perhaps for becoming a Christian, too. Very early Climacus forestalls this sort of despair and at the same time punctures any elitist tendency that might develop along the same line. From its first page the Project presents itself as a hypothesis, a thought, the type of construction that has its being in a paper currency of reflected possibility. However, so far is this from handing a religious advantage to full-time thinkers, such as philosophers, that it rather imposes on them the extra burden of converting all gains into the much heavier metal currency of living. In any event it is clear, from the title-page on, that the book is directed to philosophers.

A CROTCHETEER AT WORK

SUMMARY

A sort of paradox presents itself at the end of Socrates' seventy years. The more he strove to know himself, the more uncertain he became about how to think of himself. The challenge, it seems, proportioned itself to his effort, and so it goes in general with the thinking man, who wants more than anything else that his compulsion to think should meet its Waterloo. However, the highest possible pitch and downfall of that particular passion is not so easy to conceive, for it is no simple matter to imagine a stumbling block of which one can say: this cannot be thought.

Let us begin by assuming what Socrates dared not assume: we know what man is. Even with that assumption in his pocket, the impassioned thinker meets a further challenge, for one would suppose that in knowing what man is he would know what he himself is, since every individual is man, and would thereby know the Truth about himself as discussed in Chapter I. If he cannot produce the Truth, this throws the shadow of fresh doubt over his assumption.

But what then stops him from thinking this matter clear through to the Truth? What is this limit that thinking runs up against in questions so pertinent to the thinker himself? He cannot say, does not know. Call this Unknown *the God*.

"Is there such a something? That is, need we be talking about a *something*? In any event, why designate this 'the God' and go on to call it 'he' and 'him', with all the runaway connotations of those pronouns? No, here you must stop and prove!" Such protests contain misunderstandings. If I would prove the God's existence, I must either presuppose it or merely unpack the content of a conception, my conception of the Unknown. Unless at the outset both possibilities are open, existence and nonexistence, I would not be proving anything, for one of the alternatives is closed to start with. If both are really open, the proof can never begin.

This Unknown, this limit that thinking comes up against, may be characterized as the absolutely different, bearing no likeness at all to anything our thinking is familiar with. To represent the Unknown other than as such a limiting conception would mean likening the God capriciously to this or that imaginable oddity. If I then try to think away the capricious elements, I end up likening the God to the perfectly ordinary, a being just like myself, for instance. When I thus assimilate the Unknown to the common, I bring the God as near as possible yet no nearer than before, and so make the God appear a deceiver.

* *

"Absurd," a reader might exclaim, "I have to empty my consciousness of all likes and unlikes in order to discover such a catch."

So you must. Our attempts to characterize this Unknown in terms of recognizable differences go haywire. Thinking cannot lead to a grasp of it. Any knowledge of it has to come from the God, for its cornerstone is that man is wholly unlike the God, while thinking trades on likeness. The absolute unlikeness cannot be thought, it must be accepted. Nor is it something the God has given to man, but something man himself has set up between them. Our earlier category for that was sin (Error). There can be no consciousness of this unlikeness except as the God introduces it into consciousness, that is, becomes a Teacher.

Here we have the Absolute Paradox: the God makes himself altogether like me so that I can understand him, then lets on that I am absolutely unlike him, and finally would help me to become exactly like him.

Can a human grasp this paradox? On all sides it appears perfectly glassy and unscalable. Thought can take pot-shots at this and that about it, but thinking, as noted before, wills to be overcome, and this deepest wish is in the same key as the Paradox, although the concord is audible not in the cool middle registers but only in the moment of passion. Similarly, self-love wills its defeat in the love for another and finds its defeat when in passion it goes out to the other. It may then be tempted, of course, to betray its vows and reassert itself. We will put off until later naming the distinctive passion that goes with Reason's relationship to the Paradox.

REMARKS

The Socratic paradox that opens this chapter is somewhat akin to observations like "Plus ça change, plus c'est la même chose." In Socrates we have a man whose driving verb is 'to think', whose passion will not let him call a halt to thinking, and whose life is so favored as to permit him to think full-time. At the end of that life, or by the time one might expect such a singleminded campaign of thinking to bear fruit, he still mystifies himself. His final uncertainty is therefore paradoxical, that is, contrary to expectation.

The Socratic paradoxical uncertainty, readers should keep in mind, is bound up with what Climacus has been calling the Truth, which bears on the individual's own worth to himself, his task, and his present state. In Socrates the passion to search out this self-understanding came together with agreeable circumstances and a gift for reflection, like the rare alignment of three planets, but it culminated in disappointment, a further spur to passion, since on top of the original enquiry there is now a failure to be accounted for, and meanwhile the hourglass keeps trickling.

The thinker whose passion is to get hold of this self-understanding will have plenty to keep him busy, and veins of paradox to incite him, but why should Climacus' lay it down that every passion, at its peak, wills its own downfall? More particularly, what would it mean to say this about the specific passion of Reason, as Climacus expresses it, or of the full-time passionate thinker?

An immediate and perhaps too quick answer comes to mind. If, for example, I were to discover a life-task over and above my tasks as husband, father, postmaster, and so on, this discovery would no doubt *transform* or *redirect* my passion so that it could wrap itself around that task and in that manner enable me to be happy with myself. On the other hand, it seems evident that Climacus means something more dramatic than transference to another object when he speaks of passion's downfall. He expands the reference to downfall by introducing the concept of a supreme and insuperable challenge: something that thought cannot think. On top of that he claims to descry in human reflection a yearning to lock horns with this challenging 'cannot' and thereby come out a loser! If this picture of the thinker's passion is correct, we are indeed speaking of a paradoxical passion, but it runs so cross-grained to the way philosophers characterize themselves that one may be hard put to see how it applies. At the same time, the notion that the thinker's passion wills its own undoing is crucial to Climacus's account of the Absolute Paradox and deserves close attention.

As a first step, Climacus suggests that we reconstruct the Socratic predicament in order to highlight its key assumption: we know (implicitly) what man is. This will amount to assuming that we possess in ourselves a criterion of the Truth, that is, full power to recognize the right answers to A, B, and C, since knowing man's nature, as Climacus speaks of it, includes in its riches knowing what task if any falls to the individual man *qua* man, and similar things, even though this significant content may still need to be dug out. This will be our trial assumption, then, and the reader will note its likeness to the original Socratic presupposition of Chapter I.

As matters turn out, it is all too easy to declare this assumption at the top of a blank sheet and command it to uncoil its logical consequents. If I know what man is, then I must know what I myself am; I must know, for example, whether in my own person I have a life-task or not, and if so what it is. If I cannot come up with the answer for the man nearest me, what is the use of assuming I possess it for men the world over, down all the ages? Here my reasoning comes to at least a momentary standstill as a shadow falls over my assumed knowledge. In diagram, the Socratic adventure begins with unknowing, postulates a knowing, plucks it of all its fruit, and ends up with unknowing. Only a diffident soul would suggest, pointing to Socrates as its ideal, that the individual's task may be just to *seek* the Truth. This view would place Socrates in a flattering light but would satisfy him only if it coincided with the Truth, since his terminal predicament leaves open the chance that this view is only pretend-knowledge. In case the Truth is something quite different from an enquiry into itself, securing it will then mean *going further than Socrates*.

Before going further, however, it is necessary to catch up. The thinker's paradoxical passion (paradoxical, according to Climacus, because it senses downfall in its longing) now seeks a collision. With regard to the collision itself we have no trouble appreciating the thinker's desire to have it out with someone or something, since his failure under maximum effort to discern the Truth is a provocation, a slap. The sting of it is proportioned to his mindfulness of the kind of being he is, insofar as nothing is hidden about that: a slow or gradual learner to begin with, he is hemmed in by time, tossed here and there by the dice-throws of politics, and at every moment shuffling forward in the mortal queue. In a word, he is an "exister." Further, the Truth he is after is about himself, so that in case it should confront him with a task beyond that of mere enquiry, there ought to be time left for the task. Now, in his failure, reason presses hotly for a showdown, but if he asks himself what he wants to showdown with, he is unable to say, for the slap came out of the dark. The assumption that he knew what man is (or, what amounts to the same thing, that this knowledge lay somewhere within straining human reach) collapses, but the shattering thing is that he has nothing ready-to-hand as an intelligible substitute. At this point it will be especially tempting to fall back on possibilities whose weaknesses we remarked earlier, for instance, that perhaps there are no answers to A, B, and C, or that they are senseless or brainsick questions. If he resists these easy paths, what clear alternative remains once the postulated bit of knowing falls apart? Simply to deny that the Truth lies within man's potential reach would be tantamount to positing the Moment as the individual's last chance, but this carries with it, as we saw in Chapter I, a most ludicrous consequence: the individual is not a truth-seeker; he really thinks something quite the reverse of the Truth and is shackled to what he thinks. Whether relief or distress would issue from such a diagnosis, Climacus has made a big point of showing that it is scarcely possible for humans to discover it. With no promising continuation in sight, therefore, the passion of reason demands a showdown.

But with what? Taking it step by step once again, my failure to arrive at the Truth might wear me out, since it uses up heartbeats, but it does not exhaust reason's reserves. There remains the possibility of achieving an overview of the failure-episode, an analysis of what went wrong, and of making that the first lesson for the next generation of learners. Very well, my imagination now flings out pincers to embrace the opposing center of force. Now suppose the pincers encounter nothing, or what Climacus calls *the Unknown*, for that is just what happens; or suppose we prefer to say with Climacus that they encounter something that cannot be thought, which for tactical purposes is as good as nothing. The silence is a thunderous cue for the passion of thought to exert itself further, possibly to frame a vigorous question such as, 'How is it that my failure finds no explanation?' or even 'What accounts for my inability to explain the want of an explanation for my failure?', since no factor in the drama thus far has cut back man's power to pin new tails on old sentences. But if Climacus is correct, the failure to explain the failure is as far as thought can go.

What can it mean, though, to say that the passion of thought experiences a shuddering premonition of its own downfall? Or that it enters into that collision we spoke of with a sense of its imminent undoing? It is unfortunate that Climacus does not take time to gloss this idea since it is first of all not a very ordinary one and secondly has led a number of his interpreters to raise cries of 'Irrationalism' (and with some justice, we might add, for by itself the idea of setting reason aside or seeking a clash that betides its downfall sounds pretty much like a formula for turning intelligence and judgment over to any wisp of fancy that happens to float by).

This would therefore be as good a place as any to say a little about Climacus's use of the words 'reason' and 'passion'. Thulstrup's Commentary in the 1962 Princeton edition (pp. 222–23) rightly cautions against confusing the *Fragments*' sense of 'Reason' with this or that logically separable function of the mind, taken in abstraction from the whole life of a reflective man. The student of philosophy will have met such abstractions, and our emphasis on the thinker's passional side acknowledges this warning, but we are still left with a question: What does Climacus mean by 'reason's downfall'? What is it like for flesh and blood to experience an intimation of that? Everything in the Climacus-works, *Fragments* and *Postscript*, argues against interpreting the downfall of reason as a termination of careful thinking. Rather, what the slap-followed-by-nothing seems to suggest as a starter is that *thinking one's way to the Truth* is a doomed undertaking, not that thinking *per se* is doomed. The slap is final or, as we expressed it before, is followed by nothing. This means that whatever comes by way of a forward movement toward the Truth will be of the nature of the *unexpected*, hence there will be little use in putting my thinking-machine through practice drills in preparation for it. Beyond this, however, lies the possibility mentioned earlier and dismissed as at best a clownish idea, at worst an outrage and a lie, namely that I am not, after all, and have never in memory been, a seeker of the Truth. While such an idea would no doubt explain my failure to arrive at the Truth, and very likely supply a touch of balm to my stinging face, it would deliver such an unmerited roundhouse to the other cheek that I would be hurting worse than before. I may be a stern taskmaster to myself, but I have just enough self-love of a perfectly natural sort not to rend myself to pieces with a deadpan accusation quite *that* unexpected!

To the passionate thinker, then, hints of reason's downfall are not in the least hints that he must leave off thinking or put his critical faculties to sleep. Just the opposite. There is an enormous cache of things to think about in the somewhat unexpected hint that I must place my reliance on the unexpected. For example, this tells me that the unexpected will not take the form of a thought's occurring to somebody, which for a philosopher would be something eminently to be expected. If we may fictionalize an instance, it might occur to some fellow-thinkers, at passion's ebb but not without a certain hysterical excitement, to forget the personal slap and become very much interested in the Land of Nothing it came from, even to the extent of leading a party of explorers and sending back pictures.

To look to the unexpected, then, paradoxical as this phrase may strike us, is by no means the death of thinking. We shall have more to say about this point in the analysis of Chapter IV.

A NOTE ON PASSION

Since the concept 'passion' has a number of applications in the *Fragments*, a brief look at it may prove useful. In his fourth chapter, Climacus will draw attention to a passion uniquely tied to the Moment-hypothesis, but within the common framework of emotive life we recognize a distinction between (a) passions which are sudden gusts of emotion and can trigger spur-of-the-moment crimes, heroics, and the like, and (b) passions such as greed, joy, fear, revenge, hope, sorrow, hatred, and love which are capable of being sustained over a long period as well as of mounting by degrees to an extreme pitch. In living with such abiding passions, one has time for periods of intense concentration and serious exercise of the intelligence.

No student of philosophy who has found himself in love or in battle with an idea is a stranger to the thinker's passion, though it would be stuffy to imagine that the professorial and textbook side of philosophy gives anyone an edge in the sort of passionate thinking Climacus has in mind. In fact, the passion of a reflective individual to get clear about himself, which Climacus has been talking about from the beginning with special reference to Socrates, can be seriously impeded by the clogging effect of miscellaneous knowledge. According to the Climacian account, passion equalizes humans in the thinking department, at least in the sector of thought we are concerned with here. It does this not by an all-levelling disdain for learning but rather by focusing reflection upon a subject that is for each person equally inexhaustible as well as perfectly personal, namely himself. It seems fitting therefore to characterize this passion as an interest in himself, and an interest to which no upper limit of intensity can be assigned, since in an inexhaustible subject the challenges to passion, the setbacks and sandtraps his thought encounters, will be proportioned to his intellectual acumen and subtlety.

At first sight this may sound close to a formula for an inflated ego, even a narcissistic or pathological self-absorption. A few second-thoughts, however, dispel that impression. The interest we are concerned with is not a species of egoism seeking to express itself with indifference to, or at the expense of, other egos, but a passion to figure oneself out and get answers to a set of highly personal questions which are at the same time *not* exclusively one's own. Thus my own passion serves as a basis for appreciating the same component in any other human life. Under this equalizing understanding each one can go about his business—shopping, getting drafted, counting bank receipts, and in general giving other persons their due. This passion of thought or reason, in other words, has for its object not the good looks or fortune or health which make people unequal, but rather my own turn at existing, which obviates comparisons and leaves no room for the envy of the have-not.

What can be said about such a passion? In the first place, to say it has no upper limit of intensity (or that its object is infinite, that is, inexhaustible) amounts to saying that the world contains no object more interesting than oneself, which is a statement not about how much fun one is at parties but about this passion. In short, one finds his own self a richer property than anything else in existence. The interest announces itself as a challenge to the understanding which Climacus would no doubt want to call a contradiction or a paradox of sorts: 'This existence is mine, is mine unexpectedly, and is mine consciously, which means in a manner that dares me to get clear about it'. To the extent that this passion predominates, the individual is comparatively loosely attached to the beautiful goods and services life offers. Even if he happens to be loaded with them, his mind's center of gravity is elsewhere, so that he is in principle or spirit a poor man quickened by a dare. If a downturn of luck should snatch away whatever treasure he owns, very little of the heart's tissue would go with it, for the passion has already impoverished him in a way that no Wall Street panic could duplicate.

This passion of Reason or thought forms a sort of hinterland from which questions such as A, B, and C can emerge in a highly individuated form for each person. The fact that the answers seem nowhere to hand is a temptation to give in to passionlessness, to flag before the dare, but at the same time a sign that passion and not thought is the prime mover in the reflective life, even though thoughts form its upshot and record. Passionlessness or loss of spirit may express itself in someone's going on as if questions such as A, B, and C are silly or senseless and match up with no truths in this or any other world, yet the fact that his personal existence is the subject of those questions tells him that something is odd about the gesture by which he dismisses them. When the individual loses interest in the truth about himself, his passion may attach itself to an alternative, impersonal kind of truth. For example, he may develop instead an interest in the human subject at large, even in the religiousness of the human subject, but with the proviso that *other people's* subjectivity, religiousness, and the like shall absorb the lion's share of his passion.

Glancing now in the opposite direction, when the passion of thought is permitted to keep the thinker's own existence in steady focus, growth occurs in what Climacus calls "an eternal consciousness," a phrase that troubles many a first-time reader from the title-page on. These byway remarks on passion give us a suitable place to gloss that phrase. An individual's eternal consciousness is not an awareness that he is going to burst into endless daylight after passing through the tunnel of death. The eternal remains a facet of the Unknown, the individual's eternality nothing more than a possibility, and a bare one at that. He does not know the content of it even as a possibility except that it includes a reference to himself, but this is enough for passion to get a grip on. A question such as '*How* is it possible to come out the other end of the tunnel?' he will naturally regard as a problem beyond

57

human power and therefore a problem only for some other kind of power. Despite all its opaque veils, the possibility remains, and in virtue of its accessible content it poses a fixed question: 'Am I of one mind or two about being the one I am?'

What, though, could make such a question loom big for one person when for someone else, perhaps the man whose interest is absorbed in analyzing the subjectivity of others, it is not only a waste of time but positively counterproductive? The answer, it seems, is that passion can make it loom. Passion thrusts my own existence forward in thought and holds it there face to face with the possibility just mentioned. It is at the upper reaches of this passion that the otherwise abstract and dry-sounding question 'Am I of one mind or two?' acquires the power to cast its long shadow. Since I cannot say at all what an eternal happiness, unhappiness, or anything else is like, the question properly asks about my present state; the questioner just as properly understands eternity in terms of something he may incomprehensibly *fall* into, a little like the camouflaged pits men dig to capture large game. If eternity would isolate me with only my own thoughts for company, and more particularly my thoughts about being the one I am, the relevant question becomes: 'Those thoughts—are they happy or not?' The answer clearly depends on a prior question: 'Which thoughts are *mine*?' Despite a look of simplicity, this can be difficult for a cluttered mind to answer.

Self-knowledge, then, is the bedrock of what Climacus calls "an eternal consciousness," but acquiring self-knowledge in this sense is not equivalent to following the psychoanalyst's command 'Say whatever comes into your mind', for all sorts of other thoughts can conspire, as it were, to make themselves censors of the thoughts that I am attached to at the deepest level. The pseudo-intimate—the petty, nasty, shocking, fantastic, prurient—can interpose itself like a spate of floodwater between the individual's consciousness and the genuinely intimate. Thus a person could spend hundreds of hours on an analyst's couch without a single step forward toward confronting what he helplessly thinks and cannot unthink.

To sum up, the passion that takes my personal existence as its object is the keynote of my eternal consciousness, which is conscious of eternity only as something that can happen to it or be done to it. The related notion of an eternal happiness has for its visage a question as to

58

whether my most intimate thoughts are pleasant company. This is a reminder that the cluster of eternity-expressions such as 'eternal happiness' and 'life everlasting' point toward the Unknown of Chapter III: they make contact with a side of the individual that no one else, least of all his analyst, would be so tasteless as to inquire about. Notice that in taking this back to the individual and what he really thinks, we are in no sense demythologizing the concept of eternity in the manner modeled by Kant and elaborated by the Bultmann school. That is, the Unknown in Climacus's account remains fixedly unknown and does not surrender itself to human interpretations.

Here one can imagine a thoughtful objector saying: 'Your brief side-trip on the subject of passion starts out on familiar hard terrain, namely the dictionary, but quickly leads the reader downward into muck and marsh-gas. What my not overdelicate nostrils detect at this point is an *ideology* if not indeed a total *culture* passed along to the reader in the plain brown wrapper of a hypothesis or project of thought.

'Let me be more specific. I think you know what I mean by an ideology that promises one thing and delivers another, since you yourself have alluded to a respected theory of the human psyche which promises me an understanding of myself but confines its inquiries to the pseudo-intimate. For all its faults, however, that theory does not propose to kidnap me out of the everyday world. Can you see what I'm getting at? *What has a creature like me to do with an eternal consciousness?* A passionate interest in my own *existence* I can begin to understand, but when you peel away at that existence until nothing is left but my *consciousness*, the residue strikes me as a monstrously wizened abstraction. Who ever said my *consciousness* is the most important thing about me? Or that the most important thing about it (if it is even an "it") is whether it is *happy* or not? Can you point to a single monumental creation by a happy consciousness? Does *respice finem* mean I must lose respect for everything else? As a rule a man scarcely has time to grow into this kind of an existence before the troll bites off his head, yet civilizations do manage to come forth and to throw up the occasional pinnacle. But can you imagine a whole society devoted to sucking the poison out of the individual consciousness? Wouldn't it be the same kind of society enjoyed by a rack of sun-dried mullet? This whole business of a passionate concern about the state of my consciousness leaves me word-poor and tongue-tied. Perhaps the best I can say is that I wish to protest against it as a *man*.'

To get such an objection into perspective it may be helpful once more to go back to the starting point and place myself in the learner's shoes as regards Hypotheses A and B. The paramount concern at that point is whether the learner's relationship to the Truth about himself is as Socrates assumed or the reverse of it. We may now contrast that concern with those of the objector who feels (1) that the state of his consciousness is too gaseous and wraithlike an object to invest his passion for existence in, and (2) that a priority concern about it is the mark of a downhill civilization.

Let us consider (1) and (2) singly. First, it is Hypotheses A and B jointly which place the heavy accent on an individual's consciousness, perhaps on the assumption that he is more interesting to himself awake than asleep. The Socratic hypothesis does it by proposing that a mere forgetting stands between that consciousness and the Truth, while the Moment pronounces the tie irrevocably cut. Both A and B suppose the learner to be sufficiently attached to his memories, loves, longings, pacts, souvenirs, decisions, and convictions that they constitute for him a reality as concrete as that of, say, his thumbworn notebook or a tin of salve in his medicine chest. They are his, after all, with his fingerprints all over them. Their configurations are more uniquely his own than the key to his bank deposit box, and even more wonderfully protected against thieves in that nobody would take the trouble to steal them.

Now our objector raises the question, 'Who ever said my consciousness, this closetful of rags and bones that wouldn't bring a plugged nickel at a sidewalk sale, is the most important thing about me?', an amazing question when we reflect on it, and one with a rhetorically implied core of truth, for in all probability no one has ever said to anyone about his consciousness, '*That* is the most important thing about you'. Still, this is far from saying that an individual could not say it to himself or intimate it to another by his conduct. But supposing he does say it to himself, how will it acquire the force of a conviction when, as the objector in this instance well understands, all the drives and furies of nature set their faces against it? Could the answer be that for an individual the passion we have been speaking of gives it the force of conviction? If we assume, as we weigh this possibility, that his passion links up with the recollection that he is in Error concerning (among other things) what constitutes the most important thing about him, the possibility brightens a little more. As it picks up we can see why the objector's first point is a hair off the mark, for if I do not know whether my existence as such places a task in my hands, neither do I know that the task is *not* that of keeping my consciousness in one piece. And if my passion cannot overcome the suspicion that this consciousness is unreal, an abstraction, an illusion, or a mere apparition in empty space, whose fault will that be?

Part (2) of the objection is a shade less personal and more world-minded or civilization-minded than part (1) and expresses a seasoned conviction as to what the human consciousness ought to be busy at. A response to it in terms of the Climacian picture might begin by noting that the cartoon-notion of a whole society devoted to sweeping and dusting the individual consciousness is a polemical distortion of a task which belongs to an individual in such an unpublic way that not even the nosiest and most despotic theocracy could pretend to oversee it. Secondly, does such a task really represent a collapse of, or a lapsing from, civilization? Conceived as a task, it represents my cognizance of the unknowns of life, and only a very strange table of priorities or some highly unusual circumstance could induce a person to abandon his known public responsibilities in order to attend to his most private one, especially since, as indicated earlier, we are speaking of the kind of passion that can bide its time.

Is there a problem about the God's existence?

We come now to one of the more portentous transitions in Chapter III, where Climacus proposes we assign the name *the God* to this Unknown, this vacuity that stops the thinking man in his striving to explain his failure. This move introduces a brief but extraordinarily consequential discussion of existence-proofs. Before we attempt its decompression, a word is needed concerning what the 'metaphysical crotchet' is all about. Inasmuch as the term 'metaphysics' has been extended to take in a very diversified family of philosophical doings, it is helpful to keep in mind that Climacus is concerned with a restricted range of metaphysical issues: how best to construe the use of 'the God' and related words. The metaphysical thesis of the chapter has already been set forth: that is, the Unknown, or the God, is something that cannot be thought; it is a blank to the reasoner. The crotchet will consist in Climacus's crabby intolerance of any compromises on this point, such as one can find in the great tradition of philosophical theology or theistic philosophy, while at the same time he speaks *knowingly* of this Unknown in expressions drawn from everyday religious language. This quirk or kink or apparent inconsistency constitutes the crotchet.

The God, then, is to be simply our name for this Unknown. A rupture with tradition comes immediately afterward when Climacus says it would scarcely occur to reason to demonstrate the God's existence. In one respect this is easy to see, for the existence of *this* God, or of what we have been calling the Unknown, is established through the thinker's collisions with it, and to demand an existence-proof would indicate merely that the person had not whipped himself to the collision-point. However, this is too quick. Climacus uses a much-quoted two-part aphorism to explain the aloofness that his kind of existential thinker feels toward the demand for proofs. If the God does not exist, he remarks, it would be impossible to prove he does, and if he does, folly to attempt a proof. The first part is a sort of tautology, but the rest calls for careful unbraiding.

In what sense folly? Evidently the author means a thoughtless waste of energy, for the proof would have no use. Let us begin by supposing I, the demonstrator, desire the proof for myself. But then in starting my proof I presuppose the God's existence in my realization that if he did not exist I could not prove he did. Suppose on the other hand I set out to prove it for the sake of friend X, who does not presuppose it, and I mean to be careful not to let *my* presupposition creep into the proof! At this point Climacus's strategy begins to define itself, for if my aim is to assist a doubter, what exactly does he doubt? Does he doubt that there is an Unknown which his reason, pushed to the limit, will bump up against? If he does not doubt this, there is no use for the proof, since *the God* is just a name for that stopper.

But what if he doubts there is such a limit, and I wish to assure him with a proof? It would be wise to slow up at this point, where so many strong traditional lines intersect, for example, Anselm, Aquinas, and Descartes, who present their demonstrations with doubters, atheists, infidels, fools, and others in mind. Here one can hardly miss the fact that Climacus passes by the atheistic and agnostic positions without a word of either sympathy or reproof, as if they were unreal, contrived, make-believe, or confused positions scarcely worth his notice. It would be hasty, however, to blame this omission on oversight. That is, if the reader joins Climacus in regarding *the God* as just a name for that unknown something, then a denial or doubt of the God's existence will appear precisely as a confusion, at best perhaps an unfinished movement of thought, and the idea of answering it with a demonstration will strike him as an instance of Kant's jaunty description of folly: one man milking the he-goat while the other holds a sieve underneath.

As Climacus presents the matter, an expression of *denial* or *doubt* that the Unknown exists would be an exceedingly queer thing for a human to come out with. What could it mean to deny it, unless to say flatly that nothing exists the like of which is unknown to the sayer? But what occasion could a human stumble upon for saying that? Consider now the weaker case, where someone merely doubts that there is an Unknown. What can this mean? The concept of the Unknown in the *Fragments* comes out of an individual's striving and failing to account for his failure to ascertain the Truth. The limit in question is a limit to *his* ability to make intelligible *his* failure to arrive at the Truth about *himself*. If this is so, his doubt would amount to doubting that he would ever encounter such a limit if he tried, which is a loose recapitulation of the Socratic morning-glow optimism, and which throws it back upon the individual himself to make good the boast. At any rate it would be beside the point to offer him a proof that some generalized or metaphysical limit of thought exists, such as 'the mystical' or 'the unsayable' in Wittgenstein's *Tractatus Logico-Philosophicus*. The only unknown that matters here is the one that stands silent behind that personal slap, that is, expresses its existence in relation to a flesh and blood person's movement toward self-understanding.

Climacus, we were observing, leaves atheism and agnosticism without so much as a mention, as confusions, and this swift bypass of seemingly substantive positions may strike us as sleight-of-hand. First, if they are confusions, how can we avoid saying the same about the *theistic* position they are opposed to, and about Climacus's own version of theism which speaks perhaps too mellifluously in terms of 'he' and 'him' when it speaks of the God? The answer implicit in the *Fragments* is that theism, too, as traditionally understood, represents a confused way of construing everyday expressions that have to do with God. The philosophies that speak of God as the all-perfect being, the first unmoved mover, the *ens necessarium*, and similar things, and affirm that there exists or must exist such a one, have just as little to be said for them as do the contrary positions. Unless we bear this in mind, the radical nature of Climacus's crotchet will almost certainly escape us. He does not bypass atheism and agnosticism by declaring for a species of theism, which would simply pave the way for new stalemates, but treats them as the offspring of theism and bypasses that, too.

The violent metaphysical turn in Chapter III (and I use the term 'metaphysical' to characterize Climacus's own position, since he calls his own crotchet by that name) consists in two things. First, he helps himself to the common ways of using the word 'God' as we observed before, permitting himself to speak of the God the way Socrates does when he stays with this speech of common folk in these matters, and secondly, by insisting on using the God merely as a name for the Unknown, he dissociates himself from various forms of theism, along with their supporting metaphysical terminologies, and likewise from atheistic and agnostic denials of theism. We shall come back to this crotchet later.

The discussion takes a quarter-turn here if we speak of proving not that the God exists, but that some existent or other is the God. In this variation the demonstrator takes the existent as his starting point, its existence having been established at a prior stage, and then identifies this existent with the God. Now, if I were to attempt this by taking the Unknown, in Climacus's sense, as my given existent, and seeking to prove that *it* is the God, an awkwardness would trouble the proceedings, for this Unknown is and remains a blank. I can, of course, go the next step with Climacus and decide to *call* this Unknown *the God*. However, to speak of *proving* that it is the God would lack coherence. Would it mean, for example, that I prove a match between attributes of the God and of the Unknown? But this Unknown is characterless, else it would be somewhat known. How, then, shall I prove a match?

Let us try another way. Perhaps I have assembled in one way or another an account of some existent, call it the first in the chain of efficient causes, the source of order in nature, or something similar. May I not then coherently seek to prove that this, which does or must exist, is none other than the God? For Climacus the answer is apparently No. To begin with, we should hardly call this a proof of existence. 'Very well,' I reply, 'call it something else, but in any event I mean to prove

64

that this existent (which I will not call the Unknown, but instead the first cause or principle of governance) can be none other than the God. In other words, I aim to squeeze from our concept of this existent the unobvious information that it is identical with the God, and by so doing I will show, *contra* Climacus, that *the God* is not just a name he attaches to some fading-point of reason but is rather the name of an entity, a being that exists in its own right just as surely as the existent we start with'.

However, before investing too much of myself in this piece of work, it would be wise to look twice at the blueprint. In my right hand, I hold the concept of something, say an uncaused cause, of whose existence I am on whatever grounds quite certain; in my left, my concept of the God, whose existence I take to be in question. I now aim to show that the God must exist since he is none other than that uncaused cause. It all seems quite clear and has appeared so to more than one philosopher of indisputably first rank. Just at this point we run up against Climacus's summary judgment that to attempt such a proof would be folly. Let us begin our analysis by repeating the crotchet he places at the heart of Chapter III: *our concept of the God is correct only in so far as it coincides with the concept of the Unknown*. Expressions of doubt as to whether the Unknown *exists* are otiose, and therefore proofs of its existence have no office, satisfy no genuine need. The same holds true, then, concerning doubts of the God's existence since, again, 'the God' is just a name for that Unknown. Efforts to prove it exists brand themselves as folly in the sense of pointless undertakings since their end-products, the proofs, serve no purpose.

Now if Climacus's position here is sound, there is something very natural and persuasive about the opposing tendency of thought. This tendency may be expressed as follows: '"The Unknown" would be a seriously misleading name for the God, for it is possible to know a little, perhaps very, very little, about the God, or about the being we mean or refer to when we speak of God. In fact, men do know a little something, and precisely at this point we can invoke Climacus against himself. We have already seen how he plucks expressions like "the blessed God" out of the public air and without a word of apology. Not just the *name* "God," mind you, but *attributes* of the God figure in his reasonings, as, for example, where he says it would be a contradiction to suppose anything lower could interfere with the God's creative intention

65

(p. 18). So Climacus himself trades on some knowledge of the God! And more than just minimal knowledge, too, when you add it all up, for the Project and Poem alike treat of the God much as the common language of the religion does: as a being outside of human woes, immune to time's attritions, all-knowing, infinitely powerful, all glory and majesty. No, Climacus hardly lives up to his own crotchet, which is probably why it is a crotchet'.

Our discussion has now begun to turn on the content of those common religious expressions which Climacus simply appropriates to suit his purposes, and which the philosophers he is challenging deck out in their stiffer canonical terminologies. More specifically, it turns on whether or not having that language in hand, as we all do, and employing it, amounts to *knowing a little something about the God*. If it does, then Climacus's equation of the God and the Unknown is wrongheaded. If the equation holds, however, then laboring to prove the God's existence would be folly, a pointless gesture aimed at assuaging doubts that are at bottom confusions. If it does not hold, then theism comes back on stage to resume its shouting matches with atheism and agnosticism.

Our task now is to puzzle out a reply to the opposition along lines Climacus has already laid down. In attempting this I will be departing more than once from his ways of speaking, though not, I think, from his intent, and taking sidepaths opened up by Wittgenstein in his *Philosophical Investigations*.

To start with, it is quite true that Climacus helps himself to ordinary reverent language involving 'God' and uses it unselfconsciously wherever it suits him. He uses it as people of guarded speech use it everywhere and teach their children to use it. If this seems a risky generalization, I ask the reader's patience for now and merely remind him that it is common for parents to correct children whose speech concerning God is slighting or otherwise out of line. Now, from this it would appear that the ordinary language of religion *lays claim* (or its users do), whether justly or not, to a pretty substantial stock of *knowings*, any and every bit of which may be said to tip the scale decisively against Climacus and his crotchet. That is, the "unknownness" he places so much weight on does not at any rate keep individuals from knowing what is right and wrong to say concerning the object of their worship. For instance, one can know that words like 'mighty' and 'almighty' go

66

with seemly uses of the word 'God', but that 'feeble' and 'feckless' do not. This fact may make Climacus's stand look all the more quirky and pettifogging. Here, however, one must take special care to observe his thematic warning against haste, and above all not to take at face value what might appear to be pieces of substantive information. What is their substance, these knowings, whereof are they made? I mean the knowing that the God can do all things, is not hobbled by human hobbles, sees all things, and so on?

Here I want to introduce a possibility consistent with the *Fragments* position, though not expressed there in these terms, namely that these knowings are *grammatical*, that they are compressed or elliptical reminders of correct ways of employing language that connects with the concept of deity in everyday life. This sense of the term 'grammatical' comes from Wittgenstein, and although his applications of it in the philosophy of religion are very sparse, it may help if we begin with a couple of his remarks. At one point he writes: "*Essence* is expressed by grammar. . . . Grammar tells us what kind of object anything is."* That is, one can gather what kind of being anything is by remarking how the word for it is used, the various expressions we couple it with, the linguistic company it keeps, and the occasions and purposes of its use. So, too, with everyday religious language, and in particular the word 'God'. One can tell something of what kind of being the God is by noticing the ways in which his name figures in discourse.

In another work, Wittgenstein writes:

> "You can't hear God speak to someone else, you can hear him only when you are the one spoken to [*wenn du der Angeredete bist*]"—that is a grammatical remark.**

It is easy to imagine circumstances in which a parent might use the sentence in quotes in an informal teaching situation. In what sense, though, is it a grammatical remark, that is, a remark about what the linguistic proprieties are when one uses the word 'God'? To point this up, imagine a child puzzled by his mother's forever using such expres-

---

*Ludwig Wittgenstein, *Philosophical Investigations*, trans. G. E. M. Anscombe (New York: Macmillan, 1953), pt. 1, secs. 371, 373.

**Ludwig Wittgenstein, *Zettel*, trans. G. E. M. Anscombe (Oxford: Basil Blackwell, 1967), par. 717.

sions as 'God tells me such-and-such' and 'I asked God to give me a hint'. The child asks, "But if he talks to you, why can't *I* hear him?" The sentence cited by Wittgenstein informs the child that when 'God' is the subject of 'to speak' it can be quite in order if the speaking is unpublic and strictly one-to-one, though doubtless something would be out of order if the subject were the *paterfamilias* or the lady next door. This bit of the 'grammar' of the word 'God' is, of course, tied up with other bits, for example, that God has more possibilities than the rest of us for getting things done. This in its turn is a grammatical remark, condensing a great deal of casual instruction about what is fitting and what is not among possible expressions alluding to the power associated with a deity.

Thus a sentence expressing divine power may function in the language rather like the thumbworn sentence, 'Caesar's wife must be above suspicion', although the analogy has hollow spots as well. That is, in suitable circumstances the sentence about Caesar's wife can be employed to mean: 'Unless you're a damn fool, you watch very carefully the kinds of things you say about the wife of the high panjandrum'. Under the influence of formal semantics, where so much about language gets decided on the basis of cat-on-the-mat examples, a thinker might feel moved to insist that every indicative sentence as such purports to give information about its subject. Overriding that, it seems plain enough that the sentence about Caesar's wife can be *used* to steer someone away from employing a wide assortment of expressions and not to inform him at all about what Caesar's wife is like. It can function, in other words, to epitomize some ins and outs of prudent linguistic behavior.

If we narrow our range of examples to straight catechetical teachings, where theologians (often in partnership with theistic philosophers) have laid their characteristic patina over everyday speech, our point about grammar becomes plainer. Here the grammar, the norms of seemly and, by contrast, unseemly usage, get boiled down to flash card dimensions. With the help of such flash cards, youngsters are taught that God is all-good, all-seeing, and the like. The question, 'What *kind* of knowings are these?' does not arise for the child, nor the question, 'How are they employed? What are we to do with them?' In the main we have no reason for, hence no training in, distinguishing grammatical from substantive knowings or sorting out our knowings

68

according to their function. In philosophy it is different, and Climacus addresses himself first and last to the student of philosophy whose maturing critical faculty produces such questions in great number, the good with the bad.

To the philosopher, then, who asks, 'What kind of knowings are these?', we could reply, 'They are grammatical. They are elixirs of the grammar of the word "God"; each of them is a précis of the kinds of expressions it is appropriate for our kind to couple with that word or with thoughts of God; they are markers to show where the appropriate leaves off'. If we ask how these knowings function, or what we are given this set of flash cards for, an answer might begin: to learn guidelines for the grammar of 'God', to help keep our discourse meet and chaste.

With this much to begin on, and aware that more will need to be said about this notion of grammatical knowledge, we return to the problem at hand. How does Climacus, while making use of all the knowings compacted in those flash cards and feeling as much at home with them as any Sunday School teacher, contrive to insist that *the God* is just a name we assign to a particular Unknown? What could possess him to insist that any softening of this crotchet will inevitably misdirect our thinking in metaphysics, that is, on questions of how ordinary religious expressions are to be understood or analyzed? In order to view Climacus's position with the lights turned up brightest, let us pick one of those knowings at random, for instance that the God is all-powerful. Now if I turn my reflection to this knowing, not with a view to disputing it (since the issue here between Climacus and the theistic philosopher in no way puts the knowing in doubt), but with a view to settling what *sort* of knowing it is, I may next ask myself, granted the God is all-powerful, 'What is an all-powerful being like?' Well, what *is* it like? I don't know. I cannot answer. I haven't, as we say, had the pleasure. And with this reply I am right back with Climacus and his Unknown, for my knowing is only skin-deep.

It would, of course, be naive to imagine that we can put the issue to rest here, before the theistic philosopher has had his very cogent say. Nor is it possible for us to foresee all his possible moves in these pages. One such move, however, is quite predictable, and I would like now to imagine how a theistic philosopher might make it.

He might say, 'No more than yourself can I express what an all-powerful being is like, if by "like" you mean resembling some specifiable creature of juggernaut strength and onrush. That sort of likeness is undercut anyway by the teaching that God is not a body. I ask you, though, to remember that there are likes and likes, and we need assign no *a priori* limit to how far the notion of likeness can be stretched. Therefore my admission, namely that I cannot say what such a being would be like, does not wipe out all possibility of likeness, even to the last faint likeness of a likeness. Indeed, as some philosophers have pointed out, the notion of likeness has to be stretched almost clear out of sight in order to explain how we can infinitize an earthly adjective such as "powerful" and apply it *significantly* to deity.

'Yet we do predicate significantly, and Climacus uses those predications with as much facility as the next man. Granted, the powers they attribute to the God bear only the shadow of a likeness to powers as we know them. But—and this is the key point—the God's powers *must* be at least that much like ours, that is the very least they *can* be, if we are to regard our knowing as true or as *meaningful*. And the expedient reference to "grammatical" knowledge is of very little help, for it nowhere cuts deeply enough. Doubtless our knowings do mirror the religious language used by well-spoken people; it would be disturbing if they failed in that. However, and all the same, knowings about the correct conventions of speech are one thing, knowings about the God another. Therefore Climacus should either disown the knowings themselves, which he refuses to do, or else give up his crotchet and treat them honestly as substantive knowings, even if this gets him into toilsome disputes with the rest of us concerning the *foundations* of our knowledge about the God'.

This reply contains certain features of the primary theistic line of thought opposed to Climacus. Only a clumsy and coarse-grained sketch of that line could fit into one book, not to speak of one chapter, as anyone who knows its literature will understand. However, it is not meant as a conspectus but as the first reaction of a philosopher who thinks in theistic terms. I now want to make a few observations about it in a manner I believe Climacus would approve.

First of all, the theistic position just informally introduced is more in line than Climacus's with traditional norms of reasonableness as those are understood by philosophers. Theism, or the doctrine that reason can come to know a little something about the God over and above grammatical proprieties, is akin to the Socratic position in Chapter I, yet manages in certain schools to keep company with the Moment-idea as well. Here I would like to argue, concerning the rationale of the common use of words such as 'God', that Climacus presents a coherent alternative to the theistic position.

In the minds of many theistic philosophers, to treat the word 'God' as simply a name for the Unknown would appear to threaten or becloud the status of their knowings about God, embodied in the common language and rubbed to a harder finish by theology and theistic philosophy. How can our words be *true* of God if they merely chalk out the linguistic boundaries beyond which it becomes daring, unseemly, silly, profane, or blasphemous to say this or that of the God? Unless the chalk-lines express for us, even if only in the most pallid and minimal way, what the God is really like, unless they are in some least manner *describing* the God, how can we justify placing any weight on them, or, for that matter, on the reverent conventions they mirror?

In reply, perhaps the most straightforward approach would be this. Concerning the common teaching about God's omnipotence we ask: How is it used? Call it if you like information, truth, knowledge, Climacus does not care to dispute the point—but what do people do with it? What role does it play in discourse? If we look we shall see that it is used in various ways to chart certain coastlines of everyday human discourse. It is used catechetically and formally to teach souls where those limits lie, and on occasion as corrective, admonition, or caution against going beyond them. Once having seen this, one is measurably less inclined to think that people are doing something extraordinarily hard to do, and staggeringly hard to justify, when they 'predicate a property' of the God, for as a matter of fact nothing could be much easier to do or justify than what people actually do with such predications. A schoolboy's tongue-twister is ten times more difficult.

At this point it would be good to give the objector a few free throws. 'You yourself have described your position as slightly antic', he might begin, 'so I suppose there is no use in my asking why a person of critical bent should put on those ordinary God-fearing ways of talking. Instead let me be more direct. More than one great philosopher has expressed the thought that the whole religious thing, call it the Moment or whatever you wish, falls to pieces unless a God exists. Now you have clearly set yourself apart from thinkers who start by proving the existence of a remote something or other, say a first cause, and go on to say that that is what men mean by "God". "No," you reply, "what men mean by God is the Unknown, and since no serious person doubts that there *is* such a thing, the problem about existence is no problem at all."

'However, brave as this may sound, washing one's hands of the existence-problem is no simple matter, and to explain the point let me make use of your own terms. Time and again you speak of human reason *colliding* or *bumping* against something, or being *stopped* by it. The exact words do not matter, for the phenomenon is familiar enough: the individual's failure to reach the Truth and to account for his failure. And you think that by alluding to this experience—and calling it a collision with the Unknown—you have pretty well put the *coup de grace* to doubts about the God's existence. But, of course, there was no necessity in the first place for calling the experience a collision or anything else that presupposes a *something* encountered. How then do you make the transition from a psychologically jarring experience of bafflement to a *something* that cannot be thought? Or to *an* Unknown if you prefer, or to an unknown *one*? From the way you have expressed yourself, it seems the God is nothing but a name we assign to man's unsearchable puzzlement. This, as I read it, brings you close to positions that frankly and openly psychologize the concept of Deity and leave it at that (so close that I am at a loss to see how you square it with your tolerance of the ordinary uses of the word "God," not to mention the idea of a living God that rings through the Project and Poem)'.

These remarks, it seems to me, point up some important disquietudes that can arise when a theistic philosopher threads his way through Chapter III. The first of these concerns Climacus's readiness to use everyday worshipful expressions as if the existence of an object of worship posed no real problem. His grounds for doing this, if I understand him, can be put very briefly: those everyday expressions are metaphysically and doctrinally noncommital. That is, they embody no judgment of existence except the existence of a particular Unknown, doubts of which would be mere verbal dust-devils. It is not that people take the existence of the God (the Unknown) on 'faith'—a word Climacus has scrupulously held in reserve—but rather that the *content* of their language, that is, the concept of a God that one can extract from how the word 'God' is used, is equivalent to Climacus's concept of the Unknown.

72

The second disquietude is more complicated. While in a certain sense, as the objector points out, everything religious depends on the existence of a God, it does not follow that anything religiously important depends on *demonstrating* the existence of a God. Nor does it follow that the alternative to establishing it by means of a proof or evidence is to accept it on *faith*. Climacus's merit here lies in his presenting a third possibility which, if it can withstand objections of the sort we are considering, represents an arresting stride forward in the philosophy of religion. This third possibility seems to be coiled up in his dense remark that 'God' is not a name but a concept (p. 51). If the concept of Deity implicit in reverent ways of speaking is of a kind that shows doubts of the God's existence to be hollow and muddled, then to placate such doubts by taking them at their face value would only second the confusion. Among Christian thinkers it has been part and parcel of philosophical good manners so to regard them, and no small part of the difficulty those thinkers meet in reading Climacus can be laid to his apparent defection from politeness, his impatience with honestly meant tenders of doubt.

The third source of disquietude stems from the fact that without so much as an embarrassed clearing of the throat Climacus speaks of the thinker's failure and bafflement in terms of an encounter with a non-human *entity*. A queer sort of corrosion would appear to threaten the concept of Deity (as laid up in common language no less than in theological analysis) if on being asked 'What is this God of which you speak?' Climacus obliged himself to reply: 'The God is an individual's inability to account for his failure to get at the Truth'. For one thing, and just on the face of it, there seems no clear sense in which the words on our catechetical flash cards, for instance 'all-powerful', could be fastened on to this inability. Certainly, if Climacus is on the right track it must be for reasons that most theistic philosophers, whose watchword for the most part has been politeness, have scarcely dared bring forth.

We agree that it would be wholly out of character for Climacus to reply that the God *is* man's inability to account for his failure. The tendency to ask point-blank what the God is, or what the word means, is precisely what he wishes to turn us away from when he calls 'God' a concept rather than a name, with the suggestion that acquiring command of that concept (or, as we expressed it earlier, getting clear as to

how God-expressions function) involves considerably more than pro-
viding a description to go with a name. To use a twentieth-century
philosophical idiom, certain concepts are so enmeshed in the human
form of life that to remind ourselves of the part they play comes very
near to reviewing the basics of being a man. In this sense the concept
of God is not a very accommodating one. The analyst of concepts cannot walk around it any more than he can walk around his own life and
capture its essence in a quick diagram.

With regard to the concept 'God', Climacus aims to steer his readers
away from a spurious and primitive norm of clearness. To prepare for
what he has to say, it will be helpful to restate the objector's central
question: How does Climacus move from the experience of bafflement
(which any thinker with the heart for it may duplicate for himself,
though not necessarily within the hour) to the idea that it constitutes a
collision with an unknown *something*? Does he do so, for example, by
postulating a Deity in the manner of Kant, a God that *has to be* in order
to round out a coherent picture of human life?* By no means, and the
contrast is important enough to warrant our pausing here, for it throws
light on the tie-up between Climacus's Unknown and the common use
of God-expressions. The God of the *Fragments* does not *have* to be, nor
have to conform to any specification laid down on the principle that
'human reason demands such-and-such'. Quite the reverse. Climacus
all along speaks of this Unknown as having ways of its own which are
evidently not like the thinking man's ways, or man's ways at all, since
it first enters into man's life as a frustration of those ways. This is the
key difference between Climacus's concept of the God and what Pascal
calls 'the God of the philosophers'.

'That may be well worth pointing out', the objector might interrupt,
'and perhaps you can get some mileage out of bunching all godly-
minded philosophers together, but among the theistic ones you will
find a certain stubborn unanimity on one point. We are somewhat jealous about preserving what I shall call the *entity* of God, his substance
or reality apart from and over against any shortness of breath that
might trouble our minds. Our *minds*, I repeat, for up to now you have
not attributed to this Unknown any reality beyond that of a state of
mental panting'.

---

*Immanuel Kant, *Critique of Practical Reason*, trans. Lewis White Beck (Indi-
anapolis and New York: Liberal Arts Press, 1956), bk. 2, chap. 2, sec. 5, pp. 128–36.

By way of reply let us look further into Climacus's concept of the Unknown. Having done with the subject of existence-proofs, he returns on page 55 to this unknown something that reason yearns to think but that cannot be thought. As far as any individual thinker is concerned, it exists rightly enough as a limit to how far he can figure himself out, but since it does not give itself to him in the manner of this or that existent, common or rare, it is to that extent or by that measure as good as nothing at all, a point that is sure to raise the objector's eyebrows.* With this hint that the plunge into silence leaves nothing at all to discuss publicly, not even a blind collision, it is important to remember that the thinker Climacus has in mind will not close out his interest in the unknowings we have been calling A, B, and C. To leave off bothering himself about them would be the equivalent, in social terms, of cutting someone dead, namely himself, an act no less passional than the most ardent embrace. If his reason, at least in its custodial role of sorting out experience and tidying up its manifold, hears a rumble of its own downfall in the fact that he is left, paradoxically, with only the unexpected to count on, he will not on that account cease to have dealings with the Unknown.

Dealings with what? With the utterly unexpected, the 'absolutely different'. This is Climacus's alternative expression for the Unknown, and unhelpful as the phrase might at first appear, it puts us in a better position to answer an objector who suspects Climacus of leaning unfairly on the metaphor of collision—when there seems nothing substantial to collide with. In the first place, 'absolutely different' disavows any aim of interiorizing the Unknown, that is, of identifying it with a state of mind such as bafflement or with the brainchildren of an inventive consciousness. Classically, the most gratuitous and insubstantial of fictions, the chimera, is very far from being the blind incogitable *limit* intended by a phrase like 'absolutely different'. Secondly, even if we grant Climacus's unwillingness to interiorize the God, how does he avoid doing so? In other words, what justifies his movement from a

---

*While we are on this point, the Unknown of the *Fragments* should not be run together with *epistemological* unknowns or unknowables such as Kant's *Ding-an-sich* or the Unknowable in Herbert Spencer's *First Principles*. Briefly stated, the difference lies in the fact that Climacus's kind of thinker stands in a personal relationship to the particular Unknown that thwarts *his* chosen approach to the Truth, which concerns not the objects of knowledge in general (the quarry of the scientific community) but the answers to A, B, and C for himself.

limit to man's ability to solve himself to the habit of speaking of an unthinkable *something* totally different from man? The transition itself is
easy enough to describe. Climacus, with Socrates in mind, simply
makes use of ordinary God-expressions, which reflect a ban on man's
identifying himself or confusing himself with the God and which
speak of the God's being other than man and also having ways of his
own which are not dependent on what humans happen to think. A
thoughtless acceptance of those conventions, whose grammar, as we
noted earlier, agrees with that of Climacus's coinage *the Unknown*,
overlooks their actual uses (such as stencilling the limits of respectful
usage) and would treat them as substantive knowledge-claims that
need some shoring up. Here we may remind ourselves that it is as idle
as thumbing my nose in the dark to doubt there exists something the
like of which is unknown to me. Existence is *affirmed*, if you will, or
included in worshipful language which is aimed at its God; the question concerning existence finds itself choked off there. Similarly, the
otherness of the God and the ways he has of his own remain bound up
with the common language. All that theism could ask for concerning
the God's substance is contained in that language, but not in such a
way that theism or *knowings about the God* can be squeezed out of it.

The idea, then, is not that Climacus has a reply to the objector's demand to produce an unknown something, but that the objection lacks
cogency and should not be met directly. To make this point more
clearly, let us go back to the mother's use of the sentence 'You can't
hear God speak to someone else, you can hear him only if you are the
one spoken to'. Call that sentence S. Now concerning her use of S
much can be said. First and on the face of it, she is out to correct a
wrong expectation when she nudges the child away from expecting to
overhear God. If he grows up to be a philosopher, it may interest him to
remember how he was once flimflammed by a likeness in surface
grammar between 'I'm waiting for a hint from God' and, for example,
'I'm waiting for a hint from Godfrey'. The mother's use of S is bound up
also with the more systematic but no less grammatical teaching that
God is not a body, or is a spirit, so that in using S she is roughing out for
the child the first unshaded contours of the concept 'spirit'.

Speaking now of what *she* does with S, does it stand in need of
deeper sanction, proofs, foundational theology, a theory of predication,
or anything of the sort? Her use of S is anchored quite solidly upon the

human practice of passing on instruction to the young, in this instance grammatical instruction. If the objector asks what feature of reality makes her concept of God superior to or truer than the child's, one could answer that hers coincides with the concept of a certain Unknown to a greater degree than the child's, which leans childishly toward analogies with the known, for example, the immanent uses of words such as 'hint', 'speak to', and 'overhear'. Nor should it be objected that the mother's ways of speaking are too biblical or covenantal (in their suggestion that God takes an interest in the individual) to be typical of the everyday language of religion. Our point could be made, that is, from examples which carry no biblical overtones, for example, from the remarks of Red Cloud to a U.S. Commissioner in 1870:

> "You make all the ammunition: all I ask is enough for my people to kill game. The Great Spirit has made all things that I have in my country wild. I have to hunt them. . . ."*

What the objector demands an underpinning for, as nearly as I can make out, is a formula that in his mind captures the essential sense and purport of S and countless other sentences containing God-expressions. Formulas of this kind can be found in great number. They run something like: 'making statements about God', 'predicating properties of the transcendent', 'expressing putative truths about the supposed reality God', and (Kant's idiom) 'making judgments which go beyond possible experience'. If we look at S through one or another of these formulas, it is natural to feel that users of S ought to have on hand an existence-proof or other designative device that will certify as real the supposed reality they are talking about.

What needs justification and shoring up, it seems, is not the mother's use of S at all, but the objector's formula for what S purports to say. It would be shortsighted to call such a formula gratuitous, as if it bore no relation at all to actual uses of God-expressions. However, one could suggest that it bears to those the same relation as a person's shadow bears to his substance. That is, the formula is a sort of logical shadow cast by S and innumerable other sentences with 'God' in them, a sil-

*Dee Brown, *Bury My Heart at Wounded Knee: An Indian History of the American West* (New York: Holt, Rinehart, and Winston, 1971), p. 180.

houette thrown by those sentences *when nobody is using them.* When lifted out of their habitats and looked at all by themselves, such sentences present a characteristic shape: for the most part 'God' is a subject term, and each sentence has some words in the predicate position. What could be easier than to suppose that those sentences have the function of 'predicating something of the transcendent'? What else could one say about their function when they are not functioning? Yet it is like saying that the function of handles is to be handled, of dials to be twirled, of typewriter keys to be depressed. And this is our complaint against the kind of formulas philosophers put together to represent the everyday uses of God-expressions: the formulas never get close enough to that language to describe what we should want to call its *uses.*

To make the most of this, consider again the mother's use of S. Whether in the actual use of God-expressions a formula such as 'making statements about God' has itself a *bona fide* use or not we may leave an open question. Either way, or even if we assume it has, there is one use it does not have. Pore over it all I please, I can't make it disclose to me what that mother is doing with S. I cannot by scrutinizing the philosophical formula discern that in using S she is disabusing the youngster of a wrong expectation and thereby bringing his concept of God into tighter alignment with her own. For all the formula tells me, she might as well be concocting the coarsest or goofiest 'statement about God'—God is dead! God is out to lunch! The formula tells me nothing of how watchfully she checks her speech to avoid misleading the child. And, of course, it fails to inform me at all that what she is relaying to the child is a piece of grammar pure though not simple. To observe even this much of what she does with S, we have to ignore the formula along with the *a priori* ratiocination that went into it, for the mother's use of S stands outside of it. The formula in no way captures or contains what she does with S. It would be courting trouble to lay it down that no one ever 'makes a statement about God' in the sense of those formulas, although arguably the mother in using S does not. However, if someone should propose that she comes close to doing so in her remark to the child, our approach will be to decide by looking, but not at a formula.

To complete the case for his crotchet, Climacus finds a logical pitfall lying in wait for any thinker who consistently seeks to express the dif-

ference between the God and man in terms of the extraordinary instead of acknowledging it as a limit of comprehension. Suppose a
thinker wishes to characterize the Unknown as something exceptional
or astonishing, like a once-in-a-lifetime or just about unheard-of phenomenon. The range of human invention lies open to him and is already wildly represented in pantheons of old. When he becomes impa-
tient with himself for inventing gods, what course remains but to close
the gap between the Unknown and the perfectly ordinary, for instance,
a neighbor's child passing his window? This knowledge, too, will be
only make-believe.

Each of these two predicaments stands for a mistaken way of taking
hold of the concept of God. Commentators appear not to have noticed
their resemblance to theism and atheism respectively, although these
are evidently what the whole crotchet is about. Theism, along with
polytheistic variants of lesser importance in philosophy, forms the sentence "God is good' but, forgetting its grammatical nature, construes it
as a knowing about the God, and aims to grasp it quite naturally in
terms of what men already know. Such interpretations by theistic philosophers are much less crude than those of idolaters, taking, for example, mind or soul or governance as their ground rather than visible
forms, but the principle is the same: the Unknown (the God) in the
language of transcendence is to be characterized in terms of what is
known to us. By all odds the most exquisitely turned-out specimen of
this tendency, as well as the most hedged with safeguards against
grossness and also the most supple, is the Thomistic doctrine of analogy, which finds the ground for ordinary uses of God-expressions in
the endlessly ductile concept of Being and assigns, therefore, an important place to existence-proofs.

On the other side, atheism proposes to do away with the Unknown.
Like theism it grasps the language of transcendence wrongly as a set
of substantive knowing-claims, only it finds nothing to be said for
them. So grasped, they prod a thinker to look about for the Number
One Oddity, but like the Russian cosmonaut he discovers only the ordinary. *Ergo*, the Unknown does not exist, the God's worshippers are
wonderfully fooled, and the atheistic thinker may wear the breastpin of
the undeceived.

Both sides pay a price for the misconstruction they place on the
common uses of God-expressions. It costs them a clear view of how

that language is used and consequently how it ought to be understood. The painfulness of Climacus's crotchet lies in its injunction to theist and atheist alike to begin all over again and is proportioned to the amount a thinker has to unlearn.

With the crotchet now set forth, Climacus looks back upon it through the eyes of an imagined objector and then replies in a manner designed to make his own strategy in this chapter explicit. His objector finds crotcheteering to be exactly the word for what Climacus is doing, namely, peddling the idiosyncratic notion that there is but one correct way for philosophers to expound the concept of God. But it takes an extraordinary odyssey of thought to arrive at that conceit, which pretty well guarantees Climacus the distinction of being the only fellow who can discern the right course for metaphysics. A thinker who would keep up with Climacus must first of all empty his head of all notions of *likeness* between man and the God which might occur to him from reflecting on conventional ways of speaking. As if this were not enough, the next leg of the odyssey requires that he clear his mind of whatever *differences* he might be inclined to suppose exist between himself and the God. Yet subtracting the likenesses and differences that divide a given conception from other ones sounds like a sure way to arrive at nothing definite at all, or an X, an unknown, so the internal logic of the crotchet is consistent enough. But precisely here the objector feels impelled to protest that the resulting empty concept is not the same as *his* concept of the God.

In reckoning the force of Chapter III it would be a mistake, I believe, to take this objection lightly, or to imagine that its informal expression or the informal brief rebuttal by Climacus stamp it as a lightweight piece of thinking. Worlds of discourse turn upon it. Its arterial idea, shared by virtually the whole European tradition in philosophy, is that any well-wrought metaphysics of God that agrees with common religious language will contain some knowings about the God. To deny that idea, to equate the God with the utterly unknown or absolutely unlike, is what makes Climacus's position a reversal whose radical character cannot be appreciated unless one is aware of the profound sense of impoverishment it can generate in a traditional exponent of theism. To be in no way a doubter of the reality of God, yet to be in no way a theist either—and still to be a metaphysician—all this amounts to putting oneself forward as a thinker *sui generis*, or a crotcheteer.

Climacus's reply calls for minute study. His position, as the objector rightly observes, requires giving up a number of suppositions dear to the hearts of theistic philosophers and virtually emptying oneself of the quite modest-sounding idea that when philosophers speak of the God they know at least in some minimal way what sort of entity the God is, in case someone should demand an accounting. To have this snatched away is understandably disturbing. Aware of this fact, Climacus has ventured to characterize an alternative, proposing that the expression 'the God' is quite acceptable as a name we attach to a certain Unknown. However, as we have noted, he insists that this Unknown is the individual's *only* cognitive point of contact with the God and insists in the same breath that the Reason is wayward if it persists in trying to comprehend the God with the help of a scalar category such as *like* or *unlike*.

'What happens if you persist in that attempt?' Climacus asks. 'Suppose in your concern to know something about the God you begin with *likeness* on the principle, shared by many who seek after existence-proofs, that a proof would show at least Being in common between the eternal God and man, and that even if the God's eternal being is as different as you please from our own kind, so that the likeness *approaches* zero, its value is at any rate not *equal* to zero, and this trace-value is not only sufficient to make our talking about God significant, but quite enough besides to annul my point about absolute unlikeness. To this I would answer that it is perfectly in order for philosophers to attribute Being or existence to the God. That is, it is certainly correct to gather from worshipful language that its users acknowledge the Being of their object of worship. The mistake would lie in placing this result on file as a bit of knowledge about the God, namely that he possesses Being. If you do so, you will of course be prepared to forestall a number of confusions by saying how wondrously *unlike* our Being the God's is, though it remains none the less Being. But those unlikenesses, what of those? How will you speak of them? Well, the God's is eternal being, his power boundless power, and so on, as contrasted with ours. This, too, fits in with worshipful ways of speaking, or is, as we say, reverently *acknowledged* in those. However, as soon as we ask "What is *boundless* power like?" or "eternal being?" we again run into the glassy Unknown. That infinite sort of unlikeness is without any mark for us; we are unacquainted with the like of it. To treat our result as a case of knowing a little something is clearly overreaching ourselves. A difference with nothing to mark it off begins to sound like likeness all over again'.

Here someone might protest, 'But are you saying that to have Being in common with the God is to have *nothing* in common?'

It would be in character, I believe, for Climacus to answer in this way: 'If it matters that I have something in common with the God, well, both of us know English, and with close to parity at that, although you will quickly remind me that this presupposes we have Being in common. Precisely so, we have Being in common, the God and I. But having that, what have we? Here let us tolerate the possibility that the force of the assertion that we have Being in common is *grammatical*. In other words, 'the God', like your name and mine, has a place in language such as to make doubts about *existence* pointless. It is, for example, pointless to express doubts of my own existence and similarly pointless to doubt the God's. In the matter of my own existence my expression of doubt falls on its face, and since the only existence our *uses* of the God's name signify in philosophy is the existence of an Unknown which anyone with the time and stamina can place himself up against, doubts of the God's existence likewise lead nowhere. Thus, to say that I and the God have Being in common is to say that doubts of existence in both instances have at most a specious importunity'.

If Climacus's position is sound, one of its corollaries is of special interest in the philosophy of religion. That is, anthropomorphic elements in the ordinary (and scriptural) language of transcendence disappear altogether as a problem or as something one needs to take time out to justify. The contrary view arises from a long-lived and toughly rooted theory of language which, because its vulnerability goes mostly unnoticed, exercises imperious but veiled authority over theistic philosophies. At the heart of it is a tendency to view ordinary God-expressions not in their living features but, as mentioned earlier in this chapter, through a type of formula or sublimed logical silhouette which darkens those features. Thus, for example, observing that such and such attributes of deity turn up more or less as fixtures in common expressions of worship, one supposes the people who use those to be busy *describing* the God, or more generally *talking about* the God. If that is what people do with the word 'God', it is scarcely to be wondered that

82

philosophers ask how it is possible or what the 'logic' of it could possibly be. However, when we strip away this theory (which ranks very high among the presuppositions that Climacus chides his objector for clinging to) it becomes seriously questionable whether common religious expressions are ever used in the way the theory supposes, and indeed whether 'talking about God' goes on at all outside of philosophy. Yet so powerful is the grip of that theory and its formulas that many philosophers who are at the same time believers have felt a need to 'save' God-expressions by virtually incorporating them into the realm of poetry, or metaphor, or myth.

In the *Fragments*, Climacus is more immediately concerned with a different corollary of his position, which points straight to the Absolute Paradox. If 'the God' is only a name we assign to the Unknown and absolutely unlike, then man is dependent on this Unknown for *any and all* knowledge about itself, grammatical knowledge excepted. This is merely an alternative expression for the fact that it *is* absolutely unlike him, and this fact, too, can come to him only from the God. But even if it is handed to him that the God is absolutely unlike him, it is an eminently frictionless object he is handed—and here echoes an earlier premonition of reason's downfall. That the Unknown is simply unknown man can gather for himself; that it is also absolutely unlike him, unconditionally different from him, he lacks equipment for judging, and, if it is proclaimed to him, for understanding. Thus reason confronts, or rather collides with, something it cannot get on top of, walk around, or take in survey, so that it becomes enigmatic how man can possibly accommodate such a thing in his consciousness.

As soon as we ask ourselves how consciousness can secure a purchase on the idea of absolute unlikeness, the paradox mentioned in the title of this chapter begins to appear. What man derives from the God partakes of the God, a grammatical truism already expressed in the less comely remark that I and the God both know English, though it would be eccentric to suggest that this tells the whole story of our kinship. The source of the absolute unlikeness is therefore to be looked for in the human individual, and its category in Chapter I was Error or Sin, as applied to a creature whose distinction is that he is capable of harboring an opinion—whether it be the Truth or its opposite—on questions such as A, B, and C, and of fastening himself inexorably to that opinion. Here one can again be tempted into thinking the truth must be represented *somewhere* on earth, in the actual kaleidoscopic garden of human opinions where people are facing every which way, especially since the possible ways of answering A, B, and C boil down to a surveyable few (or so it might seem in the abstract, although there might nevertheless be something uniquely personal about each individual's Error). And here it will be particularly hard to fight off the original Socratic presupposition of Chapter I, Section A. This is part of the struggle Climacus demands of his reader.

How is the individual to become conscious of the absolute difference between himself and the God? It seems he must be informed of it, or helped to that consciousness by the God. Since man's life furnishes him no occasion for enunciating it, the question where such a notion could have come from gets answered by Climacus in terms of the Unknown, the headwaters of the unexpected, for which 'the God' is only a name we assign. This absolute difference is not something Climacus has left his reader unprepared for; it came in with the Error that had to be posited when Climacus backed off from the original Socratic assumption, and it finds new expression here in the categories of likeness and unlikeness. At this point, the intimation of reason's bankruptcy acquires a less muffled ring. What does the individual sense when, as Climacus puts it, he senses the downfall of reason? Not the negation of everyday truths about the weather or stock prices, much less the dynastic-cumulative ziggurat of knowledge built up by the scientific community. These stand off to one side, of interest here only insofar as some individual in Error thinks them the primary things his reason ought to busy itself about. The threatened element is not reason *per se* but something much dearer and closer to home, namely what the individual really thinks of himself in the sense discussed earlier. It is also his tenderest spot.

Because the absolute difference between man and the God is not a datum of perception, the consciousness of sin is indirect and shrouded. However, from steps already taken in the Project of Thought it is possible to indicate its content algebraically, that is, using variables the individual must fill in for himself. So formulated, the consciousness of sin will include these elements:

1. By self-examination the individual comes to know what he really thinks of himself and of whatever power is responsible for his existence.

2. By hearing or reading he discovers word that his opinion is a bondage and thereby learns also that another opinion exists.

3. By hearing or reading he becomes conscious that someone has presented himself as the way out of his bondage.

4. By self-examination he discovers a guilt connected with what he really thinks.

5. By examining what the other said he becomes conscious of the difference between himself and the other.

6. By confession he becomes conscious that as he persists in his own opinion he is now recoiling from the other.

7. By self-examination in the light of his confession he becomes conscious of a change in himself, such that he finds himself newly faced with a decision.

In a creature of my sort, then, Error can be such that what I really think concerning A, B, and C—questions which implicate the God in my opinion even though I abstain from naming him in the bill of particulars—is absolutely unlike the Truth, indeed, its very opposite. To become conscious that this is the way it stands with me, or to acquire what Climacus calls "the consciousness of sin," immediately puts me a full step ahead of Socrates, though hardly in a manner that does me credit.

The makings of the Absolute Paradox are now before us in full. The God makes himself exactly *like* me, a human being, in the pursuit of an understanding between us that begins with the disclosure that he is totally *unlike* me. Here is paradox or unexpectedness enough to tie the passionate thinker up in knots for a lifetime. However, there is a sequel. Now that the absolute and humanly undiscoverable unlikeness is revealed, the God who became exactly like me wishes to help me become exactly like himself while remaining the one I am.

With the question "Can such a paradox be conceived?" Climacus again weaves in his motif of warning against quick answers. This paradox contains elements quite beyond my understanding, if by that is meant not just the power to compose unprecedented word-sequences but to think them through and burn off any lingering mists in the second round of questioning. For example, this idea of becoming altogether like the God, yet remaining myself—I could not begin to say what its working out might entail, much less its culmination, since the idea has at its center the irreducibly Unknown. As for sensing the downfall of what I really think, how should such a sensing be described unless as a sort of repeated instinctive brushing away of any feelers the Paradox puts out, while yet feeling myself drawn to an understanding with it? —drawn, yet all but convinced that even if there is no happiness in what I really think, to throw my thinking-power on the mercy of the unexpected sounds unhappier still.

To fill out this picture of human thought almost but not quite willing its own demise, Climacus once more resurrects the analogue of love. In willing the other's happiness I will my own as well, but I will my own to drop to second place for the other's sake. To explain why a lover would subordinate self-love in this way, a reference to what love is like is all we need, and where a person fails to grasp the sense of it we say, 'He doesn't know what love is'. On the same principle, love's passion can go under and self-love come back on top when temptation wins out. So it is with the Paradox in relation to a human thinker, although the passion that unites them has yet to be characterized beyond this limping and spotty resemblance to falling in love.

Once Climacus gives full verbal expression to the Absolute Paradox, the crotchet of this chapter takes on a new intelligibility. The unknownness of the God, his absolute unlikeness, which is nothing more or less than the Error of Chapter I set in a metaphysician's type-font, is essential to the individual's beholding the Paradox unobscured, so that it may be remembered as having been the wholly unexpected or as something that thought could never have thought.

This is perhaps the place to take note of misunderstandings of the sort we find in the theologian Wolfhart Pannenberg, who charges Climacus with a mistake concerning the nature of thought. For Pannenberg, to establish that something is a contradiction is thereby to get on top of it. On this principle there can be no Absolute Paradox, no limit which thought cannot throw its loops around, since to establish something as a paradox or limit amounts to a step beyond it. Hence, for Pannenberg, there must be no talk of an unqualified limit, an absolute unlikeness, or the swan song of reason.* In such a response we encounter the voice of a theological *community* and can perceive the immense difficulty of shaking the individual loose from that community, de-

---

Jesus—God and Man, trans. Lewis L. Wilkins and Duane A. Priebe (Philadelphia: Westminster Press, 1968), p. 157.

tribalizing him as it were so that he may speak for himself. For there is indeed no reason in the world why a learned community as such should acknowledge an absolute or final setback or overcoming of its intellectual resources. The Paradox exists only for an individual, and if we are to keep the Absolute Paradox in the perspective of the *Fragments*, whose purpose is to enable an individual reader to see Christianity over against philosophy and as if for the first time, it would be a little on the woolly side for an individual to imagine that theologians as a *corporation* have got the Paradox pretty well indexed and laced with catwalks.

In short, it is one thing to establish coherency within the linguistic deposit of Christianity, certainly a job for the community of theologians, and something else to give the Wholly Unexpected the status of dime-a-dozen contradictions. Forgotten here, certainly, is the fact— factual to an individual believer at least—that *his* Error is what made the thing wholly unexpected, and that it is from the ranks of those in Error that one gets promoted to theologian.

THE WOUNDING PARADOX

Appendix to Chapter III of *Philosophical
Fragments*, "The Paradox and the
Offended Consciousness
(An Acoustic Illusion)"

SUMMARY

When a human thinker encounters the Paradox and comes to an understanding with it, their relationship is a happy one. However, this need not happen. The thinker may instead take offense, somewhat in the manner of wounded pride. His offense is passive, a recoil occasioned by the Paradox, even though to conceal the fact that he has suffered a wound he may outdo all the rest in self-activity. Thus, within the spectrum of passive reactions one can distinguish active and passive forms.

The Paradox, not his own thinking, discovers the offense to him. Expressions of offense which seem to arise in his own consciousness are of the nature of echoes—acoustic illusions. The reality of offense testifies to the Paradox and came into existence with it. Here again we meet the Moment; the Paradox is inseparable from it. Declarations of offense, though numberlessly diverse, all take the Paradox for their target, and all brand it foolish or something similar.

However, the Paradox puts *itself* forward as improbable, foolish, absurd, so that the witness of the offended person succeeds at most in seconding it, though unhappily. All the faults reflection claims to find in the Paradox are contained in its own self-publicity.

* *

To be unable to get the Paradox through one's head, and then to react by pronouncing it foolishness, dismissing it as improbable or beneath a thinking man's notice, or naturalizing it by means of an explanation—these are among the responses one can look for when an individual meets the Absolute Paradox. It is likewise possible to accept the Paradox yet to go on as if one were offended and thus to indicate an abiding awareness that the Paradox presents a spiny exterior.

REMARKS

When the New Testament category of Offense makes its appearance in the *Fragments*, a work addressed from beginning to end to the reflective sort of individual, it signalizes the power of the Absolute Paradox to inflict a hurt through the *intellect*. Affronted, the intellect rises up to block the rapport that the Teacher seeks with the learner, and Climacus seeks now to emphasize the *passivity* of this uprising.

If we confine the discussion to simple, heartfelt, nonintellectual responses to the Paradox, the notion of offense as something passive poses no special difficulty. The maiden's hesitant unwillingness to let herself be made happy shows her to be recoiling from the prospect of a sudden, unthinkable change of altitude. Her self-love suffered a wound from outside, passively, and this would continue to be evident even if her behavior became the reverse of passive, even if she went on to spearhead a plot against the king. The fact that the king made his unexpected offer in person, and to a person, turns every form of refusal into a personal reaction.

Passivity is not quite so easy to detect when we look into more cerebral responses to the Paradox, but assuming for a minute that it is present in those also, what is the author's stake in emphasizing the essential passivity of offense? Is it more than a tautology, after all, to observe that any rejection of the Paradox will be *ipso facto* a response to the Paradox, and in that trivial sense passive, that is, not initiated by the respondent but called forth by an external stimulus?

The author's aim, it appears, is to quell any illusions that might lead a person to suppose he can come up with a neutral, impartial estimate of the Absolute Paradox. For Climacus, the Paradox is a presence in the world that admits of two and only two responses from the person who hears of it: either acceptance of its proposal or else offense. This 'two and only two' limitation can generate a kind of offense of its own in a person who prides himself on being able to appraise a thought at arm's length. This he can do where the thought in question is, for example, a scientific hypothesis, and the kinds of possible response number more than two. There the response need not be charged with personal passion, and someone's dismissal of the hypothesis, or suspension of judgment about it, may be methodical and dispassionate all the way. The Absolute Paradox, on the other hand, disallows that kind of response. Any reaction short of unconditional acceptance betrays a personal affront.

The point is worth dwelling on, with special emphasis on kinds of offense peculiar to the intellectual life. It is easy to see, for instance, that the hypothesis of a remote civilization on another planet, proposed to account for UFO sightings, can elicit more than two kinds of reaction. (1) A hearer may first of all find it so fetching a notion that he crusades for it and will hear of no other. (2) He may see in it nothing but a romantic and vacuous extravagance that ought to be pitilessly debunked. Between these poles room exists for a range of cool inbetweens. (3) Someone might be perfectly content to wait out the evidence and leave the final verdict to the timeless scientific community. (4) Countless persons set the whole issue aside as belonging to a specialism they could hardly care less about.

The categories of acceptance or offense, happiness or unhappiness, and blessedness or hurt do not apply to responses (3) and (4). In relation to the Absolute Paradox, however, (3) and (4) as well as (2) are grouped together under offense, or as indications that the respondent has taken a personal wound in his brush with the Paradox. This is easier to see in a response such as (2), where a person brands the Paradox as sheer lunacy and would have it wiped out, than in temperate reactions on the order of (3) and (4). With the help of some examples let us try to examine the sense in which Climacus places those, too, in the class of offended moves.

In the main part of his Appendix, Climacus mentions several species of thinking-man's reaction to the Paradox, first of all one which would seek to calculate the probability of its validity and pronounce it (correctly) low or nil. A man of this tendency might reason: 'History is not exactly overflowing with precedents for the God's making himself just like me in order to remake me along the lines of himself. The Orient, I am told, has some ideas about the individual getting swallowed up in the All, but this is a different matter entirely. If you look at the thing in terms of the ratios of one kind of event to another, for instance the way we correlate sunspot eruptions with brightenings in the

Northern Lights, this Moment has no index of frequency relative to anything else, nor could we hope to assign it one since one factor is the intractably Unknown. This gives a zero probability to the whole conception, at least by any calculus of frequencies I am familiar with'.

A thinker of another sort might hold the Paradox to be beneath his notice not because of its low probability but because of the delight and satisfaction he takes in his own power of thought and the worlds it ranges over—history, literature, science, art, and above all philosophy. He might reason this way: 'The Unknown making itself known so that I (whom I know) may become like the Unknown (which means becoming God knows what)—this idea presents so many windowless opacities to human reason that the mere rumor of it poses a threat to my greatest possessions. Consider the accent it places upon myself! Myself, now, is a subject that simply cannot approach in richness the eldorados of thought I take my joy in. To imagine *myself* sufficiently interesting to interest the God and move him to venture into that Moment—no, I know better than that. Myself is a means only, a key to those treasuries I spoke of. Thank you, but I have my own carefully reckoned estimate of what ought to count for most!'

Thirdly, Climacus mentions the sort of reasoner who feels a tenderness toward the Paradox and sets out to humanize or naturalize it by giving it an explanation. This amounts to tenderly calling the Paradox back whenever it plunges off in the direction of the unthinkable, in order that a thinker may experience the comfort of thinking it clear through to its origins and causes. The importance of this move is great. It represents the supreme effort of the Socratic point of view, which takes each man to be in possession of the Truth, to domesticate this strangely forward Paradox and thus turn the Wholly Unexpected (a name etymologically true to 'Absolute Paradox') into something naturally to be expected after all. The thinker here behaves a little like the oyster, which possesses no muscles for repelling a spiky particle of sand, so lacquers it with pearl and makes it a bearable fixture of oyster life, not without some intrinsic value.

Such an explainer might reason: 'This idea that a living God took on flesh to call us to equality with him—this is most assuredly someone's idea, and if tradition assigns a date and place to its Founder I should think it captious to deny his existence. At the same time, the excited language of this Teacher's disciples stumbles very frequently into incogitable ways of speaking. If we suppose that his appearance amongst a backward people coincided with a time of oppression leavened by hope of relief, no wonder the excitement. In such a matrix every kind of flimflam can spring up, not to mention opportunism; still, it would be purblind not to see in that historical moment a matter of the highest seriousness, for it represents a giant step forward when the moral ideal latent and discoverable in every human consciousness suddenly finds words and an exemplar for itself. Let us not forget, either, the indictment we sluggish spirits must face for needing an external spur to activate our recognition of the moral ideal.

'Such a moment *had to happen*; it is as much charged with natural, developmental necessity for the human race as the appearance of breasts or chinwhiskers at the level of the maturing individual, but we should not on that account reverence its preceptor the less. On the contrary, it would be more seemly for even the best of men to acknowledge the Sin of letting self-love obscure his own moral promptings and, Repenting his delinquency, to undergo the Conversion of ranking the moral law above the blandishments of self-love, thus becoming in a significant sense a New Creature. And what better names for that Teacher than "Savior" and "Redeemer" to acknowledge the groundbreaking aid he rendered the human race? So you see, I am prepared to go just about all the way with the delirious language this Teacher inspired (which only serves to show how lethargic his disciples must have been up to the time of his coming)—provided one makes allowances for the points at which it veers so wildly from the thinkable as to leave us witless. The message was, after all, meant for us, and any hard sayings in it must be taken as freighted symbols from which scholars can extract the moral content by means of interpretation'.

These sample responses to the Absolute Paradox answer roughly to three types that Climacus gathers under the heading of "offense." While it is clear that each stands aloof from the Paradox, it is not so clear that each stands for a flinching from the kind of *personal* hurt that Climacus takes to be a sign of the Paradox and inseparable from it. There is no question but that if the word 'offense', thus understood, applies also to these more moderate-sounding responses, so that each may be understood as a personal repulse, then the Absolute Paradox has indeed laid a trap for cool heads by simply interdicting the temperate zones of human response, leaving only the equator and the poles. More than that, by characterizing *itself* as the Wholly Unexpected it treats as illusion the reasoner's sense of having *discovered* this or that sort of unreasonableness in the Paradox.

Consider response Number One, namely that the God's appearance as a human Teacher is improbable. When we review the development of the Moment-hypothesis from the opening chapters through the abbreviated statement of the Paradox in III, the question it presents to a levelheaded weigher of probabilities is this: 'What is the objective likelihood that the Unknown did appear in unrecognizable form, as a human Teacher?' Here, we may notice, the ordinary conception of probability goes into eclipse, for the sentence in question (that the Unknown has appeared in unrecognizable form) excludes any frequency-linkages with public trains of events, for us the measure of probable and improbable. For the Paradox, then, 'absurd' is a better expression than 'improbable', for it suggests the slap to reason that the Moment delivers in two ways: first, in its charge that the thinking man is in Error, and second, in the immaculate emptiness, objectively speaking, of the Moment-idea. Yet since the Paradox proclaims itself as the God (the Unknown) stepping into time and change, the reasoner merely echoes this when he ventures to discover its improbability by means of a calculation. To call the Wholly Unexpected improbable is just to repeat the idea that nothing of the sort was or is to be expected.

But why should such an echo-like reaction be called *offense*? The answer, following Climacus, is that the Paradox dares to get personal with its hearer. We have seen this in the opening accusation that I, the learner, am unsuspectingly in a state of warfare against the Truth, a message intimating in a not altogether friendly way that the sender knows me better than I know myself. It appears again in the God's offer to help me do the impossible—to unthink what I really think. This is, if anything, more acutely personal than the king's proposal to the maiden, who can at any rate continue to call her thoughts her own. The fact that nothing resembling a howl of unhappiness appears in response Number One may be deceptive, for the Paradox is manifestly personal in its address, and one way of giving it the cold shoulder is to discuss it in aseptic categories appropriate to a neutral sort of possibility, for instance that of dealing thirteen spades from a well-shuffled deck. But the Paradox, precisely to defy all objective expectancy, even the million-to-one chance, prefers to be called stupid or ridiculous than to place itself in the running with events that can be scaled against one another in terms of relative frequency. In this respect (and here the wounding comes in), the Paradox proclaims itself one of a kind, *sui generis*, in daring to let on that the learner himself is one of a kind and in daring *him* to forsake the surety of numbers and probabilities with that thought in mind.

In response Number Two, the respondent believes he has found the locus of his worth to himself in something definite and definitely worth glorying in. The splendors of the human mind are beyond one man's cataloguing, but let us pick an individual who finds their consummation in philosophy, the best of the ages. Now along comes the Paradox. Respondent Number Two perceives the element of personal dare in the Paradox, which is to say he perceives the Paradox, and it is precisely in laying claim to something visibly better that he finds grounds for pushing it away. In exalting the man himself far above his talent for absorbing the fruits of genius, and thereby differing with him as to which is his best feature, the Paradox sets itself against what he really thinks. He cannot, of course, take credit for discovering this streak of unreasonableness in the Paradox, since the Paradox spoke first in declaring him to be in Error on that same topic. Where the Paradox would thus overturn the heart's priorities, the most dashing bravado can conceal internal bleeding, and to speak therefore of offense in this instance is not stretching the point.

In response Number Three, the reasoner alters the self-image of the Paradox in order to prepare for it a well-swept chamber in the mansion of reason and to assign it a usefulness that more than makes up for its exaggerations. Foremost among those is the charge that the learner is in Error, that what he really thinks is wrong. The reasoner's abrogation of this charge forces changes all the way down the line. In short, the Moment-idea undergoes a thoroughgoing *interpretation* to make it fit in with the old Socratic assumption, and now takes its modest place in an evolutionary overview of the human race. All the Moment-categories of scripture will be retained in this interpretation. Error (Sin) becomes the tendency of human beings to fall into vices, a datum which required neither a Moment nor a Teacher to bring it to light, and the idea of permitting self-love to outrank duty as an incentive becomes an intellectual expression for that tendency. The Teacher's role is cut back accordingly to that of preceptor and exemplar of a 'way of life', the formula for which is laid up, pupate and sleepy, in each human mind. Hence the message, not the Teacher, is to be exalted. In this response, the impression of a Paradox has now been accounted for as a surge of excess voltage in the language of this Teacher's enthusiasts. Under such an interpretation, needless to add, 'the Unknown' or 'the Absolutely Unlike' would be a most inappropriate name for the God, whose nature we have no choice but to suppose is in conformity with the moral archetype we all possess.

Where Climacus would have it understood that two and only two kinds of response fit the Paradox, so that whoever hears of it and does not become a believer is offended, it becomes a reader's task to see whether he can really assimilate moderate-sounding intellectual or philosophical responses under that second heading. If we were dealing with a sensual man's response, for example that the Paradox is comfortless and an enemy of joy, the personal sting and repulse would be evident in the outcry, but it is not so easy to pick out the treble of unhappiness when expression confines itself to the middle octaves. In response Number One, for example, the passional side of the reaction does not appear in words at all but in the fact that the respondent, to whom the Paradox has something very personal to say, *changes the subject* and talks not about himself but about the Paradox, about how improbable it is. Not in the prose, then, do we find the signature of offense, but in the gesture it accomplishes.

The second response makes the Paradox out to be false in its notion that the thinker himself is unexpectedly interesting quite apart from any glow he acquires from his burnished possessions, and would be inexhaustibly interesting even if those lost all their shine. This thought, cutting straight across the grain of everything he believes, can only be false and in a tasteless way at that, for the greatness of the greatest thoughts ever thought consists for one thing in the fact that they beckon him beyond his personal horizons and in general concern themselves with more tasteful matters. He has caught the Paradox in an erroneous estimate of what his unadorned self is worth, and what he ought to rank tops in his concerns. However, the quills of the Paradox have brushed his person, and offense is concentrated in the fact that the Paradox calls him not to some new Faustian odyssey for the sake of which he might gladly have revised his priorities, but back to himself, the thing he would just as soon forget. The expression of offense, then, is the struggle to forget that he has been dared on his home ground and has refused the dare.

Kant's analysis of Christianity in *Religion* is easily the most patterned and elegant specimen of response Number Three, and its major themes continue to turn up in theological programs for purging the scriptures of 'myth'. What makes this response especially awkward to characterize as offense is the reasoner's almost glad-handed adoption of the Moment-categories into the sphere of natural beliefs. This response treats the Paradox as a sort of hysterical misunderstanding of what the Teacher's coming is all about and administers a corrective by quietly going on as if there could be nothing impertinently personal about the Teacher's coming vis-à-vis the particular learner, whose situation is so far from desperate that he needs no stronger medicine than the crisp moral reminder contained in the Teacher's message. As regards offense, the Teacher is dead, the glaze of time blurs his image. Surely there can be no question of any hostility or resentment toward so singularly well-intentioned a figure.

What then does this response come to, and in what way does it express offense? In the first place it accepts the Paradox as truth in a disguised form, a dramatic form calculated to shake up sluggards and slow-witted pupils. Though parabolically expressed as an unthinkable descent of the Deity into history, out to overcome Error with love, the Moment-narrative in actuality concerns *right conduct*. Response Number Three thus turns love into law or morals, a subject on which the morally-minded thinker can without too much difficulty align himself with the scriptures. The Paradox wishes to broach the subject of himself, and he is willing to go into that subject precisely insofar as it concerns his conduct, his score-card of right over wrong actions. The Teacher, he persuades himself, has in mind to discuss morals, which in a certain sense is nothing personal since morals can be discussed without violating the individual's essential privacy. By dwelling on that eminently worthy topic, a thinker can exert a steady force against the Paradox, which permits him to do so out of respect for his freedom, that is, by seeking an understanding rather than mounting a power play. The two may reach a cheerful concord on moral matters, but there will be no more Paradox. It is just as if the maiden were to delete everything personal from the royal proposal and instead let herself imagine that the king is no sovereign but a deputy sent by the new democratic congress to inform her—and every other citizen—that each female is now a queen and each male a king; however, because in the lowlier strata consciousness of station has become so ingrained, it is advisable to impart this by playing on the always newsworthy device of a royal proposal of marriage. The element of offense corresponding to the Paradox will thus have been done away with—unless it should count precisely as offense to do away with offense, which seems to be Climacus's point.

The easy, unaffected gait with which many a thinker has led his reader from the Moment-categories into the sphere of morals, led him, that is, to suppose that a general upgrading of morals was what the Teacher's appearance was all about, is precisely what makes the transition hard to discern. Nothing sounds safer, for example, than to opine that the Teacher came to teach 'a way of life', and then, in case someone should ask the irritating question '*What* way of life?', to follow through by saying, 'Why, love, of course'. Unfortunately, expressions such as 'way of life' and 'love', which in a vague way impinge on the area of conduct, share with melted butter the power to fit a container of any shape. The transition we are speaking of moves from the absolute to the relative, from the sphere of 'getting saved', which certainly rings with decisiveness, to that of 'getting on', adjusting to life, obeying legitimate authorities, shooting for par, and similar things. It moves away from the category of Sin to that of sins, or from the idea of hopeless Error to that of a relative weakness that strength of character can overcome.

How queer the transition is can begin to be felt when we look into the Climacian reconstruction of the New Testament. There it could hardly be plainer that nothing new in the ethical order comes in. Stronger than that, one could say that the Teacher's cutting edge is of a shape entirely different from that of the moral reformer, whose eye is on lawless, unbrotherly, or hard-hearted tendencies that must be conquered by will. The Teacher's work is represented as something he alone can do. This fact has its place also in the later analysis of Faith (Chapter IV) in which the element of volition, so heavy a factor in ethics, gets cut clean out of the meaning of becoming a disciple.

But one need not look ahead; it is enough to remark that the guidance of conduct by moral maxims and laws is the furthest thing imaginable from the "downfall of reason" Climacus associates with the Par-

97

adox. To speak of the Moment as a moral revolution is simply to pass over this aspect, to naturalize it or make it cogitable through and through. In a certain sense, the Moment idea lends itself to that, since in being made over a disciple incurs the task of imitating the exemplar; in this light it is not outrageous to say that discipleship carries a morality with it, which is not the same, however, as saying it consists in one. At the same time, the theme of morals in general, even of personal morals in general (that is, the subject of what is acceptable and unacceptable in personal conduct), can be employed as a censorship, a drowning out of the personal in another sense, the *offensively* personal, by means of a generous helping of the *interestingly* personal, the intimate, the spicy, the sudsy. This censorship expresses a refusal to take personally the offensively personal, for instance the thought that what is personal in my own Error occasioned the Moment-event, and the tendency instead to screen it in the figleaves of psychology, morals, and similar concerns. There is no *concept* so particularly personal as to be immune from this treatment; the trick is to wrap the exposed and beating heart in concepts, to put on *their* dignity sooner than countenance a total invasion of privacy, a total interview which (one likes to suppose) if it must come at all had best be the Last Judgment.

What we are looking at, then, in response Number Three, is the censorship of the Absolute Paradox, whose peculiarity and one might say absoluteness is that it *is* the Paradox only where an individual takes it personally, along with its accompanying possibility of offense. This is precisely the feature that disappears under layer after layer of humanly serious and earnest talk about morals, and all the more so when such talk outdoes itself in dredging up the embarrassing. Naturally it would be a Eureka on a rather large scale to discover that the Moment-categories have nothing to do with morals, for example, that Sin has nothing to do with sins, eternal life with earthly, or discipleship with how one behaves. It is not my aim to urge a separation but to notice a censorship, for even if being a disciple is bound up with certain parameters of acceptable conduct, it does not follow that the bond is essential; it does not follow that any conduct kept deliberately within those parameters is *ipso facto* discipleship.

Seen in this light the learner's rebuff to the Paradox need not be at all heated and direct in order to qualify as offense. Where the aim of the offended soul is to de-intensify the offensively personal, it may take the form of a muted dwelling on some very serious yet not quite so personal matter and win laurels for its avoidance of distemper.

REPRISE

The final paragraph of the Appendix observes once more that the faults one finds in the Paradox are flourishes of its own signature. Is it improbable? Yes, it is the Wholly Unexpected, the Miracle. Is it the enemy of reasonableness? Quite so, it charges that the last thing I care about is the Truth. Is it unthinkable? Indeed, for it contains the Unknown as a fixed indecipherable factor. To find such things amiss with the Paradox is to lift slogans from its own posters. How unlike each other, then, are the Paradox and what I think—but of course this remark, too, is a steal. How then over such an uncrossable distance am I as a thinking man to come to terms with the Paradox?

There is no question but that some desperate energy is required to bring us together, if an understanding is what makes it possible for two to abide together. If it were to happen, the doing would not be mine, since we are speaking of a distance only fire and light can cross—and here we perceive the sense in which Reason yields itself. If I were to chide a disciple for letting go of his brains or giving them over to unseen currents, he could perhaps still speak in order not to extinguish my hope for him, or his for me: 'Ah, do you flinch? I understand, for I still flinch myself when I think of it!' Such a reply for Climacus brings out two points: First, as an expression of offense on the part of the speaker, it acknowledges the unlikeness between the Paradox and anything that humans might be inclined to think. The speaker cleaves to this unlikeness, is happy in his dealings with the Unlike, but—and this is the closing point of the Appendix—he is not happy to the point of distraction, or better, his unhappiness does not take the form of an ecstatic transport that would hinder him from giving street directions or the time of day. His intelligence, although it could not make headway with the Paradox and think him into a happy relationship with it, but had to drop back to an onlooker's position as he gave permission and received the Paradox, was by no means tranquilized, much less snuffed out, and in fact in his new state comes back into play as wide awake as ever, only now on the best of terms with the Paradox. As is clear from passages like this, any critic who, on the strength of the "downfall of reason" motif, would fling the charge of irrationalism against Climacus ought to see to his flank.

The concept of offense will acquire a greater clearness as we look into Climacus's analysis of its opposite, Faith, in the next chapter.

6

THE TEACHER'S CONTEMPORARIES

Chapter IV of *Philosophical Fragments*,
"The Case of the Contemporary Disciple"

SUMMARY

The God himself, we assume, has appeared as a Teacher in servant form. A harbinger may precede him and point him out, but the God's coming is the central event, the central teaching. The servant/ God gives signs reluctantly since his aim is not to produce a stir but to win the learner's love. Nothing else occupies him, and this by itself commands some notice so that his appearance becomes the talk of the city. To understand this conjunction—that an historical moment should be decisive for eternity—is impossible unless one receives the condition we spoke of earlier. How then is the learner to relate himself to the paradox of this Teacher's coming? With the help of that condition, that is, by the happy passion we shall call *Faith*.

The fullest historical knowledge of this event will not produce a disciple, nor will the completest collection of the God's teachings. Discipleship or owing all to the Teacher is impossible without that passion *Faith*. It is not a form of knowledge; its object is the Teacher, not his teaching. It is not an act of will, for it depends on a condition the learner does not possess until it is given from outside himself. Because the God is not directly knowable, the contemporary or eyewitness of the Teacher's visit needs to be given this condition just as much as anyone else in order to reach a happy understanding with the Paradox. No one realizes this better than the disciple, who earlier grasped that he was in Error.

* *

It is impossible to be an immediate contemporary of such a Teacher. To be contemporary with him *as the God* requires that he hand the individual the condition for recognizing him. To be right on the scene with him can serve only as an occasion for a) acquiring historical knowledge; b) deepening self-knowledge; or c) receiving the condition. This last, though indispensable for becoming a disciple, is not a consequence of merely seeing this Teacher in the flesh.

REMARKS

With the long detour into philosophical theology behind him, Climacus picks up the story once more. The God in servant form has come upon the scene as Teacher. In this chapter the weight falls on his relationship to the contemporary learner, but a couple of preliminary points come in for discussion.

First, why would the God come himself? The royal analogy sheds a little light. The king is not seeking out this maiden to set things up for a business merger but to ask her to share his throne, a proposal of such delicate complexity that he cannot expect anyone not a king to appreciate the difficulty. In the divine analogue the point is stronger. Only the God himself *could* do what the Teacher here is prepared to do, namely, recreate the learner to the extent of restoring his forfeited ability to recognize the Truth. In this sense any human emissary could function only as herald, and the relationship between him and the learner would be occasional. That is to say, he might noise it about that something was near to happening, but he could not make it happen. More than that, *what* was to happen would not make much sense to the learner, or to the emissary either. To be informed that the Moment is close at hand would convey as much or as little as the sound of reeds shaken by the wind.

As far as his reception is concerned, the Teacher is in harm's way. For reasons discussed two chapters ago, he is bound to stay within the servant form to the last, not permitting who he is to shine through the rags or transfigure them. It will always have the ring of *lèse majesté* to suggest that the God cannot do this or is bound to do the other, but in these examples Climacus is still working within the 'if' of his Project of Thought. *If* the learner is in Error and the Truth is to come to him from Not-man, then the God, if he chooses to be the Teacher, will operate under some self-imposed restraints for the *protection* of the learner. It is only when we abrogate this 'if' that the result appears to take undue liberties with the God's sovereignty.

The brevity of the author's remarks about signs or miracles can be more than a little startling. Surely a great matter has been touched and passed over here. The God, we are told, will give signs, make wonders happen, but whether these take the form of healing afflictions and waking the dead, or controlling his surroundings in ways less often dreamed of, to see such things happen is not to become a disciple. Is the sensational event a godly one, or a swindle and an illusion? Seeing is not believing when what is seen is baffling, for the merely baffling has no indicator to determine what the learner will say next. We saw earlier that a stunning power-play would not fit in with the Teacher's plan, and where his concern is to win the learner's love he will be reluctant to do spectaculars. Still, because the learner is incapable of recognizing the Truth, wonders will be expedient to make him sit up, although the power to penetrate what he beholds does not lie within himself.

The God as Teacher has in mind only to win the learner's love. However, to have just one thing in mind from one moment to the next and day after day is extraordinary enough in itself to start tongues buzzing, since the normal load of an adult's life, from housewife to head of state, requires keeping an eye on a host of things at once, not least the provision for one's immediate creatural needs. This will be true for the learner as much as for the idly curious. Who then is the learner? What sets him off? He is one who keeps a place among his concerns for the Socratic questions we began with and for the Truth about himself. In this sense he is one who has ears. As for detecting the eternal visitor, ears are of no use unless the Teacher extends the condition, but neither is the condition any good unless the receiver has ears.

Why, with all this talk of high-minded kings, should Climacus find it more likely that lowly and depressed walks of life should produce the serious learner? It sounds patronizing, unless he means to lay a trap for thinkers who patronize with a different slant, a socially-minded rather than self-minded or religious one. For example, if discipleship were to show a great surge in numbers after the Teacher's death, flourishing in one community after another, this would constitute a much more striking social phenomenon than the localized appearance of the Teacher and his small band of followers. It might therefore occur to someone who is by profession an analyst of human disturbances to analyze the souls who became agitated over this. How shall he account for that movement? In pursuing the question, this analyst will have, besides his professional and theoretic skills, as much to go on as anyone else, namely a more or less patchy record of the Teacher's career. Now let us suppose he discovers, in case it is not common knowledge, that the early disciples include a heavy proportion of unlettered yokels. This will be a clue. Put together with a teaching about an imminent divine reign that will redress all inequities, it suggests a reason why those ignorant multitudes would flock to such a Teacher. Unable, that is, to direct their own destinies, they will know no better than to take illusory comfort and refuge in a mythical or unreal order of things that promises to overcome the old order. The less an individual knows, the poorer his grasp of reality, the more likely he is to forsake himself into discipleship.

Whether such theorizing yields hard science or slushy is a matter for time to decide, but in the meantime two points stand out. First, Climacus seems to offer a different account of why disciples from the ranks of the learned will be rare. Someone in command of much learning will find himself more or less profoundly attached to what he knows, bound to it in an erotic way such that the object of his love is not so much the learning as himself-as-learned, and he will thus be further away by several layers than the unlearned when it comes to discovering his own Error. A second point concerns several earmarks of theories such as the one we have been describing. In dealing socialmindedly, as we might say, with the relationship of early disciples to the Teacher, the theorist has really no choice but to represent Faith as a 'given', that is, as a phenomenon in the lives of other people, a phenomenon moreover in which those people are seen as holding to a particular *doctrine*, for instance a doctrine of an imminent divine takeover of human affairs, although some other doctrine might serve the same purpose. Naturally, the process, in an individual disciple, of unthinking what he really thinks and suffering the Paradox to be installed in its place is hardly among the phenomenal or public data given to the social theorist. Therefore, even the most daring theorist, setting out to explain Faith, will not dare to speak of the learner's Error (in Climacus's sense) but, to assure himself of something to talk about, will confine his remarks to 'sins' and 'guilt' in the ordinary sense. Again, his boldness in theory-construction will fall short of letting him advert to the condition which Climacus calls 'Faith'. Instead he will confine his remarks to a doctrinal sense of 'faith', or faith in a teaching. A species of theorizing which finds itself obliged by its own logic to bypass essentially personal matters in favor of speculating about what moves *other* people—is this not what we mean by gossip?

At this point the author takes us back to a question on his title-page: 'Is an historical point of departure possible for an eternal conscious-ness?' How can any eternal *result* arise from the kind of happening that comes and then fades into the past, and concerning which I could easily be mistaken in a number of ways? This question will not be wrapped up until the end of the book, but for the present only one point needs to be made. That is, this question does not present a less importunate difficulty to the Teacher's contemporary than to a learner centuries later. Either way it must be got over. However formidable a stile the fleeting, historical nature of the God's appearance places in the learner's way, it will be just as hard for the contemporary to sur-mount. Precisely insofar as an event is a bit of history, led up to by prior events and leaving its imprint on later ones, it will exhibit no mark at all that could impress a human consciousness as possessing eternal significance. A few mysterious accompaniments and scarcely intelligi-ble sayings thrown into the balance will not make the event *manifestly* decisive for an eternal consciousness. The notion that a certain heel-print is the heelprint of deity would mean, in a way that swings back and forth between superstition and nonsense, that a mark which washes away is permanent, that the ordinary is the extraordinary, that the known is the unknown. Not that the thing has to be expressed in a self-contradictory sentence; for example, 'The historically unmanifest manifests itself historically in an unmanifest way' is a sentence that might very well slip past the watchdogs of formal logic. The point re-mains, however, that the basis for an understanding between Teacher and learner, on the matter of who the Teacher is and what he is per-pared to do, does not lie in the particular reshufflings of motes and dust brought about by the Teacher's coming-into-existence.

According to the Moment-hypothesis, the learner must acquire from a particular *historical* existent, using that term in its most inclusive sense, the "point of departure" for his eternal consciousness. What does this mean? On one side of it, it means nothing more than that some instruction has to come from outside himself, or from Not-man, if he is ever to get free from his Error and position himself rightly in relation to the Unknown. In addition it means that as an earthbound organism he enjoys no access to realms other than the historical, for as long as he remains in his present depressed state of Error the Truth will have to present itself on that historical plane if it is even to be noticed, not to speak of its being recognized. This is not a very easy thought to come to terms with, for he has lived all his life in the welter of historical events, small ones and headline ones, without finding in them a very notable vehicle of the Truth. To pick out one such event as being especially pregnant with the Truth seems an impossible demand. In that respect historical events look pretty much alike, and if the Truth is supposed to announce itself in the form of some words, well, words tend to look alike too. The difficulty here is more than a simple incapacity when we recall the form that the learner's *introduction* to the Truth will take according to the Moment-hypothesis: the God will make himself exactly like him—by no means a transparent formula for helping him pick out one historical occurrence from the rest. The author's point early in his fourth chapter, then, is that the Teacher's contemporary has just as big a problem with that historical point of departure as any later learner.

In short, everything is against the learner's reaching an accord with this Paradox. That can happen, Climacus tells us, only if the Teacher himself administers the condition that will enable the learner to overcome the impossibility of piercing the historical presence to discern the eternal beneath it. To characterize that condition Climacus helps himself to another New Testament category: Faith, which he calls a "happy passion." 'Passion' refers here more immediately to the learner's letting something be done to him than to any accompanying intensification of feeling. The elements of this passion, algebraically presented, are (1) the Reason setting itself aside, and (2) the Paradox bestowing itself.

In the preceding chapter Climacus gives the reader foreshadowings of the concept of Faith when he speaks of the extremity of passion in which reason seeks its downfall. Let us now attempt to analyze this figuration. In the first place, the learner's own resources as he confronts the Teacher in person, as a contemporary, consist in his knowing with optimal certainty what the Teacher looks like and what he says. This knowledge, however, leaves the learner, even if he happens to be a genius, unable to discern anything beyond a man who looks like any number of other men, and moreover a man whose sentences, even where they slant sharply away from the familiar, are still only sentences in a familiar tongue. Now, if we may assume that the learner has discovered his Error, he is to understand from those sentences that this Teacher is prepared to give him something quite in excess of the learner's power to secure for himself, namely the ability to recognize the God in the Teacher. That is to say, he will be able to understand that the God has made himself exactly like the learner in order (if the learner permits) to help him unthink what he has bound himself to think, and to restore him to a state in which he can be happy in, with, and about himself.

In trying to specify exactly where the dereliction of reason comes into all of this, we should not assume as a matter of course that it consists in just one thing. The Teacher's unregal outward appearance may first of all raise a question in the learner's mind as to just how much like this Teacher he cares to become. Secondly, if it is a smart slap to the learner to be reminded that what he really thinks is wrong, the sting is doubled when he is invited, however tenderly, to unthink it. This plants in his consciousness not only a paradoxical thought-content such as might be epitomized in the stultifying and all but useless motto, 'What I really think is wrong', but a sense of practical paralysis as well, for what can it mean for reason to *wish* to commence thinking the opposite of what it really does think? And even if the learner cannot perform such an operation on himself, so that it has to be done to him by another and is in that sense a passion rather than an action, what can it mean for reason to approve the operation? If the learner cannot even know what he is letting himself in for when he gives the Teacher his consent, how can he ask for reason's blessing?

The last point deserves a pause. The gift which this Teacher is prepared to hand over, provided he gets permission, is not a piece of bread or a cup of water but an ability to recognize the Truth. Now is the learner, as so far described, better off with this ability or not? Perhaps if it exacts nothing in return he will be getting something for nothing, but all the signs go against that. From the instant he receives the gift, he holds it in trust, for the Teacher constitutes himself Judge, as we recall from the Project of Thought. Then what must the learner suffer in this "happy passion"? There is no foretelling. Or better say that the foretelling does not specify those details but does specify that no matter what terrors he is put through (and those will always wear the chancy semblance of everything historical and earthly), he will be expected to regard them as blessings, as steps he is being *put through* in the making-over he has signed up for. This act of giving permission, then, is not a mere matter of saying insouciantly, 'Go ahead and do your stuff', as if the Teacher were a sidewalk magician who had buttonholed him with the promise of an astounding trick. The permission is a blank cheque to the Teacher to do whatever he likes with the learner.

By putting all these factors together in a single consciousness the learner can come to see that in *this* decision reason cannot be his guide but will have to be set aside if his answer is Yes.

Climacus adds two qualifications to this characterization of Faith. Faith should not be confused with willing something. The relationship between learner and Teacher does not come into being in either of these ways. On the first point, we have already seen that the learner has no power to find out, or figure out, that this Teacher is the God. Even if we imagine him entertaining a bizarre proposition to that effect, for instance that the man he is looking at is the Unknown in unrecognizable form, the thought is too vacuous to be called a knowing. If it becomes the central fact of the learner's life that the God has come into time, this will not be in consequence of the learner's knowing anything special. In his happy passion he may wish to say he knows that his redeemer lives, but the knowing will not be transferable like a bit of science, and will signify to a third party only that he *believes* this. The point about willing is similar. The passion consists in letting something (the re-creation) be done to him. His willing can go as far as to give permission, but in order for him to will anything it would be requisite to have in imagination that which he wills. But what is there to imagine in connection with being born again? If he could imagine and will it, we would be back in the Socratic situation. All initiative therefore remains with the Teacher, and the owings point all one way.

These remarks about Faith, knowledge, and will come together in one thought: the object of Faith is not the teaching but the Teacher. We have seen the same thought expressed already in the idea that the learner will owe everything to the Teacher and that he can never forget the Teacher. In order to bring out better the notion of Faith as a relationship of this peculiar sort, we may turn briefly to another work by Climacus, the *Concluding Unscientific Postscript,* in which Faith and related categories are expounded with special emphasis on the difficulties they pose for a would-be disciple.

In that work Faith is discussed from the point of view of an existing individual. In the *Fragments* the point of view is that of a hypothetical individual, that is, a thinker engaged in the essentially communal task of developing a project of thought that the community of thinkers can put the final touches on if the thinker happens to be carried off before its completion. From the existing man's point of view, Faith is "an objective uncertainty held fast in an appropriation-process of the most passionate inwardness."*

Here it may be useful to try to fill out this bit of algebra by reference to matters already covered in the *Fragments.* If I am the Teacher's contemporary, it is first of all objectively or publicly certain that the Teacher is a man like myself, but irremediably uncertain that he is also the God come to save me from my Error. If I am to become one of his disciples or believers, all I can give for openers is my consent, and since I cannot will myself created anew, the rest is up to him. However, I do not know how much time remains for me, or what odd and unforeseeable dosages go into 'saving' someone like me (pain? poverty? injury? loneliness? monotony?). No, I do not know the first thing about saving someone from my kind of Error. True, I can give permission, but, as the saving power takes hold, this will perhaps mean laboring very hard to honor the permission I gave, fighting my tendency to revoke it or attach provisos. If it is to be serious, then, my permission includes my intention to *hold fast* to that public uncertainty, no matter what happens afterward. Further, this straining to hold fast may have its outward accompaniments, but it is for the most part an interior business. Only I and the Teacher will know if I am engaged in it with all my might or only halfheartedly. Inward, then, but in what sense 'most passionate'? In this process of being recreated, something very close to my heart, namely what I really think, is being dislodged, and something—whether one calls it the Truth or the Teacher himself is indifferent—is getting itself installed there.

*Søren Kierkegaard, *Concluding Unscientific Postscript,* trans. David F. Swenson and Walter Lowrie (Princeton: Princeton University Press, 1941), p. 182.

Here is a process in which I am helped to unthink the thoughts my heart is most attached to, thoughts which have become one with its pulsing tissue, and nothing could be more passionate, nothing of greater violence could be done to me, nothing could I want less than having to appropriate the Truth in such a way. It is clear that in a passion of this sort my reason cannot very well guide me in unseating what I really think, and as far as willing is concerned, the whole procedure goes against my will, so that I can scarcely imagine myself daring to volunteer for it short of a miraculous assist from the Teacher. Perhaps needless to add, there could be no question of even considering it until and unless I discovered myself to be in Error. Such is our expansion of the author's algebraic sentence. Some unknowns remain in it; for example, what it is like *in concreto* to hold fast to the Teacher? This, however, forms no part of the author's project.

As far as that project is concerned, we have now come far enough to explain what he means by making the Teacher and not the teaching the object of Faith.

As human practices go it is a likelihood, though not one which Climacus devotes attention to, that doctrines should begin to take form in the immediate aftermath of the God's visit. Some of these will doubtless be directly related to the Teacher's own words and life and the central Paradox, others more or less marginal. Some will be aimed at preserving the Paradox, and with it the offense, against factions that would render it unparadoxical, perhaps by blending it with this or that work of human imagination. Other doctrines will be concerned to preserve linkages with the past, to lay down sanctions for popular devotions, or to identify the original cultus over against emphases that veer away from it. I should not wish to anticipate the discerning historian as regards the variety of purposes and forms these doctrines might exhibit.

Now let us suppose it is said that believers hold these doctrines by *faith*. We can see that this by itself is a somewhat ambiguous reference to the believer. It could signify that a believer is one who in fact holds to these doctrines and abhors their negations. Or it could mean that a believer is *defined* as one who holds these doctrines. These are quite different meanings, for it is possible to cleave to a set of doctrines, and to do so by faith and not by canons of reasonableness or evidence and yet not be 'in Faith' in the sense of holding fast to the

Teacher. One could in other words be holding fast to the teaching in-stead. Now if it should occur to someone that by holding fast to the teaching one is in every practical sense holding fast to the Teacher, so that the distinction is after all not so very great, or that one can hold fast to the Teacher *through* his teaching, this description will do service for such a range of worship-styles and psychological nuances that a person would have to regard himself as something like an afterthought-Apostle to take dogmatic issue with it.

However, within the limits of Climacus's project, one thing should be stressed: since the learner is in Error, the Teacher must be granted the right to stipulate what is meant by being 'in Faith'. It is on this point, I believe, that Climacus's distinction is meant to bear. Yet it is not so easy, as Climacus has said more than once, to separate this Teacher from his teaching. In order to do the best we can for his dis-tinction, let us make one more small borrowing from the *Postscript*. There Climacus draws a hard antithetical line between a doctrine and what he calls an "existential communication"* in terms of the learn-er's relationships to these. One relationship amounts to knowing what the teaching says and the other to taking its yoke upon oneself.

Now, it is plain that the whole thrust of the Moment-hypothesis con-cerns the God's becoming a particular man, and thus we should find it easy to say that the *Fragments* has to do with an Incarnation. Doc-trinal expressions of this may take any number of forms, and since nothing is to be gained by choosing one over another, let us stay with the way Climacus puts it: "The God has . . . made his appearance as Teacher" (p. 68). Now we have a doctrine before us, and it is evident that anyone who would say 'This doctrine is false, incredible, there is nothing to be said for it' is not the disciple or believer Climacus has been talking about.

But what about someone who says, 'I have no difficulties about the truth of this doctrine'—is this person the disciple Climacus has been talking about? Could not such a person add, 'I see no difficulty ac-knowledging the truth of that doctrine—but I have not found it in my-self, and doubt I ever shall, to give that Teacher unconditional sway over me'. In point of fact, Climacus puts himself forward as just such a person. At the end of his first chapter, we recall, he remarks somewhat

*Ibid., p. 33.

lyrically that the hypothesis of the Moment carries a sort of proof or test of its own veracity as opposed to the Socratic, but this flight of doctrinal conviction comes very far short of constituting Climacus a disciple. What is lacking? The granting of permission to the Teacher, along with whatever follow-through would keep the permission unexpired and unconditional. In short, the *difficult* thing is lacking, and here the distinction we are out to capture may be expressed in terms of the concept 'difficulty'. It is only relatively difficult, when it is difficult at all, to make room in one's intellect for a doctrine, for example, the Incarnation, even when that doctrine has variant forms that express a self-contradiction. It is, on the other hand, absolutely difficult to place oneself unconditionally in the hands of another person to the extent of owing everything to that person and in such a way as to go dead against what one really thinks. The reversal that this requires was called *Conversion* back in the Project of Thought.

This is what Climacus seems to be saying when he characterizes Faith as holding fast to the Teacher rather than the teaching. Besides noting that this giving of permission is something over and above confessing a particular creed, it is important to see the giving of permission as a dialectical or logically complex action. For example, what if I were to romance myself into an expression of consent, whereas according to the Teacher the only sufficient occasion for my yielding such consent would be a conviction of my Error? Or better, the only thing he would *count* as giving permission would be an expression based on that conviction, not on an infatuation with the Teacher's charm (surely a confusion), or a preacher's trumpeting prose, or an irresistibly catchy hymn, or the sublime confidence displayed by a fondler of venomous snakes. According to the Teacher (who, since I am in Error, reserves the right to specify what will count as Faith, and likewise what will count as the permission he is after), to extend my permission on any of these bases would be to proceed from a wrong consciousness; the requisite permission is such that, except it be based on a conviction of my own Error, it will constitute in effect either an expression of willingness to give my consent at a more suitable future time or else an abandoning of myself, a throwing myself away, since the permission is among other things unconditional. (Hence there could be vehement expressions of permission which, as we say, do not get taken up, though we dare not say they pass unheard.)

To put the distinction in a different way, although the doctrine has a subject (the God) and a predicate expressing what the subject did (made his appearance as Teacher), this doctrine is peculiar in that it makes its hearer the subject, so that if the hearer replies that its subject is what is contained in the doctrine, the doctrine accuses him of changing the subject. Precisely because the God is the subject, it will be understood that the God does not wish to predicate things of himself in the manner of a celebrity but to go about the business alluded to in the doctrine, which has to do with the hearer.

* *

This chapter singles out the contemporary disciple in order to analyze his relationship to the Teacher. In light of what Climacus has said, there seems nothing advantageous or even special about the learner's contemporaneity. If the relationship turns out unhappy, this will not be unique to his generation, since the Teacher's coming is charged with offense for whoever hears of it; if it turns out happy, this will not be a result of the contemporaneity.

What remains to be said about the contemporary generation? There is first of all a *prima facie* glitter in the idea of my lifetime's overlapping with a memorable historical happening. Everyone can understand the blessed retrospect of a great-grandparent who once met Lincoln or Queen Victoria. So it will be with contemporaries of the Teacher. They, too, were on the spot and among the first to hear. However, we are speaking of retrospect, for this event is as fleeting as any other, and now the surface blessedness of having been among those present becomes somewhat faded because, in this instance, one has nothing outwardly glorious to look back upon. All of this does something to the very notion of a contemporary, something which obliges Climacus to distinguish between a contemporary in the sense of a soul who lives on the same block as the Teacher and a real or nonimmediate contemporary. The real contemporary will be someone who knows the Teacher as Teacher, having been taught by him, and whom the Teacher in turn knows for having taught him. He will be one to whom the Teacher administered the indispensable condition for becoming aware of who he is.

This is the place to bring up an important point. There are, to begin with, two senses of 'Moment' operating in the *Fragments*, first a once-for-all sense as applied to the historical, dateable advent of the Teacher, and secondly the Moment in the disciple's life in which the Teacher grants him the condition. This Moment, too, is historical, representing a time-cut in the learner's existence, although as an unpublic event it belongs to what we might better call his inward or self-history. Now the thing that for Climacus separates the real contemporary, the believer, from those who walk the same streets with him, is his receipt of the condition enabling him to "know" the Teacher. However, a conceptual mist hangs about this person-to-person transaction. We do not aim here to penetrate the curtain of privacy around Teacher and learner but merely to record our puzzlement when Climacus seems to do so, for he has some positive things to say about what it is like to receive the condition.

What is it like? It is not as though Climacus, standing conspicuously outside the Moment-religion and merely sizing it up for us, could consistently be *remembering* what conversion is like, and even if he were, he could only be remembering his own. Yet he speaks repeatedly of the learner's being given to "see the person of the God" (p. 81) and "to behold his glory" (p. 87) as the condition is granted and the Paradox bestows itself. Climacus employs verbs of vision over and over again, verbs of immediate perception that seem gratuitous and more than a little misleading because they rivet attention on a sensational experience within the episode of conversion, more specifically *a revelation to the individual learner* of the Teacher's transfigured person. Now, why should the God's granting of the condition (or bestowal of the Paradox) be described in terms of a damascene vision? With the hint of something stunning in the learner's field of perception, do we not move dangerously close to an elevation of the learner rejected back in the second chapter? Suggesting as they do that the condition conditions the learner's organs of sight, the expressions in question point in the direction of incommunicable or mystical gnosis far beyond anything the first two chapters of the book prepare us for.

How then is a reader to understand these references to private visions, unless he is simply to star them in the margin as Climacian ways of saying 'At this point something mysterious happens'? To make our difficulty plainer, let us formulate it now as a logical snag. Once Climacus chooses to regard 'the God' as just a name for the Unknown, and the predicates which convention reverently assigns to the God as parameters of comely speech, the divine names instantly empty themselves of all familiar connotation. What now will it mean, when the Teacher grants the condition, to speak of the learner's *seeing* the God in the Teacher, or *seeing* the person of the God there? If Climacus had stopped after a reference to the learner's receiving the lost power to recognize the Truth, which the reader would be prepared to acknowledge as an eye-opening event in the most decisive sense, there would be no problem, for the precise nature of the learner's Moment would be left properly to the reader's imagination. But what sense are we to make of a direct perception of the *Unknown*? Or, to change the wording a bit, what will it mean to *behold* the eternal, the nonhistorical, in the person of this Teacher?

My point in asking these questions is not at all to force a few salutary doubts into the picture, since to speak of doubting that what the learner perceives is the Unknown would be at least as tanglefooted logically as the Climacian way of speaking. The real issue concerns whether there is any need to speak at all of a perceptual experience, a vision-revelation, in which the Teacher briefly draws back the veil for one learner at a time. Why need the granting of the condition in Climacus's account be given any perceptual determinations? Instead of characterizing it as this or that kind of experience, why not leave it a variable since it is after all an experience of the Unknown? Is the function of the visual experience to remove or overcome any lingering prickles of offense? But how can a vision accomplish this where the Teacher's aim is not to dazzle but to establish an understanding?

Further, if we specify the conversion-experience in terms of a visual experience, Faith acquires a cognitive foundation insofar as the learner now *knows* that he has seen the God's person in the Teacher, and his reason can now presumably lean upon this knowing. Given the knowing, the learner need on no account set reason aside but can enlist it as an ally of 'Faith' on the strength of his having seen an unforgettably radiant face, more brilliant no doubt than the countenance of Moses. And with such comparatives in mind there is no escaping the conclusion that Faith is not a new kind of relationship with the Absolutely Different, but a matter of degree.

Here we have to ask ourselves two questions: first, what leads the author to slip into the language of visual experience? and second, how might the nature of the Condition be more appropriately described?

On the first point, as it seems to me, Climacus finds himself tempted a little beyond his strength where he slides into the language of vision.* The seeing that in common parlance gets equated with believing, the utterly convincing testimony of the sober man's eyes as he sees "the person of the God" now comes into play as if Climacus were incurably jealous of the cognitive and as if the learner would be within his rights if he merely awaited the all-conquering show of majestic effulgence. But then what has become of the understanding sought by the God in Chapter II?

Climacus offers an alternative, nonvisual account of the condition on page 79, where he speaks of the Condition conditioning or correcting the learner's "understanding of the Eternal" or his "conception of the God." This quieter and less troublesome way of describing the Condition requires a gloss of its own. It is, of course, quite different on the surface from the suggestion that the Condition conditions the organs of sight, and gives us to consider that Climacus may have been perfectly aware of possible misunderstandings tied up with seeing the God's "person." If by means of the Condition my *understanding* is to be adjusted to tolerate a new kind of fact, if I am now to be enabled "to *think* God's existence in and with" my own, nothing is said about augmented eyesight, and I shall not be tempted to confuse the new kind of fact—the Deity in history—with anything directly visible. That a glance may help set up an understanding between king and maiden no one will dispute, but this is no time to forget that the God is the Unknown and not a human sovereign. When the Condition is described in terms of correcting some erroneous conceptions of mine, it seems more in keeping with the idea of a personal understanding or an adjustment of differences, as in truces, betrothals, reconciliations— nothing overwhelming, and perhaps taking some period of time. *How* the Teacher is to make room in my understanding for this new kind of fact is not within my range of speculation, which is precisely why I find myself obliged to balk whenever Climacus lets on that a flash of the godly visage will do the trick.

To correct my erroneous conceptions means changing *what I really think*, not necessarily altering the quantum of light in my field of vi-

*Readers familiar with Kierkegaard's other writings will perhaps recall his preoccupation with looks and glances.

116

sion, and with this thought we steer a degree closer to the nature of the Condition. Now, having skirted cognitive and visual misunderstandings of the Condition (Faith), what can be safely said about it? The granting of it is to reverse what I really think of both myself and the God and to unbind me so that I may now recognize the Truth when I confront it. Plainly we are speaking here of a passion, a suffering in which all that my reason stands for gets shoved onto a siding to make room for the new kind of fact, which then (on my permission) bestows itself. But what is this like? It sounds banal to say I will now see things differently, and it would hardly help to land on fresh, lyrical expressions for the same banality.

We have now established what seems to me a clear starting point. That is, the happy passion called Faith, which takes the Teacher rather than his teaching as its object, commences with a gesture of permission on the part of a learner who is aware of his Error, and the gesture of permission is one which reason cannot sanction before the fact, although we do not predict what reason will comment in retrospect. The new "understanding of the Eternal" or "conception of the God"—phrases which come close to acknowledging a sort of *thought*-content in Faith—is clearly not to be taken as the displacement of one teaching or doctrine by another, for reasons already discussed. The new understanding, as between two *persons*, cannot be separated from the taking up of a new relationship, for that is what the understanding tends upon and is all about, and the fact of a new kind, the Paradox, is not itself a doctrine but *someone in particular*. (To profess a doctrine concerning that person, for instance 'The God appeared in history in the person of so-and-so', is by no means a weightless exhalation, but it expresses only negatively what Climacus calls Faith, that is, it expresses the fact that an individual does *not* challenge the doctrine, is *not* a dissident, and similar things.) To distinguish between this negative fact and Faith we must bear in mind again that since the learner is in Error, it is up to the Teacher to lay down what shall count as the opposite state. The taking up of the new relationship is what must therefore primarily concern us.

Accordingly, our procedure is to join together two ideas: (a) that acquiring Faith means taking up a new relationship, and (b) that the Teacher's dispensing the Condition is to be taken now as his correcting my conception of God or the Eternal. The Paradox now goes in place of what I really thought, and becomes what I really think, so that what I once really thought is washed away. But what can human brains make of this formula? Was it not given out earlier that what the learner really thinks is inseparable from his living person and that he cannot cut himself loose from it? Well, the Paradox, we are saying, is to cut him loose from it, the Paradox is to take its place. Yet this becomes a ridiculous thought when we remember that the Paradox is a person, for it lets on that a person is going to displace a particular piece of thought-content. Refute, perhaps, one wants to say, but hardly displace. Or is the Teacher to be what we call a 'living refutation' of what I really think and thus to persuade me by degrees to think the opposite of what I think? This, however, sounds misleadingly like ordinary changes of opinion; if in this instance I am one with my opinion, then I will not separate myself from it by looking very intently at a champion of the opposite view. The Condition is still required here to enable me to recognize that the opposite of my view is the Truth. No, what must happen is that the Teacher *come between* me and what I really think and, as we say, break up our marriage.

I and 'what I really think' have a quite special if clandestine affair going, which is importantly unlike my attachments to opinions on food prices, polluters, capital punishment, and so forth, although I would not have suspected its importance except for the Teacher's reminder that it is bondage. 'What I really think' makes up my opinion not of day-to-day matters but of myself *vis-à-vis* the Eternal, and reflects irremediably wrong conceptions of both myself and the Eternal, even where in my speech I have the 'grammar' of God-expressions well under control. The objective fact here is that, humanly speaking, *nothing* can come between me and what I really think, not even the thought that the God will put up with no substitute for me as his eternal friend, brother, son—equal. Such a thought is by way of being an eternal thought, with no historical phenomenon to attest it, and as such lacks the existential muscle for crowding out what I already think. In order for that to happen, the Teacher, who exists, has to come between me and what I think, so that my conception of the God, my understanding of the Eternal, can become changed to include the fact that the God is that which is *concerned* to come between me and my Error, or between me and my unhappiness.

To this amended conception of the God other thoughts, some already mentioned, fasten themselves in no particular order, for example, that I alone will satisfy the God, that I am not a make-do replacement for someone dearer to the God, that if this piece of good news is in truth news, then it is very good news indeed. As the relationship becomes happy in these thoughts I may now begin to "think the God's existence in and with" my own in my eternal one-sided debt to this Teacher. Since it is in and by means of this new passion (Faith) that I become unthinkably separated from what I once really thought, it will become unthinkable in another sense for me to confuse this relationship with merely *not doubting* something. In these and similar thoughts the Moment delivers its answers to the Socratic unknowings we began with, but I should never be able to recognize them as the Truth unless that Teacher used his existence in a self-dirtying way to break up the old liaison, shoulder it apart, and unless he also risked the unhappy reaction that Climacus calls Offense, that is, being treated as an intruder.

Clearly this chapter of the *Fragments* proposes to isolate a sense of 'faith' or 'belief' that has nothing whatever to do with assenting to doctrines. That doctrines play important roles in the community of disciples we have already acknowledged, and it is entirely in order if the community submits that its doctrines are 'held on faith' or even 'known by faith'. The Climacian move is to distinguish and preserve a sense of 'faith' that is not to be conflated with a communal agreement concerning what is to be included in a creed or confession. It follows that attempts to characterize faith in general, so as to amalgamate its several uses by means of a common denominator, can all too easily and without intentional mischief blur the Paradox-related use that Climacus takes pains to highlight. Needless to add, if that use of the word is the essential one as far as the Teacher/learner relationship is concerned, the result can be a blurring of the nature of that relationship as well.

Let us see what happens if one tries to speak inclusively of the meaning of 'faith', for instance by means of definitions. A standard dictionary lists, among the meanings of 'faith' that connect with religion, these:

. . . an act or attitude of intellectual assent to the traditional doctrines of one's religion. . . .
. . . a decision of an individual entrusting his life to God's transforming

care in response to an experience of God's mercy. . . .

. . . among Roman Catholic theologians: a supernatural virtue by which one believes on the authority of God himself all that God has revealed or proposed through the Church for belief. . . .*

The meaning Climacus assigns to 'Faith' is simply not covered by the first entry. The second definition is more flexible insofar as the category of the Absolute Paradox may be brought into engagement with it, but it contains no intimation of the paradoxical as it stands. The third has a doctrine-related tone, although its flexibility is guaranteed by the somewhat obscurantist adjective 'supernatural', but it is orientated toward what the *community* counts as a believer, so that any references to the paradoxical Teacher/learner relationship lie far in the background, to say the least. The objective lexicographer, it would seem, can only mislead us on this matter.

On a related point, no definition of 'faith' limiting itself to what the Paradox-religion has *in common* with other religions, which are also frequently designated 'faiths', will include Climacus's sense of 'Faith'. World religions may, for example, have in common that each stands by a set of doctrines, a code of morals, a cycle of observances, a sacred written or oral tradition, or a community of initiates. Such faiths, including some that make reference to Abraham's God, may have nothing at all in them corresponding to what Climacus calls 'Faith', nothing corresponding to the paradoxical Teacher/learner relationship, although they possess teachers and disciples in profusion. The question cannot, of course, be decided *a priori* whether more than one of the world's faiths honors that meaning of 'Faith', or, as Climacus expresses it, whether more than one proposes in that sense "an historical point of departure for an eternal consciousness." While historical elements abound in the spectrum of world faiths, and while it would surely be graceless to plead that any segment of humanity knows nothing of an eternal consciousness, the singular pathos that concerns Climacus has to do strictly with *basing* that consciousness on something historical. This matter promises to become clearer with a reading of the "Interlude" and the concluding "Moral," but from sections already discussed it is evident that Climacus sets his face against the too-easy conflation of religions and types of religiousness implied

*Webster's New International Dictionary, 3d ed., s.v. "faith."

in expressions such as 'world religions', 'comparative religion', and 'faiths'.

Because the influence of Kant on modern thought has been so great as to be almost inescapable, special mention ought to be made here of philosophies of religion which, like Kant's, locate the essence of religiousness in general in morally upstanding conduct, and which, when the philosopher looks at Christianity, define the relationship of disciple to Teacher in terms of that essence. That such views are at bottom Socratic shows itself at once in that they speak only marginally if at all to the reader's 'eternal consciousness', and by no means paradoxically at that, and likewise in the fact that they would urge the disciple to hold fast to the teaching rather than the Teacher. The questions they address are not the Socratic ones we introduced at the beginning but questions having to do with principled and dutiful behavior rather than with what the learner really thinks of himself as a particular self. Thus, the Teacher's role changes to that of moral preceptor, or perhaps to that of a prophet in a succession of prophets who call men back to the Law. The difference between such a view and what Climacus calls "the Moment" would consist in the former's bypassing the particular existing consciousness (and its Error) in favour of the universally human, for example, the race and its norms. A more lordly theme, indeed, but the pathos of the *point d'appui* associated with the Moment lies precisely in the fact that lordliness itself dared to summon the individual consciousness away from its efforts to forget itself in the more lordly aggregate. It dared, that is, to point to *his* Error, which could otherwise easily have been forgotten in the wider scenery of what the world calls colossal sins and wickedness; it dared to bring that particular consciousness under unheard-of magnification so as to expose the least pocket of unhappiness, proposing to clean out that pocket before it poisoned the individual's eternity.

In analyzing how the learner relates himself happily to the Teacher, we have been looking at a de-intellectualized sense of 'Faith', which Climacus explicitly disengages from knowing and willing, and which he calls a 'passion'. When we remember that from the beginning the Teacher is out to win the learner's love, it can become tempting to suggest that the nonintellectual relationship between them can be nothing else but *emotive* and that the relation is brought into being by means of emotion. To express it so would, however, risk a misunderstanding similar to the one dealt with earlier in this chapter. The relationship of learner to Teacher is, of course, not unfeeling or catatonic and could hardly come into being without palpitations of whatever sort the learner happens to be glandularly prone to, but one ought not to conclude from this that it *belongs to psychology* to explain how the relationship (Faith) is constituted, to investigate its essence, or in general to research it. Even if a psychologist throws out analytical pincers to embrace the category 'religious experience', several points have to be kept in mind to spare this psychologist needless embarrassment. In the first place, there is the question whether this 'Faith' he investigates *exists*, that is, presents itself as a datum to be classified and explained, since it holds after all between the disciple and a publicly inaccessible party of the second part. More than that, the relationship does not exist as a phenomenon in the lives of others but only as a possibility for the psychologist himself, so that to approach it as if it were the former amounts to thrusting it out of mind as the latter, a gesture that was earlier characterized as 'Offense', which can scarcely be regarded as a move in the advancement of learning.

'Well', someone might comment, 'at least a psychologist can classify Faith, group it with other human—what? phenomena?—and to that extent it will belong to psychology'. Very well, but then let him include in his characterization of Faith that the disciple comes into relation with his Teacher by suspending his reason, willing its downfall as Climacus puts it, and also that he submits to the ultimate violence of allowing what he really thinks to be displaced by its opposite, which means doing the opposite of what he really wants—and then let him name the emotion of which all this is characteristic. Perhaps he will say, 'I think it a species of love, characterized as it is by a certain tensile happiness and perhaps a bit of the proverbial blindness'. It would be hard to credit such a saying for marksmanship even if the speaker were a believer talking about his own Faith, but if he were a psychologist talking about another's, the misunderstanding would be so great as to make him ludicrous. In the last analysis, the upshot of psychologizing about Faith is either that Faith shall be assimilated to paranoia (in which the patient expresses relationships to publicly unreal objects and persons), an awkward classification if the disciple is benignly normal in all other respects, or that Faith demands a slot of its own and thus becomes a limit case of the classifying operation, or, as we say, something in a class by itself.

Passing in review the imagined advantages of contemporaneity, Climacus can find only one of substance. The contemporary will know nothing of the great build-up of gossipy theorizing that follows the Teacher's career. The obvious advantages of contemporaneity—the chance to acquire straight historical knowledge and self-knowledge— prove to be only occasions, with no power to bring him into discipleship.

7

THEMES IN THE "INTERLUDE"

"Interlude," part of Chapter IV of
Philosophical Fragments

SUMMARY

Assuming the Teacher has come and gone, let us represent the lapse of time since his death by means of an *entr'acte*, a conversation about the concepts of the actual, the possible, and the necessary. Question: "Is the past more necessary than the future? or, When the possible becomes actual, is it thereby made more necessary than it was?"

I
COMING INTO EXISTENCE

What kind of change is coming-into-existence? It is the one kind that does not presuppose an existing subject of change. It is a change not in essence but in being, a transition from not existing to existing, or from the kind of nonbeing we call *possible*.

Something necessary cannot undergo the change of coming-into-existence, since being necessary it always is.

Necessity is not a uniting of possibility and actuality. Those two differ in being, not in essence, but the essence of the necessary is to be.

Among kinds of being, the necessary is in another class entirely from the actual and the possible. The change called coming-into-existence occurs therefore without necessity.

The logical ground (that something is possible) is not enough to bring it into existence; a cause is required for that. An unbroken chain of such causes would not add up to necessity, even if we assume laws of nature in operation. Obviously, also, a freely acting cause is without necessity.

2
THE HISTORICAL

Whatever has come into existence is historical, including everything natural, if only in the fact of its having come into existence. Only the Eternal has no history.

A coming-into-existence of the natural sort may embrace within itself a coming-into-existence of the sort bound up with a personal or self-remembered history.

3
THE PAST

The immutability of the past is not like that of the necessary since the former was brought about by a change and so *could* have been different, whereas the necessary excludes all change.

The category 'necessary' is equally inapplicable to past and future history. To claim to see the past as necessary is as suspect as claiming to know the future. The idea that anything historical *has to be* would annihilate the concepts of both freedom and coming-into-existence.

4
THE APPREHENSION OF THE PAST

Whatever has come into existence has the mark of uncertainty. To try to understand the past better either by reconstructing it as a sequence of inevitable steps or by viewing it as a necessary expression of God's will is to court illusion. Even *knowledge* of the past (or future) cannot confer a necessity that is no part of what comes into existence.

The passion of wonder, in historians and philosophers, gives witness to the mark of uncertainty on whatever comes into existence. Even the most expert analyst of the *logic* of events has to *look and see* what actually did happen.

How is knowledge of the past acquired, since coming-into-existence is not an object of sense? The mode of knowing it *as* historical must make its affirmations against the uncertainty bound up with coming-into-existence. Belief or faith meets this requirement.

Immediate experience cannot deceive, as the Greek skepticism acknowledges when it grounds itself in a refusal to assent to anything beyond the immediate. This shows that the ordinary nonskeptical affirmations with regard to the historical are expressions of will, even where they are certain beyond a doubt.

Belief's conclusion on an historical matter is a resolution. In treating its immediate data as effects of a coming-into-existence, belief wills away doubt, and doubt is gone. Belief and doubt are thus opposed passions.

The noncontemporary of an event is related to the testimonies he works with in the same way a contemporary is related to what he sees and hears. In order to believe, each by an act of assent has to overcome the uncertainty attached to the event's having come into existence.

All of this supports the view that necessity and coming-into-existence belong to distinct conceptual worlds.

SUPPLEMENT: APPLICATION

The movement from nonexistence to existence belongs to everything historical. Our hypothesis (that the God has come into existence) shares this and must be believed or doubted like any other historical fact. But this one fact is also based on a self-contradiction: that which always is, comes into existence. The notion of belief or Faith as regards this one fact will mean something different from the usual since no immediate sensing or knowing goes with it, even for a contemporary.

The idea that such a happening acquires inevitability either in prospect (through intimations of its coming) or in retrospect (through its historical consequences) is a misunderstanding.

REMARKS

Our first large helping of metaphysics, in the chapter on the Absolute Paradox, had to do with construing the use of God-language. This second helping analyzes the concepts 'existence' and 'necessity' in their bearing upon historical knowledge. When Climacus asks, "Is the past more necessary than the future?" and sets himself to analyzing those concepts, it is natural to wonder how the resulting discussion connects with what has gone before. The general answer, as it develops later on, is that a thinker might find himself tempted to join together the concepts of existence and necessity, with consequences both confused in themselves and ruinous to his understanding of the Moment.

To make a beginning, thanks to the labors of careful historians a sketchily known event such as the Battle of Hastings comes to be better and better understood. Broken and anomalous reports find their places one by one in an all but seamless account that covers the prior circumstances, motives, weather, weight of arms, terrain, and key personalities. No shred of fact about it is without an agreeable hypothesis to account for it. What satisfies historians as an intelligible reconstruction of Hastings is now at hand, and even the *dramatis personae* in A.D. 1066 had nothing nearly so complete as retrospect and discipline have now made this record. At this point, suppose the historian persuades himself that, given the circumstances prevailing at the start of the battle, the outcome *followed necessarily*—it could not have happened otherwise. In putting it this way, the historian would be stationing himself (or pretending to) outside his human range of reckoning.

In the *Critique of Pure Reason* Kant declares as an "*a priori* law of nature" that "everything which happens is hypothetically necessary."* That is to say, everything historical must admit of being woven into a *wholly* intelligible knowledge of the past. There must be no remainder in a (finished) historical narrative that can "do violence or detriment to the understanding."** This "hypothetical necessity," then, has something to do with an event's being transparently understood. Climacus, it would appear, apprehends in all of this a challenge to his Paradox-hypothesis, that is, that the eternal Deity has entered into history. That hypothesis is open to challenge on Kantian or similar grounds: 'No, yours is an indefensible hypothesis. The historical episode in question, whatever it may be, must like every historical phenomenon render account of itself as a product of the physical conditions and laws operative at the time'.

Such a view would of course allow of only relative and removable perplexities in historical knowledge, not an Absolute Paradox. The view rests on a particular analysis of the concepts 'necessity' and 'historical existence' in its claim that everything historical *must* conform to the canons of scientific intelligibility or else be thrown out as non-

*Trans. Norman Kemp Smith (London: Macmillan, 1956), sec. B280, p. 248.
**Ibid., sec. B282, p. 249.

historical. With these points in mind, it is easy to see why Climacus takes time out for a look at the conceptual issues involved. Kant's position, pushed to the limit, calls for a return to the Socratic position of Chapter I by welding together the categories 'historical' and 'necessary' with at least the apparent sanction of the scientific community. Such a position would find its most dramatic expression in a structure that makes a place for each of the salient categories of the Moment-hypothesis—the learner in Error, the Teacher, the Condition, and so forth—all within an essentially *Socratic* framework, thus demonstrating that the Socratic position alone remains to us, and that the Moment-position, so interpreted, amounts to nothing more than just another instance of it. The reader who is familiar with Kant's *Religion Within the Limits of Reason Alone** will recognize this as one of the experiments Kant attempts with amazing thoroughness in that book. Reading it side by side with the *Fragments*, one may be pardoned the suspicion that Kierkegaard had one eye on Kant, who seems to have anticipated his every move fifty years before.

The Interlude, then, is not a mere musical filler between acts but is essential to the whole performance. It is concerned with whether or not our language, our ways of speaking, are so unhappily constituted as to make impossible to do in any convincing manner what Climacus has been seeking to do from the first page: to set out some irreducible oppositions between the Socratic starting point and the Moment-hypothesis. To put it another way, it is a question of the absorbency of a single human consciousness, that is, whether it can tolerate, without falling afoul of logic, *both* the Socratic position *and* the Moment in a single commodious way of thinking. If both positions can coexist in one consciousness, it is plain which one will subordinate the other, for the Moment-hypothesis comes wrapped as it were in old newspaper and reports an event that belongs to the sphere of what comes into existence and passes away—the transient. The date-stamp will prove it to be only a relative, not a decisive, moment.

I

COMING INTO EXISTENCE

Examples of new beings, or standard occasions for using the expression 'a new baby' or 'this year's peaches' and so forth, defy enumera-

---

*Trans. T. M. Greene and H. H. Hudson (New York: Harper & Bros., 1960).

tion. Nothing could be more familiar than the million new blades of grass greening on lawns or the new leaves overhead. But what of the concept 'a new being'? Or if we lean toward a more substantival mode of speech, what is the *nature* of a new being taken simply as a new being, apart from the accident of where it made its debut or what species it belongs to? When we know that something is a new being, exactly what do we know? Frequently, of course, we know that the earth or a woman has brought it forth. However, where the point of the question is to keep the notion of coming-into-existence as distinct as possible from some other notion, for example that of having-to-be, and for no other reason than that the latter may now and then get confused with it, where are we to turn for the desired distinction?

One place we can turn to is to the things we typically *say* about comings-into-existence, and one thing we can notice about what we say is how poor a fit it makes with expressions that concern having-to-be. This is roughly the way Climacus proceeds, or at any rate this is the sort of observation his shorthand decompresses into. The shorthand itself, the language Climacus employs, as Thulstrup's commentary makes very clear, comes from well-worn paths in the history of philosophy.

What then is the nature of the happening in which, say, a new baby joins the family? When that takes place we do not talk as if an older baby, who had been around for a year, had metamorphosed into a different baby. Rather the announcements and cigarwrappers would have us understand that Jimmy's arrival was in no sense a change in *essence* (as from the one we once knew as Johnny over into Jimmy), but a change in being, from *being* only a possible Jimmy to being Jimmy in the flesh. Coming-into-existence, to force it back into one sentence, is the transition from not existing at all to existing. But this 'possible Jimmy' prior to undergoing the change of coming-into-existence—what is that? Is it anything at all?

It is helpful to bear in mind that in this chapter we are not dealing with the enigmatic and unsearchable, as in the earlier metaphysical chapter, but with the commonplace, or what everyone already knows, even when our question-marks may suggest unknowings. Thus, when we ask what sort of being a *possible* being is, no extraordinary vantage point is needed; the reference is to the kinds of remark we commonly make about possibility. I hear someone speak of the butterflies he hopes to collect and mount in the next few summers, although at this time they are only anticipated, which is to say, possible. There is a point to his telling me about those butterflies. There would be no point, however, in my demanding to know where those butterflies are keeping themselves *now*. One could express the fact that we have given no use to such a question by shaking our heads at it, but also by replying (with the traditional metaphysical courtesy that answers all topical questions) that those butterflies are *nowhere* right now. Climacus in a more formal style would call them nonbeings. All of this points to Climacus's primary conclusion about coming-into-existence, namely that it is in another world from what he calls 'necessity' or 'the necessary'. To give the point a factlike expression, as he does, by declaring flatly that the necessary (whatever that is) cannot come into existence, instead of remarking in effect that the two concepts do not go together in our discourse, tends unfortunately to obscure the *kind* of point he is making.

Difficulties may arise for a reader because the concept of necessity offers fewer and slighter handholds than that of coming-into-existence. It is important, therefore, to place ourselves on a common footing with Climacus concerning how the concept 'necessity' functions in the *Fragments*. In light of the broadside fired against theism in Chapter III, it would be ill-advised to connect necessity with some attribute of the God of the theistic philosophy. Similarly, despite Thulstrup's remarks (p. 238), the author's rejection of necessity as a category applicable to coming-into-existence cannot safely be traced to "the basic Christian position" of the *Fragments* without bringing out the trump-card of revelation from quite another deck than the one Climacus has been using, and thus indicting him for a misdeal. Instead, necessity and freedom in the *Fragments* are to be understood, it seems to me, by reference to the Unknown of Chapter III, taking care not to import any distinctively biblical categories into the analysis. To sketch the main point of the Interlude under that restriction and in unelaborated fashion: When speaking of the ordinary public world of existents, of objects that come along, have their day, and sink into the past, humans have *no occasion* to speak without qualification of something's *having* to be or to happen.

Then how do these objects and events come to be if not by necessity? When Climacus proposes his one-word answer to this (in the tradition of chivalry mentioned before) he chooses 'freedom'. He might as easily have answered, 'Not necessarily', since the mere designation of a category 'freedom'* in opposition to 'necessity' does not endow us with the power to fathom anything, and surely does not bathe with light the age-old metaphysical question (recently reopened by Heidegger) 'Why are there essents rather than nothing at all?'

A helpful convention in modern philosophy would restrict our talk of necessity to the constructions of logic and mathematics.** Those disciplines, it submits, investigate and exploit the relationships that come under the rubric 'If . . . then necessarily _____'. On the same point, necessity-expressions in everyday language would typically receive *conditional* form, for example, '*If* we want to escape from this island, we have no choice but to build a raft'. Qualified in ways like this, the use of 'must' expressions in everyday discourse presents no difficulty. However, where the notion of necessity gets coupled in an unqualified way with that of coming-into-existence, then, according to Climacus, something is fishy. If, for instance, someone were to insist that owing to the logic of events and the industrial edge which England held over Spain in the sixteenth century, the Armada *had* to lose, and the channel storm *had* to come along and batter it to pieces, we would have a glaring mismarriage of the concepts of coming-into-existence and necessity. If such conclusions occur in a larger and more cautious theory of historical inevitability, as instanced say in the better Marxist literature, this would do nothing to save the bad marriage. The question Hume is celebrated for would still haunt us: What in *our* field of perceptions corresponds to something's *having* to happen? But this is merely another way of saying that humans lack occasion for joining the concepts of coming-into-existence and strict necessity or 'must'.

How could the notion of necessity come to connect itself in anyone's mind with that of coming-into-existence? The school of hard knocks, where we meet with specimens of coming-into-existence, gives us indisputable actualities and a weather-eye for the possible. Climacus asks how these ingredients could be made to yield a "synthesis con-

---

*Properly speaking, 'freedom' besides being no answer is a misleading answer. We do have occasion to speak of events freely caused, but the alternative is not 'necessity' in an unqualified sense but something like 'compulsion', 'insanity', and the like.

**Cf. Ludwig Wittgenstein, *Tractatus Logico-Philosophicus*, trans. C. K. Ogden and F. P. Ramsey (London: Routledge & Kegan Paul, 1955), 6.37, p. 180. "Es gibt nur eine *logische* Notwendigkeit" (The only necessity is *logical* necessity).

stituting necessity" since it is essential to the necessary that it *be*. Although the language of the text is philosophical shorthand at its most cramped, it is clear enough to show that Climacus can find no logic to connect them. This is a hint that the notion of the necessary, or of that whose essence is to be, when we fail to confine it to the sphere of logic and arithmetic, can only refer us back to the notion of the Unknown, the Eternal. In the chapter on the Absolute Paradox it was brought out that whatever is eternal belongs to the sphere of the Unknown, not to the human sphere. The known world (of actualities and the possibilities tied up with them) affords philosophers only what earlier we called *grammatical* knowledge of the other sphere. Accordingly, when we ask how humans could milk more than a grammatical knowledge of the necessary out of their own sphere, the answer seems to be 'In no way'.

The last three paragraphs of the section entitled "Coming into Existence" are summed up in the grammatical remark that the necessary is in a category entirely by itself. This proscribes our joining it up with categories applicable to coming-into-existence, for example by saying (with Aristotle or Leibniz) that the necessary is possible, safe and minimal though this may sound to someone practiced in the shorthand. The same point receives a *fact-like* expression when the author tells us that no coming-into-existence is necessary, and that all coming-into-existence is with freedom.

The brief reference to the notion of *causes* in the final paragraph contrasts them with logical grounds. A logical ground is a self-consistent *idea* of something, let us say the idea of a machine that can play winning tic-tac-toe. Expressing Climacus's point first in a *fact-like* way, one could say it takes a good deal more than just a logically faultless idea or blueprint to make such a gadget come into existence. The artificer has to gather materials, connect part to part, and work out the bugs. In philosophical shorthand, he has to *cause* it. Now expressing the same point in a grammatical idiom, one could say that we do not count it as *explaining* a coming-into-existence merely to look at the verbal expression for whatever it is and note that it is self-consistent.

But what of those instances in which one is, as we say, right in the driver's seat, intimate with all the workings of a vehicle and with the physical laws of force and reciprocity that govern its motions? When I put my car into gear, engine running, and step on the accelerator, is there not even a hint of necessity in the resulting movement? The knowledge of laws and intervening linked causes may indeed produce an "illusion" of necessity, according to Climacus, but that is all. The point is, necessity ('must') and coming-into-existence ('is' or 'does') belong to distinct noninteracting spheres of discourse. If all available sources of energy were bent to the service of thrusting that vehicle forward there would be just as negative an occasion for saying it *must* go ahead as if it were up to its headlights in quicksand.

The illusion of which Climacus speaks, the notion that the hard sense of 'must' which stiffens logic and mathematics has something in common with the guarded or conditional 'must' of everyday speech, can perhaps be characterized more easily if we compare it with a more familiar example, the ancient catch about Achilles and the tortoise. The idea that Achilles faces the task of closing up an infinite number of head-starts in overtaking the tortoise accommodates itself to the (false) assumption that any arithmetical expression pertaining to the hypothetical objects of that science may be expected to apply the same way in the sphere of coming-into-existence. Thus, when Climacus lays it down that the necessary cannot come into existence, or conversely that coming-into-existence is never necessary, this is equivalent to the decompressed remark: The concept of necessity, the hard logical 'must', has no more been given an application to coming-into-existence than the notion 'infinite series' has been given an application to a hundred-meter sprint.

If it is a confusion to suppose that causal linkages, for example in the operations of a mechanism, offer 'evidence' of necessity, a parallel confusion may arise if I persuade myself that *manifestations of freedom* do the same in a more oblique way. That is, one might imagine that a streak of necessity reveals itself in the *contrast* between the unswerving trajectory of a fired shell, governed by ballistic formulas, and the artilleryman's free act of pulling the lanyard. But this, too, is illusion. If Climacus's main point holds, the concept of the necessary has been assigned no clear role in relation to the world of change, and the contrast just mentioned can be made quite satisfactorily without invoking that concept.

133

2

THE HISTORICAL

In this briefest of the numbered sections, Climacus identifies the historical with the past, or with that segment of the (once) possible that *has* come into existence. Within the historical a division appears between the human being and his natural surroundings, and the author's account of this division takes up most of Section 2.

Climacus anticipates no particular strain in asking his reader to think of nature as belonging to the sphere of what comes into existence, or more specifically as having a sort of history. What would this mean? It would be quite out of step with the *Fragments* if this were to entail our thinking of nature-as-a-whole, and even more so if we were to connect nature's coming-into-existence with a biblical account of Creation. Taking nature as a whole is ruled out partly by human limitations that will not even let us see around the corner, much less take in everything at once, and partly by the fact that nature-as-a-whole is not a focal point in the book. With regard to Creation, one need not, in order to think of nature as belonging to the sphere of coming-into-existence, be concerned about how it all began or the stupefying problems of *ex nihilo* engineering. It is sufficient to reflect on what one can see from the back yard or through a single window—hedges, stars, shadows, a cat. Even if one thinks big, say about offshore oil deposits, the whole Ukrainian wheat crop, or the Humboldt Current, the quasi-grammatical point can be made that inquiries into how those immensities came into existence make sense and can prove very useful. The way in which Climacus evidently intends his claim to be understood, that is, that the natural, including both living and inanimate, has a history of sorts, does not commit him to any extraordinary judgments about the noneternity of matter or Yahweh's opening fiats.

Then what stakes ride with the reminder that nature has a 'history'? The theme of the whole work is how the individual's consciousness can bring him into relation with the Truth, and it is through this question, it would seem, and not through questions of cosmogony, that we are to view the present section. If a thinker should permit himself to forget the point of Section I—that the Eternal is in an entirely different category from everything in the temporal world—and if he should confuse the Eternal somehow with the natural, perhaps through being struck with ageless peaks and valleys, encores and symmetries, this will be a step toward forgetting what coming-into-existence means. Then if he goes so far as to enchant himself with the thought that a consciousness dimly like his own slumbers in every leaf and pebble, until the gap between nature and his own kind closes dreamily in the hammock-sway of his thought, this will take him some way toward forgetting that he, too, has come into existence. Thus, the huge idea that consciousness pervades all of nature is not so woolly after all as to be without consequences, at any rate of the sort that lead someone to crowd something essential out of mind. The danger, then, is the double one of confusing nature (more or less known) with the Eternal (which belongs to the Unknown), and then of confusing one's consciousness with nature and thereby with the Eternal. It is a species of what Climacus in the *Postscript** goes on to call "forgetting what it means to exist." The fact that such a thinker may place himself romantically at the service of a world-consciousness and pay it tribute in works of art and the like is a matter that Climacus does not go into in his metaphysical intermezzo any more than the fact that one might on the same grounds take up with rebelliousness and a devotion to evil. In the Interlude the author's purpose, it seems, is to point out a possible metaphysical confusion that can result in a crucial forgetting.

In the final paragraph something positive, though dehydrated to a dusty powder, comes out concerning the specifically human sector of nature. The reference is to a second coming-into-existence occurring within a prior one. The prior one is, of course, the begetting and birth and infancy of the human being and happens 'by nature', to use the Aristotelian expression, being historical in the widest sense of the term. The second coming-into-existence, called historical 'in the stricter sense', is by no means the New Birth of Chapter I, an interpretation that would cloud everything by commingling the categories of reason and the Moment. Rather it is the coming-into-existence of the self, the individual consciousness. It is important to consider this coming-into-existence quite apart from any and all theories of ensoulment that turn up in the history of psychology from Plato on, whether of secular or biblical inspiration, in order not to confuse Climacus's point with disputed opinions. The absence in the text of any apology

---

*Bk. 2, pt. 1, chap. 2, sec. 4B.

for what he says stands in sharp contrast to the disputatious detours of Chapter III and hints that no controversial sense is intended.

Even with that intention, what can he say noncontroversially about the coming-into-existence of a human self? Perhaps only that as a human comes along in years, he is taught language and thereby acquires among other skills that of sustaining a relationship of dialogue with himself at various levels. Humans, in other words, are language-users, and using language, as Wittgenstein puts it, is "as much a part of our natural history as walking, eating, drinking, playing. . . ."* This, it seems to me, is the quiet and unpugnacious core of the author's distinction between natural and human coming-into-existence. If it turns out to be profoundly consequential, this will not make it retroactively vulnerable, for it remains a bit of natural history so plain that to check it out would amount to a *pro forma* gesture. Climacus can hardly be said to be opting here for anything as disputable as a mind/body or soul/body dualism or a mind/brain identity theory.

This second coming-into-existence, the bringing forth of the individual consciousness or self, Climacus calls historical in a stricter sense than the bodily one. It concerns not simply the past but the individual's past as remembered, and as recorded by biographers, diarists, and the like, with emphasis on what we could call intimate or inward history. At the center of this stands an individual's relationship to the Truth, that is, the answers to his Socratic questions. There are other sides to an individual's history, but the thematic content of the *Fragments* places emphasis on the history of what he really thinks of himself and of whatever power brought it about that, in addition to being historical in the inclusive sense of coming-into-existence, he also has an inner history. This 'self', for want of a more agreeable noun, comes into existence within the life of the organism, but at least partly 'by art', as other humans teach the child to make his way linguistically and otherwise. Later this self will be characterized by the fact of having an opinion of itself, and the record of how it gets along with itself will make up its intimate history in the narrower sense of 'history'.

It is very close to a truism to observe that a second coming-into-existence comes about through the assistance a child receives from its

*Ludwig Wittgenstein, *Philosophical Investigations* (New York: Macmillan, 1953), sec. 25.

elders and from itself as it attains maturity. However, it is not so easy to penetrate the closing remarks (p. 94) that these relatively freely acting causes point to an unconditionally free one. What can this mean? Once again a tension asserts itself over the concept of necessity, and again it would be a mistake, I believe, to consider 'absolutely free' a reference to the sovereignty of the Christian God. In the preceding section the point was made that the concept of strict necessity has no application to coming-into-existence. Section 2 then appears as a corollary: neither does strict necessity figure in the individual self's coming-into-existence. Having marked out a particular sector within the sphere of coming-into-existence, the author wishes to warn us in Section 2 against applying the concept of necessity specifically to that sector.

In what way might someone come to connect the notion of necessity with the human or narrower sense of 'historical', that is, with the inner personal history of a man? When the *Fragments* was written some grand and important Hegelian concepts sought to fuse together the historical and the necessary, chiefly in the idea that history is the un-folding in time of a God's idea according to methodical stages and laws, which prefigure the inevitable outcome and may be grasped by man. If an individual becomes charmed into viewing his personal exis-tence *through* this variant of theism, then his conscious existence can take on for him the appearance of a fleeting instant within an all-encompassing consciousness, so that his personal judgments about himself or anything else will seem to possess at best only a momentary validity except where they line up with those of the circumferential di-vine idea.

Plainly an answer of a certain sort to the Socratic questions lies in the notion that the paradigm of the divine consciousness can be grasped by the individual. Here is a formula for what a human ought to place first in his life, namely understanding the great paradigm, which however reveals itself only in large trends—of world-history and the history of ideas—the *entrée* to which is omnivorous learning. Hence the individual should aspire to be like the world's most erudite appre-ciator of the divine paradigm. This view in turn implies an opinion about what it means to be in the Truth, or to have the Truth, to wit: only accidental circumstances, remediable by surges of human effort, keep me from the Truth. Humans are not in Error, after all, but in ignorance. There may even be a kind of religiosity in such a view, where the individual seeks either to immerse himself Hindu-style in the superconsciousness, or just as spiritedly to declare himself out, an upstart rebel, on the grounds that the divine thoughts are absurd, wicked, or otherwise unacceptable. In such lines of thinking, the idea of necessity comes in more or less in the following way. The thinker looks at his consciousness not as one coming-into-existence within another, but as an *aspect* or *expression* of the larger consciousness, queer as this may sound, and in that sense quite dependently bound up with the larger, so that his own consciousness is formed or determined by that of another and remains subject to the necessity of that other's logic. The key conception in such a theory is that dialectical laws analogous to laws of mechanics operate in the sphere of consciousness. The conception of laws of nature, however, is one that Climacus took pains in Section 1 to keep distinct from the conception of necessity. If the individual takes care to remember that his personal self comes into existence within the temporal span of, and bound up with, his bodily coming-into-existence, as a new self with a personality of its own and not as the determinate projection of another's, this reminder can serve to ward off enchantments which the concept of necessity might otherwise cast over the student of philosophy to whom Climacus addresses his book.

The "relatively freely effecting cause" that helps usher this self into existence is easy enough to identify in the parents and teachers who brought me along. However, it is not immediately clear how this recognizable 'cause', as the shorthand expresses it, 'points to' a cause of another sort. In line with what has gone before, the closing words of Section 2 might be understood in this way. First of all, the central fact about my self is how it stands in relation to the Truth. As we saw earlier, however, the stabs and probes I send out in that direction come back bent by collisions with the Unknown. Now this Truth concerns precisely the self that has been set on its feet and helped along by those other selves. By teaching me to use language, they opened up the *only* obvious line I now possess for purposes of comprehending my own coming-into-existence as a self. None of this makes the Unknown any less unknown, and I certainly have not at this point succeeded in comprehending the ultimate 'cause' of this self, but the *hint* so far (and 'points to' can mean 'hints at' as often as it means 'proves') is that if this blank Unknown takes any interest in furthering my relationship to the Truth, it had better brush up on its English, for if I am ever to make headway it will be through being spoken to.

But does the Unknown go in for speaking? That, of course, remains stubbornly unknown. Is the Unknown in any intelligible sense a *self*? That, too, is unknown, but owing to that very fact I dare not foreclose the possibility that this Unknown—which I ran into, we recall, in seeking to account for myself—may have up its unknown sleeve unknown resources for getting through to me on that matter. Thus, in a sense the hint comes all from my side.

3
THE PAST

Earlier sections of the Interlude try to keep the concept of 'what *must* be' sealed off from the universe of discourse that concerns history or coming-into-existence. However, in the thought that we *cannot* change the past, we find what looks like an exception, a sense in which the 'cannot' seems to stand for something more than a temporal barrier of the sort that keeps the future concealed from us until it unfolds. There seems to be a barrier that places the idea of changing the past *logically* out of the question and thus testifies to an interface between the two nonconnecting universes.

Even if we take the immutability of the past without qualification, abjuring for the moment as sophistry Climacus's reference to a "higher change" that can wipe out portions of the past, according to Section 3 this will not suffice to show that the past is necessary, for the past has come into existence and thereby declared itself outside the sphere of the necessary. As soon as we bring in a reference to change, out goes necessity in the sense of that which must always be and always in the same way. The mere fixity of the past, then, offers no occasion for concluding either that it *could* not have been different, or that, having come into existence, it must out of necessity persist in being what it is.

In his remark about Repentance (p. 95), Climacus goes further, speaking of the past by analogy with a sort of slate on which a line here and there may *in fact* be scratched out, a deed here and there *in fact* obliterated by forgiveness. This foreshadowing of the Supplement a few pages ahead succeeds in producing an instance in which people speak as if to acknowledge that the past, which came into being by means of change, honors its parentage and never becomes the offspring of necessity. At the same time, one can wonder if the notion of Repentance, or of *wishing* something in the past annulled, is of hard enough metal to support the conceptual distinction Climacus has been making, which seems sturdy enough without that extra prop.

A similar position develops in the author's remarks about freedom, which would be an illusion, he argues, if the littlest quantum of strict necessity crept into our reckonings. In philosophy, the formula 'If *that* were so, then such-and-such would be an illusion' functions typically as a vehicle for making grammatical points. In this instance the point concerns the myriad uses of language in which people expressly seek to *shape* the future—plans, pleas, requests, requisitions, cries for help, and so forth. That we do have uses for innumerable forms of speech like these is an unchallenged observation about how we employ language and makes up the minor premise of the *reductio*. That having freedom *means* being the kind of creature that has such forms of language woven into its way of life is, speaking again syllogistically, the major premise and nerve of the argument, from which the reality of freedom follows. Now, Climacus employs an argument of a very different style rhetorically, though to the same effect, namely a sort of thought-experiment calculated to dramatize the repugnancy between the concepts of necessity and coming-into-existence. Consider the most remote and trivial state of affairs one can imagine, say the position of a fallen leaf on the surface of a pond in some unmapped woodland. If we persuade ourselves that the leaf floats where it is by strict necessity, or *could* not be positioned otherwise, then every particle that touches the leaf would have to lock into place around it, and every particle farther out follow suit in deference to the eternal-historical hybrid we have posited, chilling the world down to a temperature of absolute zero. This is something like the picture Climacus offers us, though indeed the thought of a germ of necessity taking over the world is an impossible image to work with.

These two pieces of reasoning, the one plainly about language, the other a conceptual experiment dealing fancifully with the physics of 'possible worlds', make the same essentially grammatical point: we do not, in fact, apply the unqualified logical 'must' to things that come into existence and pass away.

To introduce necessity at any point in a time-sequence, the final paragraph of Section 3 remarks, would wipe out the distinction between past and future. This figuration, too, can set a reader spinning. What would that calamity be like? Again one can weave a piece of fancy. Perhaps the smallest fleck of necessity on our tongues would put a check to all discourse, for if change and, more particularly, coming-into-existence froze up completely, what would be the point of telling anybody anything? Although fictions of this sort may have their charms, it would be at least as telling to repeat the grammatical point mentioned above. Then, in place of a reference to monstrous illusions and images of a paralytic universe, one could remark in a prosier style that the absence of a convention for applying a hard-line concept of necessity to historical matters leaves it completely up in the air as to what if any turn of events would compel us to institute such a convention.

4
THE APPREHENSION OF THE PAST

In his opening paragraph, Climacus takes *uncertainty* to be a mark of everything that has come into existence. This important move, which leads a little later into the concept of faith or belief, repeats the theme: Necessity and coming-into-existence have no part of each other. Because they do not, there will always be on the side of the knower or apprehender of a past event, no matter how unchallengeably it sits in the history books, a residue of uncertainty. Climacus does not advance this as a psychological fact, as if historians experienced a quaver of doubt with every reference to the past, although he does see in *wonder*, the passion of being struck by something in existence, a proper passion for historians. The fact is rather a grammatical one, struck off from the point already laid down, that we have, in fact, no use for expressions of unqualified necessity in relation to matters of existence, although such uses are plentiful where we deal with hypothetical entities as in mathematics.

This point comes out most clearly when set over against mistaken ways of trying to understand the past. Suppose, for example, that I seek to enlarge my understanding of a past event by reconstructing the circumstances that led up to it, perhaps on the Kantian principle that "everything that happens is hypothetically necessary." The device by which I propose to augment my understanding is, let us say, a massing of facts about the 1940 German strategy and preparations on the one hand, and Allied weaknesses on the other, until the situation takes on the look of a poised avalanche. By gathering this data, I can in a certain sense drain the 'wonder' out of the fall of France. The more I learn about it, the less anomalous or unexpected the event appears. Still, what would it add to my understanding if I climaxed these researches with the flat-out remark, 'France had to fall'? This, according to Climacus, would introduce an element of intellectual illusion, or better say forgetfulness, helped along by the intervening stretch of time. What could sanction the words '*had* to'? Surely not the mere fact that between 1940 and today I pieced together a great many facts. My knowing a great deal *now* can scarcely have made something happen back in 1940!

Perhaps, someone might argue, *God's* knowing and willing the event made it happen or would not permit it to happen in any other way, and my reconstructing the circumstances is a way of enlarging my understanding to something nearer divine completeness. Climacus calls this manifestation-theory another form of the illusion, which lies in the idea that someone's *knowing* something has the power to forge a marriage between the concepts of necessity and coming-into-existence, or has the power to institute uses for words like 'must' in the historical sphere.

Here Climacus takes a problematic turn on the issue of *how we acquire* knowledge of the past. Since coming-into-existence is not an immediate object of knowledge, by means of what organ or faculty, he asks, do we arrive at certainty about yesteryear? The question has an odd, strained ring to it. Why, after all, say flatly that coming-into-existence *cannot* be sensed or cognized immediately? If indeed the 'what' of an event, say the flowering of a jonquil, may be known immediately, if one can witness it from beginning to end, where is the catch in claiming to know immediately that it has taken place? From the way Climacus goes on, it appears that his point is a first cousin to the dictum he cites several times: immediate sensing and cognition cannot deceive, while coming-into-existence has about it the obscurity that goes with any transition from nonbeing or possibility to actuality. Does he intend us to understand that, while immediate cognition of the 'what'—the fact that this jonquil is *now* in bloom—is something I cannot be mistaken about, can know beyond challenging, the same does not hold for past-tense expressions of that fact, for example, that the jonquil *has* come into flower? Are we to understand that the former is a report of what one perceives straight on, the latter an inference, hypothesis, or presumption?

To take the easiest part first, the notion that immediate sensation or cognition "cannot deceive" is philosophical shorthand for the following grammatical point. Knowing that the plant before my eyes is a jonquil in full bloom amounts to (a) knowing how the English expression 'jonquil in bloom' is typically applied, and (b) perceiving in my immediate surroundings a typical occasion for applying it. To express doubt in relation to this pair of correlates would come perilously close to saying— in fluent English—that I doubt I know English, a remark which, if not exactly a self-contradiction, seems at any rate to swallow its own tail. The more difficult side of Climacus's point concerns my knowledge that the jonquil *has* flowered. Suppose it flowered yesterday, if memory serves me. *Qua* past event, this happening stands outside the range of what I can presently see. There would be something out of sorts about calling my memory of the flowering an *inference*, as if I had worked my way to the judgment by excluding some clear alternative, yet it expresses more than what I can apprehend at this moment, and with that distinction in mind Climacus seeks a category-name suitable for our apprehension of the past.

Much about the past is known with certainty, but where do we get our certainty, since uncertainty is the earmark of anything that has come into existence? What makes us in many instances doubt-free? The will, says Climacus, and his references to ancient and later scepticism show that he is not about to let loose an unheard-of opinion. The "organ", as he puts it, for apprehending the past, the category-name he has been seeking, is *belief* or *faith*, not to be confused with Faith (the condition for recognizing the Teacher) as described a chapter earlier. Belief or faith keeps the uncertainty at bay and harmless, *as if* by the individual's constantly repeating to himself, 'Well, there is no point in raising doubts about *that* event'. This repeated negating of an uncertainty sounds psychologically queer as a description of how people typically apprehend a past event, but the message seems modest enough: I can choose to dismiss any question as to whether the jonquil bloomed yesterday, or as to whether Hitler's armies overran the French and British, at least until I am persuaded that doubting will serve some purpose. I have no such option concerning what Climacus calls "immediate sensation and cognition," the impressions of my close surroundings and my knowledge that this is *called* a pen, a desk, and so forth.

Belief or faith, then, in this nonreligious sense, comes into its certainties by *willing* doubt out of the picture or by *refusing* to acknowledge doubt's pleas without a sufficient positive reason for reopening the closed case. By using these expressions of volition, Climacus means to keep our apprehension of the past distinct from the passive sort of apprehending that he calls 'immediate', where the knower is helpless but to acknowledge what he perceives, and distinct also from the apprehension of what *must* be so, for example, the relations between signs—or 'essences' in another terminology—within a calculus.

In the last paragraphs before the "Supplement," Climacus begins to connect the distinctions he has been making with matters that bear on his Teacher-narrative. The thesis sounds at first quite bold: the man who later hears about a past event by means of eyewitness testimony is related to that event in the same way as the witnesses. Thus, their testimony is for purposes of accurately apprehending the past as good as if he had been present himself at the event. That is, they relay to him the immediacies of perception, more or less what he would have gathered for himself had he been there. At first sight one can hardly avoid thinking of this thesis as somewhat overstated for the sake of compression, for example, where Climacus chooses not to mention the kinds of mutilation and touching up that testimony can undergo. Even if we add a dash of that to the mixture, however, the point stands: contemporary and successor alike have to apprehend the *coming-into-existence* aspect of an event by *believing* it, whether the occasion for affirming the event happens to be a witnessing or a yellowed writ of testimony.

SUPPLEMENT: APPLICATION

How do these distinctions apply to the hypothesis that the God has been involved in one of those comings-into-existence? Up to this point, the author has applied it solely to historical events of the ordinary sort, whose only 'contradiction', as he puts it, is that they have come into existence. In what sense is that a contradiction? On the side of the individual the hint of something contradictory comes in, apparently, whenever by means of the passion of believing he takes as certain some happening which is chronically and essentially uncertain, adopting it with a passion into his certitudes. On the side of the event, the contradiction-like aspect goes with the notion, already discussed, of a *new* being, which comes into existence out of a state, if we may call it that, of never having been, or comes along at such and such a place and time from having been a nonentity everywhere and always up to the hour of its coming-into-existence. Its existence in this sense 'contradicts' its former nothingness.

From the content of the Moment-hypothesis it is perhaps easier to generate expressions that look stubbornly self-contradictory: That which always is, or is eternal and changeless, at a certain date commenced to exist, that is, became a particular human Teacher. This historical claim, with its references to a specifiable individual and calendar date, is something to be believed or disbelieved in the same way as any other claim that involves a coming-into-existence. In this instance, however, the *risk* of believing what cannot be directly cognized—a risk which as far as commonplace historical events are concerned can be overcome by weights of evidence and testimonies until the possibility of doubt gets pushed into a very small corner—finds itself prodigiously accentuated by the element of self-contradiction. Reason is deprived of sensible occasions for conjecturing that the Eternal (or the Absolutely Different) has come into existence, and as a result questions such as 'How do you known *that* happened?' leave reason stammering. The contradiction blocks all normal avenues for alleviating a historian's kind of doubt. This can also give us a hint that questions like 'How do you know?' as well as doubts and demands for evidence are somewhat misleading and wrong-headed, but for the present it will be more useful to look into the special risk attached to believing the Moment-hypothesis.

The risk here has very little to do with the off-chance of accepting a factually inaccurate or erroneous historical report and a great deal to do with the fact that this belief—that the God has entered existence as a human Teacher—has, as a piece of history, a peculiar emptiness about it. To other persons it can appear that one who believes it is not so much mistaken or ill-informed as radically and pathetically unfortunate, in that his central belief is a mere mock-up of a belief, hollow through and through. Under a certain kind of bright lighting it looks very much like a belief that *nothing unusual happened*. That is, if the Unknown appeared in history as an ordinary man (in unrecognizable form) and after a time followed all men before him to the grave, the ordinary course of events would look to every waking eye unruptured and undisturbed. Climacus seeks to highlight the peculiarity of his hypothesis by rewording it as a self-contradiction, a knotted Parmenidean sentence. In that form it delivers a hard logical rap to any head that seeks to assimilate it into the common run of facts. The effect is the same if we reword it as an empty hypothesis. Reason is undone either way, or consents to its own undoing, when in order to believe one is obliged to let his guard down and admit conceptions that are, objectively speaking, hollow at the core, for example, the invisible-historical. Part of the risk, then, lies in the reaction of *other* souls to this believer who, though he has not gone mad in any of the standard ways, assembles his thoughts around an empty central historical thought, empty in the sense of being absolutely equivalent to the historical thought that 'on that date there was nothing outside the usual to report'.

Here a further word is in order concerning what it is that enables a person to set reason aside in precisely this manner. In the preceding chapter, Climacus spoke of the condition first mentioned in his Project of Thought and identified it with "that happy passion" he proposes to call Faith. The fact that reasoning offers the believer no organ for apprehending this event's happening, much less the 'how' of it, puts him under a tremendous handicap and fixed disadvantage when he comes up against expressions of reasonableness in his fellow-men, so that he risks at every instant looking for all the world as if his critical powers had fallen into a strange captivity. Thus his situation partakes, in the manner of a constant risk, of some of the pathos of the Teacher's situation in Chapter II, where a failure of understanding threatens the relationship. For example, reasonableness might inquire of the believer, 'What leads you to believe that that event took place?' It would be more direct (and no less reasonable) if the asker asked, 'What induced you to place that empty, vacuous thought at the center of all your thinking?' It would then be possible to reply, 'It all began with the discovery that I was in Error', which reply, although it would not make discourse easier for either party, would make clear to both that the pathos surrounding the believer's situation had some of its roots in the asker's own situation, inasmuch as according to the Moment-hypothesis the asker himself would be in Error. And such a reply would also lead in good time to a vital distinction. The expression of faith or belief with regard to a simple historical proposition consists in keeping doubts at arm's length so long as there is no positive occasion for doubting. But the expression of Faith with regard to this special historical belief does not involve the possibility of doubt at all—only belief or offense, as re-marked earlier—and its typical inward overture-expression will consist in giving the Teacher permission to install himself in the learner.

8

AFTER THE TEACHER HAS COME AND GONE

Chapter V of *Philosophical Fragments*,
"The Disciple at Second Hand"

SUMMARY

Assume the Interlude spans 1843 years; the Teacher's disciples include not only some contemporaries but numbers who come along much later. How do these two groups differ? In order not to overlook any distinctions within the second and presumably larger group, let us first attend to that.

I
The class of disciples at second hand considered with respect to the differences comprised within it

For our purpose it will suffice to compare briefly the first with the latest generation of secondary disciples.

A. THE FIRST GENERATION

How great a value shall we put on being so close in time to the Teacher's own generation? Suppose a tyrant of the first generation used every possible device to determine from witnesses precisely how the Teacher's career went, and put together a seamless and richly detailed account. To what advantage? Historical precision, surely, but this is not a move in the direction toward discipleship, which would presuppose among other things a sense of sin.

The advantage of being nearer to the shock-event means at best a less dilute awareness of the decision facing anyone who hears of it. This decision, however, can go either way.

B. THE LAST GENERATION

Furthest removed from the shock, the last generation has the seeming advantage of being able to survey the consequences of the Teacher's coming, which appear to lend probability to the belief that it happened, although its paradox-character does not make a very good fit with ordinary senses of 'probable'.

If those consequences are taken to be such that, for example, an individual can be born into a Faith-endowed family and come into his second nature before he has discovered his first or heard of the second, confusion is sovereign.

Even if every detail of life bears the stamp of those consequences, this could have happened only by means of individuals in successive generations relating themselves to the past event through conversions.

C. COMPARISON

If the first generation of secondary disciples can boast a less encumbered view of discipleship, a sharper fear goes along with this appreciation of the difficulty. However, for the latest generation the situation is only seemingly less fearful.

2

The problem of the disciple at second hand

With the historical fact posited in our hypothesis, no generation is luckier or unluckier than any other in being born closer to or further away from it in time. Historical knowings such as the testimony of contemporaries can serve only as *occasions* for someone's becoming a disciple; in every instance of discipleship, the God himself must give the condition. If a contemporary of the God as Teacher could pass on the condition to later comers, he himself and not the God would become the object of Faith, but in our hypothesis the learner owes everything to the God and nothing to other men.

Then what can a contemporary do for a successor? He can put himself forward as one who believes against reason, that is, he can make himself an occasion for the other to make up his mind about it. In what

way might the credibility of a contemporary properly concern a successor? Again, only as an occasion for bringing to his notice the central
historical fact, that the God appeared in human form, a proposal that
in its emptiness hides any marginal inconsistencies that might creep
into a contemporary's account.

Thus there is no disciple at second hand with respect to *this* fact. As
far as concerns any advantage from being a contemporary of the God's
visit, it would be just as well for him if the God left the earth.

*　*

These remarks, some of them borrowed from the New Testament,
seem to cut back to zero the advantage of contemporaneity. Yes,
the result is the equality of all men when, one by one, they fetch up
against the difficulty of becoming a disciple. But does this not point to
a triumphant generation at some later age, when the seeds of the first
generation come to fruition? Perhaps so, but will this be a believing
generation? What believer would find himself at home in a triumphal
procession?

Concerning my use of scriptural expressions, let me conclude by reminding the reader of the questions on the title-page. Christianity
alone, and nothing else in history, has proposed itself to be an historical point of departure for the individual's eternal consciousness, the
same Christianity which I have treated here as a hypothetical conceit,
but which could never have arisen in my own heart.

REMARKS

In the snippet of conversation that opens this chapter, the author
proposes to take a gamble by raising the question of a disciple at some
remove in time from the Teacher's generation. The question, which he
suspects is a fishy one, is something like this: 'With the discussion of
the contemporary disciple behind us, how does this option of becoming a disciple differ for persons of later generations?' What if one cannot ask such a question? In other words, what if asking it presupposes
a distinction that turns out to be unreal? Not only is there a real issue
here, replies the other side, but a spate of possible issues arising from
countless differences between any one generation and another. But
can we not, the author asks, treat all those differences under a single

class-heading, the secondary disciple over against the contemporary? This is what he proposes to do.

I

The class of disciples at second hand considered with respect to the differences comprised within it

By limiting discussion to the first and latest generations of second-ary disciples, spanning 1843 years, Climacus can save a lot of space. The possible loss of perspective in using an historian's fine-grained style lies in an embarrassment of riches, an absorbing cumulative tap-estry of social history and the history of ideas from one century to the next. If, as the author suspects, the distinctions between *disciples* of one period and another turn out to be insignificant, what a waste it would be in a chapter on the nature of discipleship to pass in review every little nuance in the history of ideas!

An algebraic style is to be preferred over a cumulative one, on the grounds that the communal-scholarly drive toward completeness of records can easily create a swamp around the concept 'disciple' by going on as though mastery of the manifold distinctions were a pre-condition for understanding what being a disciple means. In "The Case of the Contemporary Disciple" and earlier, Climacus has made the point that individuals become disciples in virtue of the God's grant-ing the condition to one at a time. It makes no important difference, then, if an individual happens to be born before or after Darwin pub-lished his theory, or in a decade that saw great ferment among the op-pressed classes, or during a revival of Pythagoreanism. As Climacus has set the matter up, such factors cannot enter into the *reasonable-ness* of becoming a disciple, in which becoming "reason is set aside and the Paradox bestows itself."

A. THE FIRST GENERATION OF SECONDARY DISCIPLES

A reader can boil the algebra of this section down to one formula, though with a degree of ease that can be misleading when one consid-ers the areas where the formula is to be applied. The formula states simply that historical precision has nothing to do with Faith, hence that any edge in precision the first generation might boast cannot be

151

turned to the account of Faith. This will mean that the pursuit of word-for-word accuracy in reporting the Teacher's sayings, and the effort to fix up any anachronisms, inconsistencies, and unkept promises in the Teacher's message, would amount merely to marking time in relation to becoming a disciple. Verbal snags in the sources of testimony are, for Climacus, eddies of turbulence on the fringes of a central event whose very conception is self-contradictory, and are not only minor but positively to be expected on other grounds, for example, that any testifying disciple of old would be expected to have his mind on the central event or, expressed in another way, on the Teacher rather than his teaching.

However, the mystique that has come to surround the idea of self-contradiction in the twentieth century, for example, in the dictum 'A contradiction implies any proposition whatever'—which may hold true within some particular calculus but should not on account of that be confused with senses of 'contradiction' in public use—tends to make any inconsistency an absolute stopper and its removal a number one priority. Let us therefore pause long enough to ask the following: Suppose the Teacher had made a remark which could only be taken as promising his return to earth within the lifetime of one or another contemporary disciple. His failure to do so would constitute, at least for some persons in the first and second generations of secondary disciples, an inconsistency between word and fact striking enough for anyone to notice and baffling enough to make at least some of the surviving contemporaries, in their appeals for patience, cast wide and deep for possible explanations, leaving a tangled record for future generations. The original disciples would have acknowledged the inconsistency in their efforts to make it into only an apparent one and to keep it on the periphery of what was to them the cyclonic heart of the matter.

Thus, our question becomes: What was the role of that inconsistency for the surviving original disciples? How did it look to them? Why would they have done everything possible to shrink its apparent magnitude in the minds of converts? Issues of this sort can grow into fixed question marks for the scholarly community, whose members at a given time cannot do everything at once but must wait for new documents to turn up or for a colleague to complete his research and submit it to the corporate gaze. In perfect freedom, for example, a colleague might theorize: 'There was never any serious possibility of the Teacher's return, but the original team had a good thing going. They had the concessionaires' job for the new movement, plus control of all tithes and gratuities, and did not want grumblers out in the remoter cells to kill the goose, so naturally would send off letters aimed at quieting them with far-fetched explanations'. Nor will it prevent someone equally enterprising at a still later time from giving that theory a new lease, with or without crediting its originator. It is perfectly to be expected that a particular theory should go through moon-like phases of light and dark in the eyes of the scientific community.

In all of this, however, it is important to keep in mind the main point Climacus makes in this section: historical precision, though attainable in principle and more directly for the first generation than for any afterwards, is stored along side-paths, not the path of discipleship, not the path of Faith. This will mean, for one thing, that *for a disciple* inconsistencies within the reportage, or between reported promise and fact, stand outside the task appointed for himself, that is, to keep fast the bond between himself and the Teacher. Besides being a bond with the Unknown, which keeps its dark side toward the individual, this bond involves his signing over permission, then paying on demand, and treating even his worst troubles as blessings, no matter what his reason has to say about it. The bond, then, whatever else one might wish to say about discipleship, entails a certain amount of uncaring about textual inconsistencies or the tidying up of the divine appointment-calendar.

The same holds for another kind of inconsistency, this time between some bit of the reportage and the common understanding of the Teacher's character as an historical person. Suppose one paragraph of the report described an incident so outrageously out of joint with the rest that it constituted an odd little cankering presence, for instance if the Teacher had reportedly cursed a certain fish for not growing big enough, or got his annual tax money by opening a fresh fig. Too far off the norm even to be called a miracle, such an event could strike someone as an occasion to get busy in quest of historical precision, at least to the extent of shifting all the obviously unhistorical surds and clinkers out of the testimony. So it might seem, and even to a disciple, but only in some capacity which has nothing to do with being a disciple. That is, relating oneself to the central event of the Moment-hypothesis means relating oneself to the Teacher, who can be recognized only if he himself extends the condition. This relationship of Faith in the capitalized sense presupposes that the learner has understood himself to be in Error, and his part in the relationship commences when he grants the other party permission to correct the Error, whatever that may entail. This is identified as the hard initial thing for the would-be disciple, inasmuch as it goes against not merely the faculty of reason *per se* because of the Paradox, but against what he personally really thinks, the Error that dyes every cell of his heart. Now to be of the opinion that the hard initial thing for a disciple is something different, and consists let us say in the task of achieving a luminous portrait of the historical Teacher, or of putting the testimony of an earlier generation through a critical filter so as to incorporate it into the wineskins of reason, would amount to giving the floor to one's Error.

This is why it must be said that inconsistences of various kinds within the reportage do not add up to difficulties for the disciple as such. This is not to deny that they may challenge someone in his scholarly capacity and run his imagination up against brick walls. The point is that the disciple as such is not commanded to *imagine* anything. Stretching the imagination to accommodate a queer bit of text, filing away at the text to make it agree with one's powers of imagining—these are not tasks one acquires in virtue of one's discipleship. Even if we allow that such projects have to do with historical precision and must be granted the same high esteem we place on every serious effort to approach that ideal, they still have no decisive bearing on discipleship or Faith.

'On the other hand', someone might ask, 'are we not to expect, in the historical portions of a chronicle of the Moment-event, and in whatever details the chroniclers of the generation left to us, enough intelligibility so that we may incorporate them into our understanding? Are we not to expect the several sources to say the same things, and the personality of the Teacher to emerge as integral? And by bringing the reports into line with one another, and finding paths around the inconsistencies and bafflers, can we not hope to make their content clearer and above all more relevant to our own time?' Out of such questions as these, scholarly projects can take form whose value is not to be judged *a priori* or sight unseen. More than that, it is not self-evident that Climacus's main point (that such projects have no bearing on Faith, or that they bear on Faith only in virtue of some misunderstanding) can hold out against them.

It is not self-evident, for example, that systematically constructing *interpretations* for hard sayings in the original testimony is a project rooted in a misunderstanding and has no bearing on Faith. For Climacus, himself no slouch at rendering interpretations, the question with regard to a given interpretive project would turn on whether the interpretations, in their reasonableness, call attention to the downfall of reason in the decision to become a disciple, or whether instead they obscure the Paradox under a whitewash of human categories and talk. The fact that this downfall of reason, this forsaking of human guidance, is something nobody normally wants, should put us on sharp notice that the problem of making the original testimony relevant to a later generation may very well prove to be a phony problem. It would arise, presumably, when individuals complain that the testimony is irrelevant to their lives, or simply treat it so, with the result that making it come alive for them presents itself as a necessary preliminary to any decision on their part.

However, we have to remind ourselves of exactly what such an individual is calling irrelevant. It is first of all the charge that he himself is in bondage to Error by his own fault, and that his maker, out of love for him (since his maker has a hardheaded streak that will not let him make do with substitutes, he must win that individual personally) has come into existence to lead him out of this fix if he will allow it. Of all the expressions one might pick to characterize this historical claim, from 'the Miracle' to a howl of offense, 'irrelevant' seems the least applicable, unless we are speaking of an individual who is irrelevant to himself. For this reason the task of making the original testimony relevant defines itself as one of *repeating* rather than *interpreting* something. If it should in fact come about that an individual greets the repetition with a blank stare, or even shouts out the word 'Irrelevant!', the disciple is under no obligation to take such expressions at face value, unless it has slipped his mind that what he is repeating to the other person includes a note to the effect that the person is in Error. None of this takes away a dram from the merit of venturing interpretations of the original testimony but only from the merit of imagining that such a project is on the way to Faith. The principle Climacus appeals to in severing such projects from Faith is straightforward enough: in the

Moment-hypothesis it belongs to the God alone (since the learner is in Error) to lay down what shall count as a Faith-relationship between the learner and the Teacher.

B. THE LAST GENERATION

In dealing with the subclass of disciples on earth in the 1843rd year after the Teacher's birth, Climacus effects a radical change of scenery under the heading of "consequences." We are now to imagine that our peculiar historical fact, the God's visit, has made itself noticed in every corner of the world that word of mouth can reach, even to becoming the zero-point in a calendar-system so that no one can refer to the year of his own birth without a half-remembered reference to that event. Disciples number in the millions, and over most of the globe every town has a spire consecrated to the event. For a member of this last generation the question then arises: can this person come into the re-lationship of Faith by means of those results? Can they mediate him into that relationship by ushering him into a life-matrix in which it will seem perfectly natural to suppose that the Moment-event really hap-pened just as the ancient testimony described it?

To begin, no more than smatterings of historical learning would be needed for a reflective soul to remark: 'Clearly the world was not al-ways like this. Something hugely consequential must have happened about 1843 years ago. As regards what it was, keener brains than mine have seen no reason to doubt that the first witnesses told accurately what they saw and heard, which when you come right down to it amounted to some strange phenomena and even stranger sentences. I see no reason for headshaking over whether I would have seen and heard the same had I been there'. Up to this point Climacus would have no quarrel with this individual, who merely finds in the report of that event something to arouse his attention. His not-doubting expres-ses the relationship of faith with a small 'f' discussed in the Interlude. He has not yet made a move toward naturalizing or probabilizing the event. That would begin to happen if he went on to say, 'That which announced to the world that it would change everything, has changed everything. Could greater authentication be asked? I thank the God for bringing me along after his mighty leavening had done its work, for in virtue of being *born into* discipleship I myself am one of the conse-quences. If this is not so, at any rate the God has left his flank open to such an interpretation by permitting the consequences to perfume the air of whole nations'.

The naturalizing of the Moment-event, as expressed in these remarks, would consist in the person's entering into the Faith-relationship unconsciously, more or less like a man who wakes up with a hangover and finds out that he has enlisted in the army. However, if by our hypothesis a learner must set aside his reason in order to appropriate the Paradox, he must first have come into his reason. In the same way, if awareness of his Error is the only circumstance commensurate with the dread act of setting reason aside, no such dread act is required of him in order merely not to doubt that a profoundly consequential event occurred 1843 years before. All of this is summed up in the observation that his readiness to align himself with the multitudes who do not profess doubts of the *teaching* is very far indeed from a readiness to extend the *Teacher* a free hand over himself.

In that personal and conscious granting of permission an individual encounters the Paradox-character of the event, which Climacus fears will be obscured by what he calls "probabilizing" and "naturalizing." That is, the Moment-event can be represented in a sentence which is *not* self-contradictory as easily as in one which is, and this guarantees that an individual can accommodate himself quite comfortably to a *sentence* or *doctrine* without in the slightest degree setting reason aside. He can also discover, as he comes of age, that he has grown up with it and adjusted his mind to it with little or no strain. The Paradox-character manifests itself in quite another way than in a self-contradictory chain of words. One way of expressing it is in terms of the historical vacuity of the Unknown's appearing in unrecognizable form, a happening as juiceless as a moth's wing for purposes of news-hawking, yet a nonevent which for one person at a time changes everything. That is, if a sober and waking person hands himself over body and soul to another, and that other is the Unknown, everything is changed for him and continues to be new and changed and can never become custom, even if the other assigns him to nothing but waiting. No one would say he is in a *cognitive* relationship to the historical event that made it possible. On the other hand, to infuse the event with probability, for instance by suggesting that other events dating from it make it more and more likely that such and such a man, indiscernible from other men, was in fact none other than the Unknown, would amount to *adopting* a cognitive relationship in preference to one in which the individual cuts loose from his cognitive faculty, his reason, and takes it up again only in the service of the one to whom he owes everything.

In the present day a more suitable expression of Climacus's point might take for its premise not the all-pervading consequences of the Moment-event but the subsequent erosion and fading out of these. For example, a century or so later someone might compose his thoughts in this way: 'For a time, I must confess, the consequences of that event 1943 years ago, it seemed, had just about sixty-five percent overcome the world and were bidding to make a clean sweep of it. Now, though, it seems the center cannot hold, cracks are opening up in the walls, millions declare the whole thing unworthy of belief. Yes, it is almost as if some lordly figure, the rallying-point for all those millions and the altarlight of every consecrated edifice, had simply died. And there is no pause, either, for residual innocence to hold a funeral with drum-taps and mourning reeds. The sustaining arm has gone limp, and everything it used to support is picking up the momentum of downfall. One would at least have thought that a visit from the Eternal would have eternal consequences, that it would check stampeding nihilism and spavined lives, in short that it would—overcome. I for one feel grateful and liberated for having come on the scene at the right time to perceive that this Moment-idea had from the outset no real staying power. It should be obvious that time and eternity cannot couple, as obvious as the fact that consequences admit of more than one explanation. How did the great consequences come about? A king joins the band of disciples and by fiat makes all his subjects do the same. Then the king next door, the first one's brother, does the same. An institution builds up real estate and power, makes alliances, homogenizes opinion, gains millions of yea-sayers. Well, the erosion happening before our eyes shows that the Moment was an idea that came along, caught fire for a time, and now takes its place in the records under the heading, "This too was formerly believed".'

The point of view just expressed judges the event of 1843 years ago to be an episode (now just about over) in human *thought*, a little like Ptolemaism in astronomy, and thus to have no eternal root but only the root of human ideation. Climacus's point is that consequences of the Moment-event have no decisive effect *one way or the other* on the individual's relationship to that event. Thus, a vanishing or dissolution of the consequences, as the moss grows over them like lost Yucatan cities, would approximate a return to the original situation in which there were as yet no consequences to speak of and the option to become a disciple was much more stark. The author of the view just expressed is speaking of consequences with a worldly-wise Aurelian melancholy such as we find in the famous lines:

> The Sea of Faith
> Was once, too, at the full, and round earth's shore
> Lay like the folds of a bright girdle furl'd.
> But now I only hear
> Its melancholy, long, withdrawing roar. . . .*

The trap Climacus sets for this observer consists in several things, first of all in the earlier principle that since the individual is in Error it is up to the God to lay down what shall count as getting out of it, that is, what Faith is. Secondly, if the Moment-event *exists* for Faith alone, it is something essentially different from its consequences, which exist for anyone to behold. Therefore, the observer in question, when he speaks of "Faith," speaks of consequences such as the fact that at one time a whole sea of people affirmed a particular teaching or doctrine. Even if the consequences were on the upswing, it would be absent-minded to forget that the event of which they are consequences is historically vacuous, so that the hungriest historical appetite as it gobbles up the consequences will bite down on nothing at all when it gets back to the historical fact that generated them. But Faith is precisely the individual's happy relationship to *that* historical fact, not to the fact that millions affirm the fact or that millions have left off affirming it.

To express this in another way, those millions are without exception *other* persons, not to be identified with the observer himself. For him to survey them and watch the ebbing away of something called "Faith" is indeed a possibility, only it is quite certain that this "Faith," even if he assigns it a capital 'F', is very far from being the Faith that Climacus talks about. In the *Fragments*, Faith is by no means other people's affirmations, which exist to be sure, can be written out, studied, and seen

*Matthew Arnold, "Dover Beach," in *Poetry and Criticism of Matthew Arnold*, ed. H. Dwight Culler (Boston: Houghton Mifflin Co., 1961), p. 162.

to wax and wane over the centuries, but is rather whatever the God counts Faith to be. This, as we have seen, consists in a relationship in which one person receives the condition and turns *himself* over to the Teacher. If by the God's reckoning anything other than or less than that counts as offense, then so must the observer's point of view in our example. That point of view will also contain a misunderstanding. That is, the Faith-relationship takes on a peculiar feature from the fact that one party to it is invisible, nowhere to be seen, so that even from a headmaster's rostrum with its full view of everyone in the hall, one cannot keep check on the state of another's Faith-relationship, only one's own.

Further, still assuming that the consequences have crumbled during the stretch between 1843 and 1943, or become barely differentiated from other consequences, Climacus has laid another sort of trap for this observer. In waving goodbye to other people's once steadfast affirmation of this or that package of doctrines, which affirmation he mistakenly identifies with 'Faith', the observer regards the content of those doctrines as products of human ideation. Now, the package of doctrines may contain a number of particulars by which early disciples signified the self-identity of their band over against one or another breakaway faction. In addition, the package will include a reference to the Moment-event, the God's appearance on earth in unrecognizable form, for otherwise we depart from the Moment-hypothesis. Here we have to ask: whose piece of ideation is the Absolute Paradox? Next we hark back to the closing remarks of the Project of Thought, where Climacus reflects that the Moment-idea is not at all the sort of idea that humans come up with. Yet the God as Teacher and Saviour is precisely the *point d'appui* for Faith in the eminent sense, or an individual's happy relationship with the Teacher rather than the teaching. When this is kept in mind, it becomes straightway impossible, except in a romantic mist where anything goes, to view the decline of the consequences as the decline of Faith.

C. COMPARISON

The alterations in circumstance from one generation to the next are too many to sift and examine when the aim is an account of discipleship. Climacus settles for a brief comparison between the first and last secondary generations, with emphasis on the relative ease with which an individual can become a disciple depending on when he was born. If early disciples ran the risk of being thrown to the lions, and in a later age the lion becomes all but extinct, this represents an accidental easing of the situation. On the other hand, if the practice of feeding prisoners to wild animals gets abandoned because of things the Teacher taught (a claim which takes a good bit of proving), it could be called a consequence of the Moment and one which clearly makes discipleship easier for later generations.

Still, the whole option of discipleship presents itself in the first instance as a difficulty arising from the fact that the individual is in Error and loves his Error and cannot let go of it, so that unless the God extends the condition, there will be no disciple. In this sense there is no such thing as a *would-be* disciple. The late comer, we may suppose, enjoys the probability that his reception as a disciple will be free from any looming threat to life and limb and may even be the occasion for a local celebration. The transition is thus placid, and after a number of placid years the anniversary will perhaps slip his memory. Where, then, is the difficulty if this thinking individual (since the book is addressed to students of philosophy) is not put to the ordeal? Wherein lies the parity between his transition and that of some persecuted early disciple?

Would it not lie in the awareness that he is signing a blank check and handing it over to someone else? The difference between generations balances out on reflection. The apparent ease of a transition to discipleship in 1843 as compared with the year 50 conceals a peculiar danger. Suppose the payoff on my blank check has nothing to do with lions or with anything that springs and kills in a matter of seconds. The early disciple had a hard choice, I do not deny that, but he did not face the difficulty of paying and paying, or living with the haunted consciousness of one who has agreed to pay and pay, or having to keep at bay the ravishing thought that he is the victim of vampirish appetites and merciless shakedowns.

When, thanks to the consequences, it is no longer a disgrace to become a disciple, this ease is the new form of the danger and gives rise to a difficulty which corresponds to that faced by the first generation. But what precisely in this new situation could seize someone with the same awe and fear that seized the first generation? We are not speaking now of exaggerated anxieties and scruples which can overtake someone of any generation but of a primitive reaction to an Absolute Paradox which has, however, been sufficiently triumphant to carve out zones of tranquillity here and there, zones in which someone's transition to discipleship may be greeted with brotherly understanding.

The answer in briefest form is that what does not occur in the actual order can still occur in the order of thought or possibility. In a savagely inimical climate, disciples of the first generation were spared one danger, namely that congenial circumstances and the placid tenor of their environment would enable them to forget what the move was all about, as if the transition were like a successful surgical episode that can acquire the blessed aftermath of being completely over with, leaving him as good as new, or, in short, a trial he has *passed through* so that it will be as pardonable thereafter to forget the Teacher as to forget the surgeon, with whom he stands in a Socratic relationship. That this is a danger special to the more sheltered generations is not a dramatic enough fact to evoke primitive awe in the new disciple. Climacus's point is that when this special danger is brought into reflective link-up with the individual's knowledge of his Error plus his understanding of the Moment, a difficulty just as heavy as the first generation's will seat itself upon him. It will not do to characterize this difficulty in a way that holds true for everyone, but remarks of the following sort might occur to some disciple or other in that 1943 situation:

'A disciple is assuredly something that no one who clings to his powers of reason would wish to be, and now I am a disciple, I have signed a blank check and am ready for anything. But day after halcyon day goes by with no demand for payment. What then was all the earthquake and urgency about? Can it be that the thing dividing my generation's experience from that of the earliest is the present rarity of lions? Signing the blank check meant I would happily pay out my last drop of blood. In a sense I can be thankful I am still alive, but I certainly had in mind something other than this whopping dose of monotony. Isn't my money as green as the next fellow's, my blood as red? Why am I not wanted on more desperate fronts? Am I being made a fool of, handled with the kid-glove solicitude we extend to the immature? Am I being spared the blushes of discovering that I would back out of any 20th century lion's cage and take to my heels? I expected trials, but not this terrible one of remaining untried'.

A disciple of a different sort might follow this line: 'The aftermath of my becoming a disciple is not entirely what I had in mind. That, to put it in a word, was *results*. Why, after all, did I go beyond becoming a disciple to becoming a full-time servant of the Teacher if not to help accelerate the pace of results and take a modest and minor hand in overcoming the world? That is what I propose to see to, no matter how painfully it tweaks the authorities—the civil ones as well as any spirit-less captains placed over me within the band of disciples. Let them jail me or cast me out. My own fate matters little so long as the tide of results rises toward flood'.

In both these examples a questionable element begins to define it-self in the disciple's treatment of the condition entrusted to him by the Teacher, and in terms of examples like these it becomes clearer what Climacus means in his clipped remarks about a new difficulty (p. 124). In each case the disciple is on the point of tumbling back into 'what he really thinks', earlier characterized as Error. The fear corresponding to the new difficulty thus identifies itself as a fear and awe in the face of *judgment*, an adumbration of a judgment which will hold him to task for how he treated the condition that the Teacher held out to him, and whether he let go when the voltage ran too high (or too unexcitingly low) between the God's will and what he himself was inclined to think. The first-generation disciple had less opportunity to sink back into his Error, whereas relative ease makes demands of fortitude that stretch yawningly over years and years.

It is easy to see that the disciple belonging to a hounded and per-secuted generation, with no cushion of consequences to lean on, does not suffer the dangers that come with having to outwait himself. He does not have to contend through monotonous summers and winters with the scoffing grin of 'what he really thinks' as it seeks with patient cunning to displace the Teacher from his heart—not with dogs baying on his trail and bone-crushing hatreds at the boil. His journey is quick, foreshortened by human enmity; the fear of judgment, of having to confess that he cast aside the condition or could not long tolerate a new existence that grated so against the old, shrinks in proportion. All the temptations, for example, that grinding monotony can generate— the idea that the Teacher finds me useless, has marooned me far from the action, and so forth—temptations which, remember, I had for-sworn in signing the blank check and promising to take whatever hap-pens as something absolutely made-to-measure for myself alone, temptations I forswore precisely because they form part of 'what I really think', and for yielding to which I will most certainly be judged, not least by myself, are spared me.

Considerations like these project a certain silhouette of the Moment-event in terms of *the human material the God is up against* in becoming Teacher and Savior. The God is constrained from communicating himself directly, from "elevating the learner" as an earlier chapter expressed it. As a result, the God is constantly up against what the learner really thinks, yet the God cannot pull his rank, the badges of which he tore off in order to approach the learner. This vaunting self-opinion on the part of the learner has not been annihilated once for all, and this fact is an expression of the God's genuine lowliness, that he remains permanently on the scene and in his lowliness sets off to stylish advantage the very thing he is out to overcome: 'what I really think'.

2
The problem of the disciple at second hand

The considerations leading up to this problem condense very easily. First, in establishing knowledge about an ordinary historical event, nearness in time offers an advantage by way of consulting eyewitnesses and the like. Second, with an eternal fact, if we may so stretch the meaning of 'fact', there is no question of relative nearness. If it is a fact, for example, that the God is almighty, whether we are inclined to think of it as a grammatical fact or some other kind, everyone is equidistant from it; the eternal does not swim in and out of visibility like a comet, depending on what century one gets born into. Similarly, if it is taken as a revealed fact, as doctrine, that the God has appointed a Redeemer from eternity to save men, this has not so far been specified as an historical event but only as something the God has had eternally in mind.* A whole people could bend the knee gratefully in acknowledgment of the God's eternal intention, but there would not be in their kingdom even a mustard seed of what Climacus has been calling

*This is G. E. Lessing's point in "The Proof of the Spirit and of Power," in *Lessing's Theological Writings*, trans. H. Chadwick (London: Adam & Charles Black, 1956), pp. 51–56.

'Faith', a category that engages in an essential way with the concept of coming-into-existence.

A final consideration brings in the Moment-event, which differs from an eternal fact in having come into the crooked streets of history, left tracks, and so on. As we have already seen, it is not an ordinary historical fact, being indistinguishable publicly from the fact that nothing unusual took place, for it expresses that the Unknown once appeared in unrecognizable form. How, then, does belief in this special *historical* fact place an individual in a different situation than if, say, he acknowledged an *eternal* fact, for instance a revealed doctrine to the effect that the God had appointed a Redeemer from eternity? For there seems no question but that a person who accepts that doctrine could not only confess his sins before his God, but also give the God a blank check as it were, keeping strenuously in mind that he has submitted himself body and soul to this eternal Redeemer—whom the God holds in reserve.

This is a pivotal issue, ringed with possibilities for misunderstanding and essential for a grasp of the *Fragments*. It is the issue raised on the title-page, and it asks in effect: What difference does it entail for a learner to be in relationship to a dated *historical* appearance of the Redeemer/God rather than to a doctrine that possesses every bit of the conceptual content of the former relationship *except* that historical element? Here, surely, cool or querulous appeals to *fine* distinctions would be out of place; we are at a juncture where the question can be put in the opposite way: Why, if one is prepared to accept the *doctrine* as described, should *offense* declare itself as soon as, but no sooner than, the dated historical Teacher comes into the picture? Why, when the historical element gets pieced in, does an Absolute Paradox emerge and the potential for an individual's unhappiness shoot up? It should also be clear, I believe, that the answer must not come as a surprise but rather must spring from the original hypothesis as outlined in the early chapters. To clear the ground for this discussion, it would be misleading to imagine that some determinate *moral* demand comes into the scene with the historical Redeemer but is absent where one merely holds to the 'eternal Redeemer' *doctrine*. It would be equally erroneous to imagine that the lowliness of the Teacher's servant-rags in some way makes for a greater shock than if he had come in kingly robes, although, to be sure, this may jar a traditional expectation in one faction or another.

What then has Climacus included in his original hypothesis to help us grasp this point?

To begin, the Absolute Paradox corresponds in the sphere of reflection to the wholly unexpected in the historical domain. In terms now of an *individual's* total reaction (for he will not be a 100 percent reflective being, yet in being reflective he will not be a 100 percent historical being either, in the sense that a castle or a cathedral is, but rather will be one that can monitor his own history), the wholly unexpected has the effect of making him take his own person in a light in which there was *no* prior sanction for taking it, otherwise the development would be halfway expected. With this in mind it becomes easier, in terms of the categories Climacus gives us to work with, to express the difference we are seeking. As long as the Redeemer/God keeps his place in eternity, there is never any question of his *seeking out* the individual, positively shadowing him; hence the individual can be quite comfortable with himself, with his doctrine, and even, be it noted, with his Error, which it may please him to identify with his faults, sins, or vices, inasmuch as the contrasting Truth, which would reveal it more frightfully, keeps itself in another sphere altogether. Whatever troubles may come his way, he can remain enviably untroubled and carefree in the thought that, should the God desire to tap him as a prophet or messenger, he will be ready to jump to his feet since he has submitted himself to this God. As for anything wholly unexpected, no one of course can expect him to have any notions in stock.

Now, the wholly unexpected will express itself in words, thereby (it might appear) doing away with itself since the words themselves will be common enough no matter how puzzling their arrangement. In one combination they will say: He who is absolutely unlike me has made himself exactly like me in order to help me become exactly like himself. For any kind of understanding of this the individual must bring to the situation some sense of the absolute unlikeness in the opening clause, and therefore a cultivated power of remembering himself, a sense not only of his own humanity but of what he really thinks of himself and of the God, so that it will not draw a blank stare when the Teacher proposes to change precisely *that* about him. (Notice that it will not matter here whether the individual is a contemporary or whether the Teacher died thousands of years before. That the God became his equal eclipses all such differences, and with the God once is enough to make the point. To express the matter *pianissimo*, it would go against the grammar of 'the God' to suggest that the God had exhausted himself in the first go at it, or that it all happened so long ago that he has since found other mighty acts to occupy him.)

Now lights and darks begin to emerge as in a photodeveloping tank. It is no longer possible for an individual so besought to stand at ease with his tribe or with a whole people of catholic belief, because the historical Teacher, as opposed now to a Redeemer eternally promised, will have no one but that individual himself, will accept no substitute. If it were not for that one particular, namely the individual himself, the whole point of a historical Redeemer would disperse itself in a vapor, since the God, if I may make a further grammatical remark, must be held completely free to make anything he wishes out of men, even so many million soda crackers if the notion pleases him, *without* going through the historical weir of getting born and dying. Unless, that is, he would have no other than that one individual personally, in which case the complications of unhappy love come into the picture as outlined in the chapter called "The God as Teacher and Saviour."

It thus becomes plain that even if our individual possesses a doctrine to the effect that the God notices men, and possesses it not as a personal conceit but as a revelation cherished in the educated bosom of his people, this is something very different from being personally sought out by the God. Once that idea comes into the picture, it will make very little difference to the individual how many other individuals there are. The fact that he by name is one of the hunted is enough to turn his life upside down. How is this individual to look at himself once the Teacher has appeared? For there was nothing whatever in his doctrine to ameliorate the unexpectedness of *his* being singled out as indispensable to the God's desires. There was no sanction for taking his own person in such a light, even though in a certain sense he and his people 'knew all about' the Redeemer/God, knew it exclusively, and knew it, moreover, from the God's own words. Now let us add to the doctrinal deposit and to this people the belief that the God, although he might temper his wrath and stay the rod of punishment, would never place himself at the mercy of some human in Error. With the advent of the historical Moment-event this rock gets bent all out of shape, and with it, if we may put it so, much of the very grammar of the expression 'the God' as this people has received it. This has nothing in particular to do with the Teacher's servant form, although that may indeed have had other meanings and purposes. The decisive thing is that (a) the God came *himself*, and (b) that he came as this individual's *equal*. He came, in other words, as one exactly like me, exactly like one of those in Error, leaving majesty behind.

Let us take time out to be very particular about the sense of 'wholly unexpected' that applies here. Suppose that this individual not only 'knew all about' the Redeemer-doctrine in the sense earlier described, but honored a certain prophet who once declared, 'The God himself will come and save you'. This intimation, we may note, says nothing about the God's forsaking his majesty, and specifically nothing about his treating me as an equal or making himself into the equal of me. In a word, the prophetic promise is not specified in terms of the God's becoming historical; the 'you' it speaks of can be a nation, it need not be the 'me' that could unsettle my own mind, and the God's coming in his own person could just as easily be taken to signify some stupefying flash-event that would shake off a people's captors, a long-prayed-for event which would not be wholly unexpected and which would scarcely leave the God at anyone's mercy.

In the Moment-hypothesis, then, the God's severance from power and glory has much to do with the total unexpectedness of his coming. In this sense the event dares to alter *downwards* the individual's conception of the God, or at any rate let us not rule out the possibility of a misunderstanding along these lines: the more sensitively the individual appreciates the God's measureless altitude, the deeper the wound produced by any hint of its diminution. For the individual had, as we might express it, *uses* for the distance between himself and the God, and this does not mean merely that it enabled him to take a lighter, less rending view of his own Error. More immediately it served to stabilize his way of looking at himself, his manner of navigating the straits of life, its remote but readable pulse of light unaffected by the most tumultuous seas. If that star winked out or tumbled from its place, disorientation would result, but as a distant, unchanging presence it enabled the individual to steer and to see his hand before his face.

All at once this time-honored and suffered-for conception of the God dissolves into perplexities, for the God has to all appearances relinquished his majesty in order to become exactly like me, to become my equal. It will certainly not occur to me as a natural inference that this is perhaps the *only* way in which the God could bring off whatever he is about, for it is not part of my conception of the God that he is ever cut back to only one possibility. It would be much more likely (assuming I do not dismiss the matter out of hand as a freakish contretemps) that I would try putting my conception of the God together with that of monkeyshines or the whimsical, although the two conceptions will repel each other.

Then, too, majesty expresses itself in *taste* as well as in its tendency to keep its distance from the touch of coarse familiarity. What a potential for misunderstanding lies in the thought that this majesty should go to such an extreme in order to enjoy my company! The more clearly I respect the difference between us, in comparison with which the gulf between an emperor and a poor maiden is a mere two fingers wide, the greater the potential for my personal unhappiness in this thought. A God whose majesty is a cast-off garment, whose taste has failed him, and who thereby becomes, as we say, capable of anything, is not the easiest conception in the world to get happy with, especially if I have been happy for a long time with the contrary conception.

So much for the shaking up my conception of the God receives in this wholly unexpected development. Now what does it do to my conception of myself? This very self of mine is, after all, the occasion for the God's impoverishment and desolation. If I find myself at an extremity in having to suppose that the God would have no one in place of me (and here it makes no difference how many other places he may have reserved), I will not say I understand the God's intent in the sense of finding it intelligibly commensurate with this or that intention of my own, since we are speaking of the Unknown, but on the other hand I can hardly fail to apprehend the 'what' of the God's appearing as my equal. It signifies a certain delicacy of tread that he does not simply *turn me into* some kind of twinkling gem to go with his temple fittings, for even if that hurt it would soon be over, and of course there would then be no nonsense about equality. So it is not just another bijou he wants, but myself and in such form that I do not cease to be the one I am.

Even so, it would appear to me (and this can be uttered with all reverence) easy enough for the God to preserve me as I am without going to the tasteless extreme of making himself exactly like me. All he needs to do is balsamize me just as I am in his pellucid gaze, like a mote in a sunbeam in a very quiet room, and in this way I, too, could be warm and happy, while putting out of mind that unthinkable revision upwards in my conception of myself which would follow from the madness about equality. What I can't bear is to see the God's taste sink below the level of my own, seeing that I do not care for the thought of being eternally on exhibit before my own eyes in a sea of light. But it is even worse than that, for what the God wants (if we may for a moment go along with the unexpected heartbreak about equality) is my *consent*!

Consent changes a great many things, for it means he does not want merely to keep me on permanent display as a minor triumph of *ex nihilo* engineering. No, consent has enormously to do with equality. I don't ask consent of the dough I want to bake into soda crackers or the interesting bug it pleases me to mount on a pin. Consent has to do with equality, and equality goes both ways, equality has just as much to do with the God's jacking me *up* as jacking himself down. As regards the former, it can be a gratifying thing to escalate a notch or two, but to escalate to God knows what—why, this is synonymous with being swept clean away so that every level-headed distinction between upward and downward gets blotted out. Of course, it is not as though this Teacher has left me completely in the dark about the escalation he has in mind, for unless I misunderstand the meaning of the word 'disciple' it will consist in my becoming more and more like himself. Let me ponder this just long enough to observe that becoming more like himself, more nearly equal if you prefer, is not what would ordinarily be called receiving a leg up in the world. Even if we exclude externals entirely, what he calls happiness could very likely be in another world from what I mean by that term. Yes, no wonder he asks my consent, for the hint of unthinkable altitudes leaves me with no clear picture of what I shall care about and what I shall cease caring about in that new state, which comes pretty close to not knowing at all what will become of myself in his hands. Of course there is no doubt that expressions such as 'eternal happiness' have a resonance of goodness and joyful promise, but all of that is so very far from knowing what I am letting myself in for that I would have to be in a state of near hysteria to let myself imagine it stood for something definite.

So, then, whatever I may decide, this Teacher has at any rate succeeded in making me resemble him in one respect, his acquaintance with ulcerating grief. Of the crushing suggestion that the God emptied himself because he would have no other in place of me, I have already said enough to indicate that even if he wins, he loses. It would be far less shocking, this touching down of the God in the historical stream, if I had not been so happy—and happy with that very God, happy in a lawful, godly way—before this wholly unexpected overthrow of all my old ways of thinking about him and me. For I cannot imagine, much less requite, that much love.

Now that these distinctions are behind us, says Climacus, we are ready to begin discussing the disciple at second hand. The key to this problem lies in the condition extended by the God to each individual who becomes a disciple. Since every individual receives it at first hand, there is no disciple at second hand. The alternative, namely that the Teacher/God imparts the condition to some contemporaries who in turn pass it to their successors, Climacus calls inane. The immediate logic of his stand is capturable in one sentence: Our original hypothesis departed from Socrates precisely where it specified a new relationship between the individual and the God, in which the individual would owe nothing to another human but everything to the God. To imagine on the other hand that in receiving the condition a contemporary of the Teacher could then impart it to others would lacerate the original hypothesis. Still, one could ask, why is it so patently out of the question, so "self-contradictory," to conceive that the God might entrust the first disciples with not only the condition but the passing on of it?

In order to decompress the two paragraphs in which Climacus deals with this issue, it will be helpful to remember the equivalence between the condition and Faith, whose object is the Teacher in person and not a teaching that can be passed on to others. The concept of Faith came into the original hypothesis with a distinctive 'grammar' or set of conceptual ties identifying it as a relationship between the individual and that one-and-only Teacher who is at the same time the God. Now the relationship can commence when the Teacher imparts the condition, but the relationship is something over and above the experience of receiving the condition, though connected with it. The same logic applies as where Climacus spoke earlier of the God's having to come himself rather than delegate his most trusted minister. By hypothesis the God alone can bestow the condition.

But what is the condition? It is the power to recognize the Truth and to acknowledge that the Teacher is the God who can bring me through a second birth. If by receiving the condition and going through that second birth I received also the power to enable others to recognize the God in the Teacher, and likewise the power to re-create them, then by my second birth I would become not my own self restored to newness but a second God, and thus all categorial dikes dividing divine from human, known from Unknown, eternal from temporal, and the Socratic from the Moment would collapse. In passing on the condition to someone of the next generation I could not very well show him the Teacher, who has vanished; I could only show him myself, and if then I empowered him to recognize the God in *me*, and acknowledge *my* power to re-create him, what real need would he have for that other Teacher? He would attach himself to me, and this would tumble the pair of us into a confused variant of the Socratic relationship.

There is a further reason for calling the possibility in question inane, a reason tied up with what Climacus calls "the autopsy of Faith" or awareness of having received the condition that a disciple always carries about with him. That is, if I have become a disciple, owing everything to the God, it will not escape my memory that I was once in Error, or that I am one thing and the God another, or that equality is not at all the same thing as identity. Thus when I venture to communicate with another human, unless carelessly I mislay the autopsy record, it can never seriously occur to me that I myself am the Teacher to another human. If that other person undergoes the change called Conversion, I can never seriously imagine that the power effecting this change came from me. I would have to lose all awareness of my own past before I could lead another up that garden path.

Granting that Climacus may have shed light here on a point of logic, one could readily ask: How might an actual confusion along these lines express itself? What would it be like *in concreto* if the conviction spread that contemporary disciples could hand on Faith to later ones? In order to obtain the clearest possible fix on this question, it seems to me, we must first scout Climacus's responses to the pair of questions he regards as central in this section.

First, what *can* a contemporary disciple do for a successor? He can put himself forward as believing that the God came to earth in the person of such and such an historical teacher, and acknowledge that in believing this he has set aside his reason. Such guarded witness, turning the successor off as much as on, betokens respect for the logical point just discussed. The successor's Faith-relationship, if it comes to be at all, will come in consequence of his receiving the condition from the God and not from the contemporary, even if he performs miracles. The contemporary can, of course, do the one thing any human can do for another: say something to light up the other's attention, leaving it uncertain, however, as to whether the other will come nearer or recoil. In doing this he can also repeat the content of the Moment-fact, but scrupling to repeat it in such a manner that the other shall not be invited to take his word for it, although as regards eyewitness-features of the event this contemporary's testimony may be as good as anyone's. For again, when we remember what 'believing' means as applied to this event, the other person cannot believe it happened just on the strength of my claim to have believed it. Uniquely among historical facts, this one does not exist at all for an observant *public* but only as a possibility related to some individual in terms of what he can do with it; that is the gist of all that Climacus has said about the Condition.

The second question concerns the *credibility* of a contemporary witness, and here it makes no difference whether the testimony is oral, on paper, or chiseled on a rock. The only fact about which credibility could make a significant difference is the Moment-event: 'The one who came was the God' or 'The one this witness knew was the Unknown'—sentences with numbing logical stings in their tails. However, this is the same event or fact that was said a moment ago not to exist at all for a public and to exist for an individual only insofar as the God extends him the condition for apprehending it.

These last considerations, we had hoped, would throw light on the question: What would it be like if the idea *caught on* that the condition is transferable like an heirloom, so that contemporary disciples could hand it on to successors and so proliferate Faith somewhat as in olden times the housewives of each generation passed on their stock of ever-budding leaven? What manner of disciple would be tempted to put himself forward as the dispenser of Faith or as anything but a witness to the God's own tidings? Specifically, how would such a one advertise himself, and what might his entourage look like in actuality? Here the occasional aberrant individual who falls for the "inanity" (p. 129) would hold little interest for Climacus, who in all probability had in mind a thinker of some importance.

The thinker who comes readiest to mind is once again Kant, in whose Enlightenment classic *Religion Within the Limits of Reason Alone* we can find in full flower the salient points of the view in question. Kant regards himself first of all as in some sense a disciple. Yet the sense is a guarded one, for he does not think of himself as having received the condition historically, so as to place him in a relationship with the God dating from some remembered time, but as having possessed it all along, so that one foot of his thought stays firmly on the Socratic ground of truth by recollection. With the freedom his other foot gives him, though, he wishes to touch all the bases of the Moment-hypothesis— the Learner/Teacher dichotomy, the Learner's Error, the God as Teacher and Saviour, Conversion, Faith, Repentance, Redemption, Atonement, and Judgment. To each of these conceptions, however, Kant gives an *interpretation* consonant with the fact that he has not broken cleanly with the Socratic presupposition that all men possess the Truth.

Although the following brief account of Kant's *Religion* is hardly more than a footnote which the interested reader can follow up on his own, it deserves a place in this chapter. For Kant, the Learner's state of Error is presupposed as an inherited radical propensity to evil brought on by the individual himself and expressing itself in frailties, impurity of motivation, and sometimes wickedness, all in the sphere of actions, though it is not so desperate a state as to place the individual in total bondage to what he really thinks of himself, for he possesses a good will along with it. So far from being destitute of the Truth, each individual possesses it in the form of a Moral Law in the recesses of his consciousness, but he must undergo a Repentance and Conversion in order to rank it tops among his maxims of conduct. The Teacher, coming *as if* from on high, matches up in all essentials with an archetype of the good man already obscurely present in the individual consciousness, so there can be no question of the individual's 'owing everything to the God'. What he does owe this Teacher is thanks for a timely tip, a spur to his laggard consciousness, which he might have received from any morally alert citizen *without* the Teacher and even if the Teacher had never been. The Teacher's roles as Redeemer, Savior, and Judge are thus to be interpreted as essentially Socratic relationships between man and man and in no sense as going beyond Socrates in the direction of any new or unheard-of God-relationship. In Kant's picture, Faith (the condition) can be nothing other than a species of knowledge (in this instance, knowledge bearing upon moral behavior), which as such can be passed on from contemporary to successor without any first-hand dealings between that successor and the Teacher, if indeed we may speak at all of 'passing on' that which everybody possesses *ab initio.*

In Kant's presentation of the Moment categories, all talk of the Teacher's being the God incarnate must be interpreted as figurative language aimed at emphasizing the importance of the Teacher's *message* by aggrandizing his *person.* The presence in Kant's account of the very same key locutions employed in the 'Project of Thought' (and lifted out of the New Testament) can convey the misleading impression that the Kantian hermeneutic is to be grouped with Moment-philosophies, although a closer look will make plain that it departs from those by 180 degrees, beginning with the opening Socratic presupposition. While it may seem very queer to speculate, as I have done, that Climacus has in mind a work as important and richly figured as Kant's when he dismisses the so-called "inanity" with short shrift, nevertheless Kant comes as close as anyone to the embodiment of such a position.

On a reading of Kant it becomes clearer, too, what might ensue if that position were to triumph or at least win a handsome following. If, following Kant, Faith is a form of knowledge, and the Teacher's message the clearest historical expression of that knowledge (at least up until his coming), then it will become a priority matter to figure out *exactly what that message says*, bringing to bear every linguistic tool and skill that man has developed. Such an undertaking a lone individual could scarcely set in motion, much less consummate. It is a collective task for an ongoing community of trained persons. The stage is thus set for the scientific community, or that portion of it devoted to theology, to commence its analysis of the sources, with the emphasis in one century on sifting out their straight historical content, and in the next century on penetrating the Teacher's verbal message with understanding. Where the *message* is assumed to be central and decisive, every possible question about its content must be dealt with in the careful, unhurried manner characteristic of this community, with the result that scholarly productions mount in volume beyond any one person's power to assimilate them.

Other consequences of the communal analysis will not be quite so direct or inevitable. Consider, for example, the fact that the community, as a multiplicity of persons, constitutes a public. Now, if the sources it examines are as Climacus has presented them, if they make up a testimony to the Teacher as the God, then, for reasons already discussed, those sources are not only not addressed to a public but cannot even exist for a public so far as concerns their central historical fact, the God's coming into history. This situation *vis-à-vis* the communal analysis thus contains a gaucheness that would perhaps be paralleled if we imagined a civil servant intercepting and opening an individual's personal letter, aiming with the best will in the world to interpret its message to him. Yet if the crux of that letter for its addressee consists a great deal less in its hometown news than in the fact that it comes from nobody else but Julia and is addressed to nobody else but himself, the official interpretation will constitute a broken cloud-cover over the essential content, and if the interpretation should run to two or more volumes, a total blackout. The community is barred as such from discovering the Paradox in the sources, and the same will hold true of an individual if he is reading the sources *qua* member of the community since in that capacity he is bound to report only what exists for a public.

In Climacus's view, the primitive witnesses address themselves to an individual in bondage, whom the Teacher proposes to set free if he consents to be brought into a Faith-relationship. Whatever the scientific community may be, it is not an individual in bondage. This may be expressed in various ways. The Community is subject only to the kind of error that washes itself out in the long run; the community as such is sinless, hence cannot enter into Faith-relationship, being immune to the sort of lesion it is intended to heal; the community has nothing to be forgiven; it cannot be reborn as a community; at most it may be a community of the reborn. Each of these clauses is a grammatical remark in Wittgenstein's sense, reflecting the way Moment-expressions are used in Climacus's hypothesis. Since the kind of Sin or Error the Teacher is out to conquer is vested in the individual *per se* and personally, the learned community will naturally find no trace of that in its own corporate self, and since it can behold only what its corporate lens is designed to behold, it must translate that side of the Teacher's message into sins or errors in the ordinary sense, of which the literature of paganism offers a full catalogue.

Serious consequences trail these points of grammar. For one thing, they mean that the community as such does not possess what Climacus calls an "autopsy of Faith" by which to remember a former state of Error, since it had no such state. To go further, this autopsy, which can belong only to an individual as a memory-record of his own abandoned and forgiven Error, works as a constant reminder of the Absolute Paradox by whose bestowal he became himself again. Now, if we are correct in saying that the community cannot centralize the Paradox (its range of acceptable discoveries being limited to those which can be incorporated into a *collective* understanding), then what will the community make central? The answer can only be: the Teacher's message and its linguistic-historical matrix.

It is not within an outsider's competence to anticipate the richness of research possible for this trained community. However, a pair of observations will be in order bearing on our main line of discussion. First, at some point the team investigating the Teacher's message will venture—hopefully without fanfare and with the cupped ear of the learned community in mind so as not to disturb the faithful at large— an *ordering* of the concepts in that message, as to which ones are primary and essential, and which are derivative, conditioned by local circumstances, or otherwise secondary. Thus, people trained in the historical background and original tongues can key in on the main themes of the Teacher's overtures and the discourse of those he authorized to speak in his name, and in this manner identify one theme or another as the dominant. If the theme hammered over and over happens to be an opacity, an extremely dark saying, this will not escape the community, who sooner or later will put forward the opacity as the dominant theme on the basis of, for example, the frequency of its repetitions.

Let us suppose, for no reason worth going into, that the communal consensus picks as the dominant theme: 'The Unknown has taken a decisive hand in things'. This will not be so far from saying 'The Unknown stepped into the historical stream', or even 'The God came into existence', as to fail to connect with Climacus's point that the central Moment-event does not exist for a public but solely for Faith, that is, for an individual who has come into accord with the condition. (Should the communal consensus be satisfied for a time that their chosen form of the opacity is less opaque than the original, this can be expected to correct itself in a century or two by the normal self-corrective tendency of every learned community.) Very well, the *Leitmotif* of the Teacher's message has been isolated and given fresh expression in the community's chosen idiom, which captures and preserves the opacity found in the sources. Now the message in its entirety requires to be interpreted as a body of knowledge that can be passed on to others.

With due respect for the influence and power of Kant's effort, it is not inevitable that the community interpret the message strictly in terms of moral rules and maxims. One alternative, as Kant himself hinted late in his life,* would be to place *love* next to duty at the center of the message, or even to make it inseparable from the stiff commandment to shape up morally. Still other approaches could interpret the message by welding it to a current secular philosophy of life conceived along Socratic lines, that is, unfolded from the brain of a first-rate philosopher. Since every nation boasts its top ten thinkers, there is no end to the possible variations.

In fact, since each of these communal endeavors develops from the Socratic starting-point cited in Hypothesis A of the Project of Thought, there is only one sort of approach ruled out from the start. That single proscribed line is to make *the Teacher in his own person* the dominant theme of his message. By this I do not mean that the community will begrudge this Teacher the kind of acknowledgment that every learned community reserves for its great inspirers. In that respect the Teacher will receive credits left and right in the same way that every logician after Aristotle acknowledges a debt to that name. Rather, the community cannot permit the Teacher *in his own person* to be the dominant theme of his message. To be more specific, it cannot permit such a notion to shipwreck the community's Socratic starting point. Above all, the Teacher must not be featured in such a singular way that he can turn everything upside down by making *me the individual learner* the dominant theme of his message (which would among other things make my stepping out of the community for an hour, abandoning its eyes and ears and using my own, a *sine qua non* for my getting the

*In *Religion Within the Limits of Reason Alone*, trans. T. M. Greene, and H. H. Hudson (New York: Harper & Bros., 1960), p. 6n.

178

message straight). To take such a view of the Teacher would be tantamount to confessing that the community had smashed up against the Absolute Paradox and contrived its own downfall insofar as the community stands for Reason in these matters.

To return for a moment to the style of the *Fragments*, featuring the Teacher in this way would place the individual member of that community in a new and unprefigured relationship with the Unknown, which would have to be understood as having made itself exactly like him in order to seek him out privately for the purpose of winning him. Once the individual member has taken this bruise—and this point is decisive as regards his connection with the community—he can no longer take the dominant concept in the Teacher's message to be a mere opacity on a par with something Hamlet might have said to befuddle Polonius. No, the community in this man's eyes immediately becomes mistaken about what the dominant theme is, although not culpably wrong, since even though other opacities may exist all over the place, the Absolute Paradox does not exist for a community. The Paradox is indeed an opacity, but not just any opacity constitutes the Paradox; that particular opacity, unlike the one starred by the community as the dominant theme, carries explicit reference to the God's *daring*, underscored by an equally explicit reference to *what the God is up against* in daringly taking a hand, namely, myself and the possibility of my being capitally offended. Apart from these references, the mere idea that the Unknown has taken a hand in history is hardly enough to signalize the downfall of anyone's reason, standing as it does for any number of wonders and bafflers attributed to a power not of this world. If the God's daring extends to this liaison with *me*, then any account of the dominant theme which speaks only of the God and not of me (except insofar as it includes every person in the historical stream) is thus indicted for changing the subject.

Our question of a few pages back was this: What would it be like if the conviction spread that one generation of disciples could pass Faith on to the next? This would make a disciple capable of doing immeasurably greater things for a successor than Climacus would allow, unless of course Faith came to mean something much less than Climacus makes it out to be. At any rate, we singled out Kant's pioneering interpretation of the Moment-categories as a classic expression of the above conviction and observed that in displacing the person of the Teacher from the central place, it effects a restyling of the whole Moment-hypothesis back into Socratic and secular relationships. In these, Faith becomes a kind of knowledge, for example, an understanding of existence which one man can educe from another by playing midwife; the Teacher becomes a ground-breaking enunciator of that knowledge; the community's *interpretation* of the sources becomes the approved vehicle of instruction by which Faith-as-knowledge gets passed from one individual to the next without the God's direct ministering. The result of such a trend, then, would be a secularization (what Climacus calls "naturalization") of all the key Moment-categories and, along with this, the gradual censorship of even the *rumor* of a new relationship between the God and the individual.

As far as Climacus is concerned, the only view of how the first disciples relate to later ones that is compatible with his initial hypothesis is expressed in a troublesomely compressed way on page 130. All that the contemporary disciples would need to leave behind them, he says, would be words to this effect: 'We have believed that the God appeared among us as a servant in the year _____, lived and taught here, and died'. This single sentence would be "more than enough" to serve as an occasion for a later arrival to confront the option of discipleship. This is Climacus's opinion, but when one remembers that it took Climacus two or three chapters to articulate the Moment-categories in their barest essentials, that solitary and not very trumpet-tongued sentence looks very slight. To reconstruct the rest of the Moment-hypothesis from it, as a paleontologist might work from a single tooth or skull fragment, may be possible for someone trained to a keen edge in dialectics, but most of us would face the task with a vacant stare.

Could a successor detect a personal reference to himself in those few words? Could he, for example, turn that single sentence over in his mind and conclude, 'This can only mean that the God had in mind to consult *me* about something!'? Yes, he could, Climacus seems to be saying, for this is what the Moment is all about. Could any given successor, working from that slightest of sentences, gather for himself the essentials of Hypothesis B in the Project of Thought, including its anti-Socratic starting point, whose immediate consequence is that he, the learner, is in Error by his own fault? Yes, he could. The sentence in question is a gesture of emphasis, jabbing a finger at the single central fact of the God's coming as a human Teacher. If the contemporary left word of his belief that the God came himself to tell him something, this would be enough to make a successor look twice at himself with that core-testimony in mind, or else later nail himself for his uncaring heart.

The least we can take away from the concluding chapter of the *Fragments* is that contemporary testimonies are not decisive for a successor; required for Faith is the condition received at the God's hand. Climacus characterizes the testimony of a believer as delivered in such a way as to *forbid immediate acceptance.* Thus the one-sentence testimony that a page or two earlier we were told would suffice as an occasion is now to be understood as trailing a clause such as: 'We have believed . . . although it is manifestly a folly and counter to reason'. This rider is at any rate enough to prevent a successor from confusing the rumor of the God's coming with any other sort of wonder that in his own tradition might reverently be attributed to deity.

Flatly, then, there is no such thing as a disciple at second hand. Nothing essential about discipleship hinges on the piece of fortune involved in being a townsman of the Teacher during his ministry. A contemporary believer conscious of this, in order not to let any psychological shock resulting from that fact be confused with matters of eternal consequence, could just as well wish that the cause of it should depart.

While we are on this last point, it is interesting to observe that the *Fragments'* analysis of the role of contemporaneity, looked at through the Kantian interpretation we sketched a few pages back, would exhibit a monstrous flaw. That is, even allowing that the contemporary is no luckier than his successor, it would seem that both of them are inestimably luckier than all the persons who died *before* the Teacher appeared. This expresses Kant's deep and repeated concern that the essential Truth be of a sort accessible to all men, hence that the Truth *have been* on earth ever since a man existed. Otherwise deaths prior to the Teacher's coming would constitute an arbitrary cut-off that clashes with our human norms of justice. Kant's position, no matter how vulnerable it may turn out to be in the final analysis, cannot be taken lightly or passed over. It involves to an intense degree what Climacus in his first chapter calls "the pathos of our project," a tension that goes with venturing to "base an eternal happiness upon historical knowledge."

The *Fragments* is silent upon this point concerning those who died before the Teacher came, perhaps grouping it with "petty difficulties" (p. 130), more likely leaving it as a matter to be pronounced on by whatever doctrinalizing body the band of believers might happen to set up. Such a body might incorporate word, for example, that the Teacher's coming was announced to the dead as well as the living. This might provide an anxious individual with whatever succor it was meant to provide, but since it contains an element that cannot be thought straight through to a transparency, it could not very well satisfy a philosopher such as Kant, who confines himself to ideas acceptable to a communal understanding. In that event, though, the flaw would lie not so much with the doctrine as with the philosopher's all-too-willing submergence of his personal faculty of understanding into the communal one, and in his choosing to respond to the doctrine *qua* member instead of in his own name.

There is a more fundamental reason, however, why Kant's interpretation of the Moment could not accommodate that bit of doctrine. That is, if the Kantian interpretation excludes all save Socratic relationships between any teacher and any learner, then it excludes them just as much for the dead as for the living.

* *

In the concluding section, Climacus replies to a single opposing thought, which, however, is not precisely an objection since the thinker challenges nothing that has gone before: 'May we not look for a future generation in which the Moment-event has won out? And will that new and happy generation not be different from the first and all the ones in between? If this were so, the equality you have sought to establish between any two generations would be compromised'.

Climacus unleashes his scorn at the thought of this sort of millennium, and the rationale behind his scorn is not far to seek. It runs through his whole account of the relationship between the Teacher and every generation, and it may be summed up by saying that a generation as such, that is, as an aggregate or a public, stands in no relationship at all to the Teacher, even if 99 or 100 per cent have joyfully seized the condition from his hands. He administers the condition to one at a time, and in each one by himself is where the passion is, where the Teacher who is the Truth displaces the learner's Error. My Error, or the wrongness of what I myself really think, is not so frailly linked to me that it comes loose at one yank, and consequently I have to be vigilant *in* Faith to keep from recoiling back into it. For reasons like these, a victory-parade with myself in its ranks, to proclaim that *I* have won out and *my* task is done, is indeed a riotous idea. If all or most men are like me in this respect, such a parade could properly enlist mostly corpses and not be much of a parade.

In the final page or two of the *Fragments*, Climacus adverts once more to his many borrowings from the New Testament. Christianity, he remarks, is the one historical phenomenon that actually fits his description of the Moment. Of no philosophy, mythology, or piece of historical knowledge can this be said. This exclusiveness-thesis is not self-authenticating, nor is it a working assumption, but offers itself as a bit of contingent knowledge in the History of Religions. Viewed in this light, it is a claim that can best be considered together with the questions on the title page of the *Fragments*, along with the concluding Moral.

9

RETROSPECT AND "MORAL"

"Moral," the concluding statement of
Philosophical Fragments

In the trefoil of questions back on his title page, Climacus sets the theme for his piece: Under what assumptions would it make sense, when all is said, to speak of basing one's eternal happiness on something historical? In its most compressed form, his answer might read: That would make sense only if the 'Project of Thought' represents the actual state of things, only if the learner is indeed so completely destitute of the Truth that, if he is ever to possess it, the God must position himself to impart it along with the ability to recognize it.

This question-and-answer ensemble ties together the title page and the closing page, but not without some leftover problems. Consider first the empirical-sounding thesis that Christianity is the *only* historical phenomenon which, in spite of its historical nature and also by means of it, puts itself forward as the point of departure for the individual's eternal consciousness and the basis of his eternal happiness (p. 137). Climacus has no intention of arguing for his uniqueness-claim, perhaps for the very good reason that its truth, if established, would not be decisive for the individual's "new decision," or because the task of establishing the utter singularity of any phenomenon would require a long-term team effort. Still, it is a little misleading to preface the claim with a phrase like "it is well-known."

How are we to understand it? Orthodox wings of Christianity have certainly maintained that the coming of Jesus Christ was and is a *sine qua non* of any individual's eternal happiness. However, this is not quite the same as maintaining that Christianity is the *one* voice in the world that has intended itself to be taken in that way. Coming up with an unguarded uniqueness-claim about anything under the sun is a pretty sure way of tempting scholarly spoilers, well within their rights, to make mincemeat of it. It seems out of place, therefore, for Climacus to include in his peroration a claim so vulnerable to learned comparisons, yet on the last page he wishes to give the claim all possible force by insisting once more that the unique idea "did not arise in the heart of any man." No such idea is to be found in philosophy, mythology, or straight historical chronicling.

Let us consider these one at a time. First, no system of philosophy, Climacus tells us, has ever contained the idea that an individual's eternal happiness has been made possible by something's coming-into-existence. Here the range of reference, 'philosophy', is hard to take in survey, and the rhetorical "it is well-known" on the preceding page is not enough to carry us safely past the quicksand of Pickwickian meanings. May we not call to mind certain Asiatic philosophies of life, which some may prefer to call religions, in which a Buddha or Vedic sage or founding guru gives it out that the individual can hope to achieve a timeless bliss if only he will attach himself to the wise man's teaching? Hitting upon that teaching is surely a calendar event, something historical. Why should it not fit Climacus's description of the Moment just as well as Christianity does?

On this point Climacus has provided us with a few resolving distinctions. The historical, first of all, is the sphere of that which comes into existence. Now if the guru passes on to me the doctrine or teaching that a specified course of life will land me in an everlasting bliss, there is no doubt that the guru himself is historical, but is the teaching? The fact that the guru has come into existence does not guarantee the same about the teaching, which may have emerged from Socratic reflection (recollection) with the help of all manner of influencing pundits and mentors. Even if tradition hotly ascribes the teaching to this one guru's searing insight dated 3000 years ago, this would still leave its origin ambiguous and ourselves uncertain as to whether it came into existence in the paradigm-manner of this or that chicken, bee, crocus, or man, or was fetched from some recess of the guru's consciousness. If the latter, then my counting on the teaching as a basis for my eternal happiness would not amount to basing it on 'something historical' in the sense of a coming-into-existence.

Suppose we alter the picture and imagine the guru saying, 'Before I appeared no one could tell you how to achieve eternal bliss. All by itself my soul stormed the unknown and brought this teaching into history'. Still, even if the enlightened one cured the sick and raised the dead, this would not suffice to make his teaching 'something historical' as that expression is employed by Climacus, nor would my becoming the guru's disciple offer an instance of basing my eternal happiness on something historical. Whatever we might want to say about the guru's Promethean exploits and messianic flights of speech, a teaching is simply not the sort of thing that fits the grammar of 'coming-into-existence', for the claim that 'It never was till now' is subject to the qualification that it may have been arrived at by recollection, imagination, or construction, like a psalm. In short, the guru may have enlightened himself. The one idea (or teaching, if we prefer) that does not appear in any philosophy is the idea of basing my eternal happiness on something that is *not* a doctrine, a philosophy, or anything of the sort, but is rather the kind of existent that I myself am, or a dog, or a tomato plant in someone's garden. It is this sort of historical existent that no philosophy, according to Climacus, has ever put forward as a basis for the individual's eternal happiness.

For example, suppose a philosopher were to say: 'Thinking will get you nowhere, but you may assure yourself of an eternal happiness by keeping yourself tied every minute of your life, by a string as long as you please, to the tomato plant in the northeast corner of a plot owned by J. Smithers of Canton, Ohio'. Or, '. . . by stroking a dachshund named Fritz that lives at 8 Potiphar Street, Liverpool, England'. Or, '. . . by placing yourself eight paces to the left of one Oliver Faversham, a soldier of fortune whose last known address was somewhere in the Congo, and keeping that precise distance for nine days'. The mere strangeness of such proposals is not what excludes them from philosophy, nor the uncertainty of one's ever finding the dog or tomato plant or soldier. Rather it is the fact that no mark or sign has been agreed upon as indicating that one tomato plant or man is linked with the eternal more closely than other plants or men. Nothing in the historical sphere, therefore, could cue an observer to label some specific existent a conduit of life everlasting.

So much for philosophy as a source of the idea in question. When we turn to mythology, where fancy has unbridled play, it might at first seem an overstatement to say that no mythmaker has ever had that idea. Yet it would hardly be controversial to remark that myth is characterized in part by its indifference to the historical in its particularity, for example, the birthplaces and dates of Prometheus or Sisyphus. Thus, even where a myth is based on some actual experience, as is

186

said of many myths, and even where a people receives it as an historical account, archetypal personages and objects suffice for its role as myth, which remains unaffected by questions about what has or has not in fact come into existence or about what exists right now. On the other hand, the idea of basing my eternal happiness on something historical, as Climacus understands it, has everything to do with such matters. If I am not to base it on the mere conception or archetype of something historical, then I am referred to the sort of particular that mythmakers do not take seriously. It is for this reason, and not because Climacus plumes himself on discovering some unsuspected limit of human imagination, that mythmakers may be said to address themselves to the imagination and would treat as foreign to their concerns the idea of basing one's eternal happiness on something historical.

To make this point clearer, consider the following Gnostic myth. A person of the world of light, a god, becomes a victim of the powers of darkness. The light in this person is shattered, and sparks of it are imprisoned in human individuals. A redeemer, sent by the highest god and disguised as a poor earthling, tries to awaken those separate sparks and teach individuals the password for the way back to a reunion of those sparks into the primal person of light after the death of the individual.*

Arguably, someone could accept this account as bearing hard on the Socratic questions, and by taking it to heart, joining the Gnostic brotherhood, and similar acts, base his eternal happiness on it. Does he thereby base his eternity on 'something historical' in the *Fragments* sense? It would appear that the answer is, 'No, he bases it on a teaching', for the Lessing distinction once more applies. The peculiar pathos of relating oneself to *that one* is missing here, whether the 'one' be taken to be some poor man (in the Gnostic formula, a divine pathfinder in disguise) or whatever historical particular you please. In the Gnostic account, the object of belief, as indicated by the teaching, namely the emissary or redeemer from the world of light, remains undesignated historically, so that the individual must attach himself to the teaching, the passwords, the preceding generation of disciples, and so forth. The example thus runs parallel to that of the

*Cf. Rudolf Bultmann, *Theology of the New Testament*, trans. Kendrick Grobel (New York: Charles Scribner's Sons, 1951), vol. 1, pp. 166–67.

Redeemer-*doctrine* we discussed earlier. The factor of coming-into-existence is left out, and even if one believes that the event of the emissary's coming-into-existence has already taken place, the question of *which one he is* gets treated here with an unconcern typical of the mythmaker.

On the other hand the pathos of basing my eternal happiness on something historical is tied up with the importance of not confusing one historical particular with another, for this is precisely the realm in which such confusions abound, where resemblant countenances and false prophets and cases of mistaken identity trick us. This is enough to show either that the emissary is not intended to be taken historically in the sense of being tied down to a particular existent, or that the individual in the Gnostic sect is basing his eternity not on something that has come into existence in the hard sense but rather on sharing the teaching, for his eternity is based on the password that one man can impart to another regardless of who introduced it.

If mythology does not trade in historical particulars, then what of history itself, that is, the discipline practiced by historians? The work of chronicling and connecting past events by reference to documents and other indicators ties back at every point to the kind of historical particulars Climacus has been talking about. But what does it mean to assert that no historian has ever come up with the idea of basing an eternal happiness on one of those? Again, what appears to be a straight generalization founded on a survey turns out to be nothing of the sort. The mythmaker does not bind himself to what has come into existence, but the historian does; what, though, would serve the historian as a criterion for deciding that one existent manifests the eternal more than another, so as to command more than his historian's interest? Here we ought to keep in mind the Interlude, where it was said that "the Eternal has absolutely no history," a shorthand and substantival expression for the grammatical fact that talk of the eternal is empirically vacuous. The historian, who may be expected to have developed an eye for historical particulars, does not thereby sharpen his eye for benchmarks of the eternal in those. Without making the concept of eternality useless or fake, this deprives it of a role in any empirical discipline that sets itself to articulate past sequences. In short, the historian sets his face against the gratuitous. In the absence of a criterion for judging that one coming-into-existence is more blazoned with the eternal than the one next to it, any judgment to that effect will carry the embarrassment of pointlessness. The historian will confront neither the occasion nor the temptation to come up with it, since the criterion it presupposes is not built into his science.

By cutting off the idea in question from access by thought, imagination, and memory, Climacus reinforces the remark in his Project that the Moment-hypothesis is not a human product. The whole discussion may be given a quarter-turn by recalling that the concept of an eternal happiness is empty, a doughnut hole with no specifiable content except perhaps to those for whom the face value of the two words is content enough, or who operate from the apriorism that an eternal happiness must have something in common with the earthly kind, else we could not understand the term. My point is that we do not understand the term in the sense of grasping what an eternal happiness would be like, although this fact does not get in the way of our knowing how the expression functions in the New Testament and elsewhere.*

If, now, it may be assumed that the philosopher, the mythologist, and the historian have no part in the genesis of the idea in question, or even that it is not a human idea, from none of these assumptions would it follow that Christianity is the world's only specimen of that nonhuman idea. In particular, we have yet to consider other *religions* in which one finds, in one form or another, both historical content and the idea of an eternal happiness.

In the religion of Islam, for example, we find a paradisal concept joined with that of a dateable historical revelation given to the God's prophet, through the angel Gabriel, along with the idea that the believer is to base his eternal happiness on what the prophet learned from the God. Why should this not come as close as anything to being an instance of the idea in question? The answer lies for the most part with matters already discussed. That is, the coming-into-existence of a

---

*The grammar of the expression 'eternal happiness' is a little like the following. Imagine a vague alarm rippling through a crowded theater, setting people on edge. On stage an announcer declares, 'If you will make your way to the Egress, you will be all right'. Only no one knows what an 'Egress' is. No one knows if it's a person, like an ogress, or a dispensary, a shelter, a hole in the wall, or what, although 'Egress' connects in their minds with a very advantageous thing to locate. Now if a sign flashed on at that moment, 'This way to the Egress', even a child would get the point of it, even though he would be as much in the dark as the others about exactly what an Egress is.

divine *teaching* does not yield a 'something historical' in the sense employed by Climacus. Lessing's point is well-taken: the ideality of a doctrine or teaching, even the teaching that the God became a flesh-and-blood redeemer, places it in another category from that which comes into existence in the manner of a plant, rock, or man.

Now what if a tribe held that by touching a certain rock, which fell from the sky in a blaze of light within memory of the oldest shaman, the individual acquired an inpouring of beatitude sufficient to assure his personal eternal happiness? Here, in the area of primitive beliefs, we seem to find a kind of instance of the idea in question. Even if we resist the temptation to classify it straightway as myth, or as a mixture of myth and ignorance, there remains room to ask whether it offers a clear instance of basing one's eternal happiness on something historical. That is, the fact of something's falling out of the sky on a given date is not exactly a paradigmatic instance of coming-into-existence. Aside from that, this is not at all a case in which something historical *intends itself* to be taken as a basis for an individual's eternal happiness, howevermuch the shaman intends it to be so taken. The uniqueness-claim, as Climacus words it, depends explicitly on the manifest intention of the historical phenomenon, which narrows the field significantly, excluding all manner of phenomena which do not go in for intending, and indeed any phenomenon that lacks an accompanying expression of salvific intent, such as the rock.

What kind of thesis, then, is the uniqueness-claim? It is meant to express something "well-known," that is, that Christianity alone proclaims the Moment. This is, however, only in a very limited sense an empirical claim. It is bound up with a complex and elliptical piece of reasoning which concludes that Christianity makes a singular and decisive breach with human powers of ideation, imagination, and recollection when it requires that the individual, for the sake of his eternal happiness, secure himself to something which, like himself, has come into existence. Ideation, that is, lacks an avenue to the historical particular; imagination does not trouble itself with drawing the line between actual and fancied comings-into-existence; and memory, like the other two faculties, lacks a criterion of the eternal within the historical, and so is kept within immanence.

What do these riders signify, then, unless that Christianity alone ventures to base an individual's eternity on a particular historical *per-*

son more or less like himself in the sense of not being an archetype but having a body, conceiving and expressing intentions, and so forth? Here the uniqueness-claim approximates a sort of truism with an empirical kernel: Christianity alone proclaims the Moment-idea. That idea, as the Project of Thought showed, can be unpacked of a considerable wealth of consequences, so that the uniqueness-claim would admit of fuller expression in the following way: Christianity alone intends that the individual base his eternal happiness on an individual rather than a teaching, and in such a way as paradoxically to go against his powers of reason.

To be sure, then, Christianity alone is Christianity, that much is "well-known," is a truism, and Climacus's avoidance of argument concerning this point is a sign that the uniqueness-claim is not something an individual can put to use in relating himself to the Truth or in making the changeover from Error to Truth.

With the foregoing in mind, we can see better the author's strategy in using open-ended expressions such as "basing an eternal happiness on something historical," although the effect might have been more direct if he had said "on an historical individual." It would not do, for example, to have called Christianity the only phenomenon that summons the individual to base his eternal happiness on a *divine incarnation*, the description of which could in all likelihood find handsome parallels in many a pocket of human lore. The same holds true of any other *event*, however wondrous, or any specific doctrine, sacramental observance, fulfilled prophecy, and so on, historical though these might be. The center of gravity of the uniqueness-claim is its reference to the sort of historical thing that comes into existence and passes away on some existing strand, accessible to whatever locals might be contemporary but not to even the most brilliant probe of thought from afar. In short, an individual. Instantly the conception of basing an eternal happiness on such a one flashes its paradoxical side, since my reason can furnish (a) no way of discerning the keys to an eternal happiness in such a one, even if I enjoy the questionable privilege of being a contemporary, and (b) no way of cementing myself to such a fly-by-night kind of being.

Only in retrospect, after Climacus has completed his account of the relation between Christianity and philosophy, can we properly raise the question: Is his presentation of Christianity true to the sources?

Does it accurately present the core content of the New Testament? No one can fail to notice the major omissions. The Old Testament inheritance, prophets and all, goes with hardly a mention. The Apostles come up only in his discussion of the contemporary disciple, and their work along with its historical setting is left to the imagination. Nothing is said about the Teacher's resurrection and ascension beyond the slenderest possible reference to his "leaving the earth." The manner of his death is passed over except to say he is forsaken. Not a word appears anywhere about the founding and future of a church, or about the Trinity. These and perhaps other weighty matters which have place in the ancient Christian creeds have been left out. Even so, omissions make up the least queer feature of Climacus's account and can be readily explained. He sets out to expose the chasm between Christianity and human thought by tracing out the consequences of Hypothesis B, the Moment. Central among these consequences are the God's coming in the form of a Teacher and the exalting of the Teacher over his teaching. For a thinker who asks merely how men could hope to relate themselves to the Truth if the Socratic position were overturned, the idea of the God as Teacher will be an essential part of the answer, but New Testament elements such as baptism, the resurrection, and the doctrine of grace, among others, no matter how much they may signify for a disciple, contribute nothing to that question.

It is the narrowly targeted Project of Thought, then, that determines what shall be omitted, and in this light the omissions are not so strange. Still, those make only one oddity in the *Fragments'* picture of Christianity. In the following restrospect I will confine myself to three:

1. The Absolute Paradox with its corresponding 'downfall of reason', vital to the *Fragments* account of Christianity, seems not to be a scriptural conception at all, nor indeed to have been the *point d'appui* for conversions reported in the New Testament.

2. The surprising sense of 'Faith' that comes out in the *Fragments* as the primary New Testament sense seems not to be scriptural at all.

3. Matters such as 1 and 2 raise the general question: Why should the *Fragments* picture of Christianity not take its place as merely an interpretation *inter alia*, along with those of Reimarus, Lessing, Kant, and the rest? Indeed, what *could* it be but another interpretation, with all the risk of idiosyncrasy entailed by that?

Let us first consider the suspicion that the Absolute Paradox is unscriptural, a brainchild of the author. Here the first point to bear in mind is that the *Fragments* is addressed not to everyone but to students of philosophy, and more particularly to the sort of philosopher who finds it in himself to accommodate Christianity to human thought. Working against this tendency in its manifold expressions, Climacus seeks to isolate a feature of Christianity that comes into relief only for one person at a time, and not at all for the loose aggregate of thinkers who make up the philosophic tradition. One way of expressing that feature is by putting words like these on a disciple's lips: 'The God, absolutely unlike me, has come into existence in a form indistinguishable from the most ordinary, and sought my permission to make me into something as nearly like himself as a son is like a father'. Such words reveal plainly enough that the disciple has let go of the leading-strings of reason in permitting the nonevent to change everything for him.

If now one refuses to take the author's repeated word for it that the New Testament is where he found this idea, and instead wishes to ask how well it fits in with the scriptural account of what took place in the coming of Jesus Christ, the question, needless to say, will not be settled by an effort of learned teamwork on the texts, since the scriptures do not address themselves to teams. However, even if generations of scholarly referees, believers all, stood fast on the claim that no Absolute Paradox appears in holy writ, this would not rule out its being present and at the very center of things when one learner at a time comes up against the texts.

We confront a more formidable difficulty in the happy passion Climacus calls "Faith in the eminent sense." Is it scriptural or not? In the journals of 1850,* Kierkegaard writes in a somewhat self-congratulatory way: "It is clear that in my writings I have given a further definition of the concept faith, which did not exist until now." Such a remark invites misunderstanding. How odd if it should have taken eighteen centuries and more before anyone got the main New Testament sense of 'faith' right! Here again, however, the air begins to clear

The Journals of Kierkegaard, ed. Alexander Dru (New York: Harper & Bros., 1958), p. 201.

if we remember the intended addressee of the Climacus-works. Climacus is very far from suggesting that nonphilosophers are incapable of grasping the primary New Testament meaning of 'faith', but on the other hand nonphilosophers may discern in themselves no need at all for a compendious *definition*.

In its one-sentence form, Climacus's definition reads as follows: "(Faith is) an objective uncertainty held fast in an appropriation-process of the most passionate inwardness."* Here it becomes possible to specify a sense to go with Kierkegaard's claim in the 1850 journal entry. The thing that "did not exist until now" is of course the "further definition" of 'Faith' that we have just cited. In what does its novelty consist? In the packaging, I want to suggest, of several New Testament components, in their colligation or perspicuous arrangement for elucidatory purposes in the Climacus-works. A reading of the 1850 entry that suggests invention or fresh discovery will not bear examination. The task of matching up this definition with New Testament references—to the God's public concealment, the individual's Sin, the suffering in its healing process, the ambiguities of outward religiousness, and the Teacher himself as the Truth—may be left as an exercise for any reader who sees a need for it. He will find, I believe, that this definition of 'Faith' is quite as conformable with the New Testament as any one-sentence definition can be. Its peculiar molecular arrangement is a result not of idiosyncrasy but of the fact that the intended reader of the *Fragments* and *Postscript* is a philosopher, a thinking type who, although Faith is by no means a contemplative relationship to the Teacher, would pardonably be inclined to see his own Error as residing in what he really *thinks*, and to see its cure in terms of the humanly impossible task of unthinking it.

We turn now to the more general question: 'Even allowing that the *Fragments'* picture of Christianity, as far as it goes and apart from omissions already noted, hangs together with the New Testament, it is far from being the only picture that does so. For the record, let us mention only the scandalous H. Reimarus, then Lessing's miniature in "The Education of the Human Race," and finally Kant's masterful development of the same theme in his *Religion*. Well, then, what is the

---

*Søren Kierkegaard, *Concluding Unscientific Postscript*, trans. David F. Swenson and Walter Lowrie (Princeton: Princeton University Press, 1941), p. 182.

Fragments if not one more interpretation? It is true that Climacus does not aim to make Christianity agreeable to reason, and in this respect his interpretation differs from those others, but does it thereby cease to be an interpretation?'

This way of speaking is on the surface a congenial one, but calling this, that, and the other picture or account of Christianity an 'interpretation' presupposes that one has paused somewhere along the way to distinguish between an interpretation and something else. Otherwise, if 'interpretation' means essentially the same as 'picture' or 'account' and the like, it becomes redundant or worse to call the *Fragments* an interpretation.

If I may propose such a distinction, the Moment-hypothesis offers itself not as an interpretation but as a re-expression of the New Testament core. The wording changes—Jesus becomes the nameless Teacher, 'the God' merely a name for the Unknown, and so on—but the result is not an interpretation if by that we intend any measure of accommodation to secular categories of thought. Lessing offers such an accommodation in his aforementioned essay, where the dogmatic category of divine revelation becomes softened and pluralized into stages in an educational development of the human race, with new educational plateaus still on the horizon. Whether this is true or not is of no concern in a discussion of what is meant by 'interpretation', but it marks Lessing's picture as an accommodation in a way that cannot be said of the *Fragments*. Here it will perhaps be tempting to see this issue as a logomachy to be settled by negotiating an agreeable definition of 'interpretation'. Yet it would be hard to formulate one that nobody would call tendentious or stipulative.

Perhaps the following partial definition will be of use: Where an author, seeking sympathetically to extract the elixir of the New Testament, comes to his task with the Socratic presupposition that men already possess the Truth, the resulting effort will be an *interpretation*; where he does not raise a hand against those texts that declare him to be in Error, then we may look for a *re-expression*. Alternatively: where in quest of that elixir he takes as his object the Teacher's message, the result will be an *interpretation*, and where he takes instead the Teacher's person, a *re-expression*. The small merit of this partial definition is merely that *in case* the New Testament intends a gesture of fatal violence against immemorial habits of human thought, that gesture shall not be lost in the shuffle. At the first hint of it the private reader will take it upon himself to let the scriptures have their say, if only to avoid the chance that someone in Error will be doing all the talking, for if it is foremost in his mind to have his own say, or to come up with his own interpretation, the first casualty will very likely be the remark that would bid him listen.

The inescapably personal component in the charge of Error deeply complicates the question of where re-expression leaves off and interpretation begins. The personal element, that is, raises the question for each reader of the New Testament just how far he is prepared to tolerate an "advance upon Socrates" which places not only Socrates' thought but his own in limbo. In order not to intellectualize this matter too much, let us add that it is also a question of how well his consciousness can make room for the idea of the God's coming in person, as a human Teacher, with its hint of some passionate personal business afoot with the reader. At any rate, it is a question which gathers the whole of the *Fragments* under its shadow and brings us directly to the 'Moral'. Let us turn to that, and afterwards come back to the important distinction between re-expression and interpretation.

"The projected hypothesis indisputably makes an advance upon Socrates. . . ." So begins the Moral. To my knowledge no commentator has stopped to cavil with Swenson's choice of the valuably ambiguous idiom 'makes an advance upon'. It carries the sense of expressions such as 'goes beyond', 'moves forward from', 'outstrips', and the like, but it has a military or pugnacious sense as well, as conveyed by General Grant's message to the Confederate commander at Vicksburg: "I propose to advance immediately upon your works," a reminder that the Moment-hypothesis gets off the ground by upending the Socratic assumption that men already possess the Truth. In any event, the former sense of "an advance upon Socrates" is primary, since the Moment-hypothesis contains features that Socrates was in no position, or had no occasion, to come out for.

Those features severally and collectively place the Moment-hypothesis *beyond* Socrates. Whether the denial of the Socratic presupposition, along with its coil of consequences, is truer than its affirmation is for the present undecidable and is made so by the novelty of those startling features. First of all, when one throws out the Socratic starting point and cuts man off from the Truth by saying that he lacks the condition for apprehending it, then a new organ (Faith, or the condition) has to be posited if he is ever to possess the Truth, an organ so new, in fact, that no man has heard of it prior to the God's historical bestowal of it in the Moment, although men may earlier have possessed 'faith' in other senses of the term. Small wonder, then, that the truth of the hypothesis is harder to discern than the mere fact that it goes beyond Socrates.

The second feature that takes some getting used to is a new presupposition: the consciousness of Sin, which includes but is not limited to a consciousness that even if the Truth (the true answers to the Socratic questions) were printed on a card and propped up beside my breakfast eggs, it would evoke no recognition in me. This was a possibility for Socrates, as remarked in the opening paragraph of the *Fragments*, and one that gave him troubled hours, but it was not one that he could make room for as a presupposition, if for no other reason than that it ran counter to his own.

The next feature Climacus calls "a new decision: the Moment." In what sense is the Moment a *decision*? Here we may usefully recall that the Moment as an historical happening is equivalent, objectively considered, to a continuation of the ordinary run of events, as indicated by the stultifying words 'The Unknown has appeared in unrecognizable form'. That is to say, in the contemporary public's field of view, it created no big ripple. That Moment does not exist, or rather it exists only insofar as this or that individual comes into relation with it, either by permitting that which publicly does not exist to change everything for him, or by becoming offended in the rumor of it. That is where the decision comes in. The option to believe or be offended, with no room for anything in between, is just as foreign to Socrates and to the natural man at large as is the consciousness of Sin, and in the face of such disturbing novelty one finds it much easier again to pronounce this feature un-Socratic than to decide about its agreement with reality.

Climacus lists "a new Teacher: the God in time" as the final feature of his hypothesis. Like the others, it has no place in the Socratic picture of things. What need had Socrates for a divine Teacher if the Truth lay within him?

To go back now to the question we left dangling, which concerned the relationship of the Moment-hypothesis to the New Testament, let us imagine a reader responding to the 'Moral' in this way:

'Those four features listed in the "Moral" are certainly presented in the New Testament wherever it speaks of faith, sin, the "fullness of time," and God's acting in the ministry of Jesus. For all I know, they are features unique to the New Testament, although I am not altogether sure how that could be conclusively established. But will you not agree that Climacus gives them an arrangement peculiarly his own, an emphasis different from what they receive in the source, and a linguistic rigidity far beyond what they receive in the less contrived prose of the New Testament? No doubt this is what Climacus feels his philosophical reader needs in order, as you put it earlier, to see Christianity as if for the first time, and if it pleases you to call this not an interpretation but merely a studied juxtaposition of uninterpreted factors, I do not wish to be unreasonable. My point is that our author is arranging and emphasizing and rigidifying for a purpose, and that purpose, I take it, is to reinforce a presupposition all his own, namely, that there *just is* a total break between the New Testament and human reason. Before one can assess the relationship of his Moment-hypothesis to the scriptural source, do you not see grounds for a separate inquiry about his presupposition?'

To get our bearings on this question, let us recall that in order to contrast philosophy and Christianity, Climacus sets up opposing diagrams of the individual's relationship to the Truth, (a) as conceived by philosophy under the Socratic presupposition, and (b) as conceived under the opposite presupposition. Under (b) it comes out that the individual, if he is to get the Truth, must do so by establishing a rapport with something that has come into existence. Very well, Christianity is at all events something of that sort and dares intend itself, according to Climacus, to be taken as "news" or "new wine" in respect of the quartet of features in the 'Moral': a new organ, presupposition, decision, and Teacher. Now, does the New Testament give those features the same weight and centrality they receive in the diagram?

Normally it can be legitimate and important for the learned community to discuss whether a particular diagram, drawing a path through a somewhat disorderly matrix of texts, shows a skewed emphasis and perhaps betrays a preconception of the diagrammer's. This is an issue in nuance-scholarship. Unfortunately, however, the question of whether Climacus is presupposing, as opposed to merely noticing and pointing out, a clean split between the New Testament and human reason is hardly the sort of question that yields to even the most accomplished scholarship. It is the question of the Absolute Paradox all over again. Precisely because the scriptural mode of address is to persons one at a time, the grounds for deciding lie with the addressee. This is not to claim, of course, that the individual subject be formally installed as the authority on what the New Testament is all about, since any pretensions along that line have to be reviewed in the light of his Error. What I am saying is that collegial-exegetical talent is not equipped to recognize the downfall of reason: it has no occasion for supposing that its procedures, conceived as self-corrective over the long run, might be hopelessly off the track. The individual subject, on the other hand, is granted such an occasion along with the personal indictment delivered by the New Testament. While this does not make him a scriptural authority, it certainly authorizes him to announce that his own reason has been brought to a standstill by something scriptural.

Thus the learned community as such, in lacking machinery for uncovering an Absolute Paradox in the Christian sources, lacks also the wherewithal for judging whether Climacus's position originates with Climacus himself, as a flight of personal fancy, or with the New Testament.

Without those four novel features to back him up, the 'Moral' continues, Climacus could not seriously claim to have made an advance upon Socrates. This is a suitable place to remark that the sort of novelty Climacus ascribes to those features does not lie in the confounding fact of their having nothing in common with anything else in human thought, whatever that might mean. Rather, their novelty over against the Socratic position shows itself in the threat of ultimate violence they direct against the individual's vision of himself as thinker or philosopher. The opening bid of the "new presupposition" is that I, the individual thinker, do not want the Truth, and that I must begin by acquiring a consciousness of that fact. Whatever else may be new or old, this is at any rate a new start for a philosopher! Once I acquire such a consciousness it becomes easy enough to surmise that something wonderfully uncommon and improbable would be needed to put me in possession of the Truth (though not necessarily a miracle of the sort that would set crowds agog). For one thing I should require a new organ of sight, perhaps even a new heart, in order even to recognize the Truth, and since a transplant is by no means minor surgery, a decision as well. And who if not a new Teacher is to guide me in such crucial matters? Thus we encounter once more, in the briefest retrospect, all four features of the advance upon Socrates. The fact that this or that feature creates sympathetic vibrations with this or that sector of human thought is of small concern since human thought in general resonates with everything linguistic.

Does the 'Moral' shed any light on our earlier question: Is Climacus offering an *interpretation* of the New Testament? It is true if trite to observe that the answer depends on what we mean by 'interpretation'. If we mean an attempt by reason to ride herd on the four "new" elements summed up in the 'Moral', perhaps by demonstrating that they are all immemorially older than the New Testament and very nearly as old as the creation, then Climacus's book is not an interpretation. If, on the other hand, we side with a noted theologian who writes, ". . . every understanding (of the scriptural word), even if it is not mediated by way of explicit interpretation, still tacitly includes interpretation,"* then we stretch 'interpretation' to mean pretty much the same as any sort of understanding, a prelude perhaps to drawing helpful distinctions between dissimilar kinds of interpretation.

Viewed within that eminently flexible guideline, the *Fragments* emerges as the kind of 'interpretation' aimed at underscoring what is new in the New Testament, doubtless on the principle that nothing can be heard as good or bad news unless it is heard as news. In short, it is the kind of interpretation calculated to quicken a jaded ear for news. In addressing the differences between philosophy and Christianity, the *Fragments* speaks repetitiously to the ear of the philosopher as the man most likely to have persuaded himself that he has *heard of* no new organ for apprehending the Truth; of no presupposition except the old Socratic one; of no decision beyond the decisions of immanence respecting virtue and vice; and of no Teacher other than Socrates, Prodicus, the servant girl, or himself.

*Gerhard Ebeling, *The Problem of Historicity* (Philadelphia: Fortress Press, 1967), pp. 11–12.

The final sentence of the 'Moral' directs its irony in scattershot fashion against whole tribes of philosophers who let it be understood that they have gone beyond Socrates. What exactly does that mean? Here it would be untimely to fix attention on the Hegelian schools of Kierkegaard's day and perhaps more useful to ask: "What would it be like for a philosopher well into the twentieth century to 'make an advance upon Socrates, yet to say essentially the same things as he'?" With this question, naturally, we are confining ourselves to thinkers insofar as they speak to the Socratic questions, and not insofar as they ponder quantum mechanics, logical syntax, the higher parsing, the *époche*, or other recent matters of note.

Jean-Paul Sartre, for one, at least *seems* to direct his mind away from those topical issues toward Socratic ones:

A. Is it a great or little thing to exist as myself?
B. Have I a task just for having been born a human and independent of any tasks set for me by my social station?
C. If so, exactly what is it, and as of this date how far along have I carried it?

For example, in remarks that connect with Question A, Sartre speaks of man as "a being which is compelled to decide the meaning of being."* To be compelled to decide, however, is to proceed from a state of unknowing, so that on this particular question, if I read him correctly, Sartre says essentially the same thing as Socrates, namely, 'As for myself, I don't know if it's great or little'.

In remarks that look as if they might engage with Question B, Sartre describes a fundamental task or project that every human is actually busy at, consciously or not, and despite the fact that it is a ridiculous task: "The best way to conceive of the fundamental project of human reality is to say that man is the being whose project is to be God."** In dealing with these issues, Sartre speaks from a postulated atheism, the logical sister and spitting negative image of theism. The conception of God he negates belongs to a species of theism that would predicate of deity the inert fixity of nonconscious beings and, at the same time, the

---

Being and Nothingness, trans. Hazel Barnes (New York: Philosophical Library, 1956), pt. 4, chap. 1, sec. 3, p. 556.
**Ibid., pt. 4, chap. 2, sec. 1, p. 566.

volatility and flux of consciousness, the two predicates corresponding to *l'en-soi* and *le pour-soi* in Sartre's ontology. When a thinker proposes, as doubtless some have done, to attribute permanence to the individual's flighty consciousness, Sartre pronounces this an impossible and absurd mismating of concepts. In consequence of being born a human, then, the individual finds himself committed willy-nilly to a task whose accomplishment, even in part, is ruled out by logic. This takes care of Question C also, which promptly aborts itself once Sartre reminds us that the task we are all engaged in is impossible.

If we take Sartre's ideas as responses to Questions B and C, they give every appearance of a big push beyond Socrates, but it is at least doubtful that a closer look will bear this out. To begin with, even if we allow Sartre the highest marks for discerning that every human is *in fact* going all out to become something logically impossible (since it would miss the point to cavil here at the validity of his discovery), by no means does it follow that the task Sartre has caught us doing is none other than the task hinted at in the Socratic questions. The task Sartre describes could very easily be one that we chose in default or perhaps in ignorance of the one intimated in Questions B and C. If so, Sartre has not prescribed answers to B and C or even spoken to those questions, and therefore cannot be said to have stolen a march on Socrates.

If the example of Sartre is at all representative, it may be no easy thing to find a philosopher who in a barefaced manner professes to go farther than Socrates. How one is to apply the closing words of the 'Moral' thus becomes something of a riddle. This riddle is our cue to break off the discussion and let the last shaft of Climacus's irony follow its own parabola and strike where it will.

A RETROSPECT

Looking back at the reading just completed, it seems to me that Kierkegaard has performed a major service in bringing to light once more the radical distinction between philosophy and Christianity. *Philosophical Fragments* offers a refreshed perception of Christianity, enabling us to see it for the first time, even when we have been exposed for decades to its teachings and traditions. Needless to remark, clarifying one's perception of Christianity should not be confused with comprehending it, or with deciding to become a Christian in case one is not already a Christian. Kierkegaard's service in the *Fragments* is directed toward neither of those ends but rather toward enabling his reader to perceive where human devices leave off and a radically different sort of mentality makes its presence felt.

To see Christianity through the *Fragments* is to view it as the detonation on earth of something not of this world, and part of Kierkegaard's achievement is to have hit on a way of characterizing the central event, a way which does not presuppose that its author is himself a Christian. When Christianity is characterized as the absolutely unthinkable paradox, the likelihood of someone's confusing it with philosophy or some other indisputably human composition is much reduced. Equally significant, it seems to me, is the fact that Kierkegaard, for the purpose at hand, abstracts the central event from church traditions, the New Testament, and much of the deposit of doctrine, all of which have been associated with Christianity from its beginnings. When the question 'What is Christianity?' arises, many are inclined to reply, 'Why, it is the church' or 'It is the New Testament' or 'It is the ancient doctrine'. In the *Fragments*, Kierkegaard presents a more primitive vision of the matter, enabling us to answer the question in a way that looks past those institutions and all the debates that surround them. This is liberating. To be able to say what Chritianity is and to distinguish its categories from those of philosophy, mythology, poetry, history and morals—this, too, is liberating and would be enough to earn a place for Kierkegaard in the front rank of philosophers even if he had written nothing else.

Besides highlighting the Absolute Paradox, *Philosophical Fragments* also seeks to clarify our perception of Judaism at least to the extent of restoring to the God-concept its Old Testament majesty after the erosion it suffered in various forms of theism and deism. Here, too, Kierkegaard's movement is in the service not of winning proselytes but of clearing away philosophical cobwebs.

Finally Kierkegaard has shed a rather unusual light on the individual's *cognitive* relationship to Christianity. It would not be alien to the mind of his pseudonym, Johannes Climacus, to refer to the New Testament as 'The Book of the Rumor'. New Testament narratives show people caught up in the turbulence surrounding the shattering Rumor—turbulence in the spoken word, in private lives, in official circles, and in the natural order. Let us suppose that historical studies, aimed at working closer to the original turbulence and to the persons caught up in it, achieve a spectacular level of success. Independent evidences come to light, let us imagine, establishing the authenticity of one New Testament character after another, as recently happened when someone uncovered a stone pedestal inscribed with the name of Pontius Pilate. However, as more and more of the *dramatis personae* are authenticated, does our cognitive relationship to the Rumor grow stronger? Does the Rumor creep up the ladder of probability until at some point it ceases to be the Rumor and becomes the Fact?

Not at all. Because of its singular character, the Rumor remains the Rumor no matter what turns up to enrich our knowledge. Trickles of evidence over the years can gradually confer probability on the improbable, but those same trickles can do nothing to probabilize the unthinkable. This is why the author of the *Fragments* shows little concern about the findings of historians. This particular Rumor, which carries no human fingerprint or signature, made its initial appearance in a distant corner of the Roman Empire and proceeded to spread, as rumors often do. But, instead of either dashing itself to pieces against the hard coral of knowledge or getting itself confirmed and incorporated into that stony mass, it remains afloat in the air, out of anyone's cognitive reach, the undying Rumor.

INDEX

ABC Questions, 4, 9–17, 26, 33, 46, 52–53, 57, 75, 83–85

Absolute Paradox, the: analysis of, by the learned community, 176–78, 182, 198–99; and Christianity, 192–93; conception of, 85–87, 117; definition of, 21, 50, 85, 89; as a doctrine, 113; as element of Faith, 106; and the Eternal, 118; exists for the individual, 87; gives Offense, 88–100, 119, 155; grammatical knowings about, 176–77; human grasp of, 50; and the Moment, 88; and necessity, 127; reactions to, 88, 90–92, 166; replaces what I really think (Error), 118; secularization (naturalization) of, 180; as *someone in particular*, 117; and the Wholly Unexpected, 91, 93, 99, 166–69

Acoustic allusion, 88

Agnosticism, 62–63

Analogy, Thomistic doctrine of, 79

Anxiety, language of, 36, 40–41

Arnold, Matthew, 158n

Atheism, 62–63, 79–80

Atonement, 7

Battle of Hastings, 127

Being to Non-being, 19. *See also* New Birth

Belief, nonreligious sense of, 143–44

Bultmann, school of, 59

Bury My Heart at Wounded Knee (Brown), 77n

Cause, 132–33

Christianity: Climacus's presentation of, 191–204; historical phenomenon of, 150, 184; and philosophy, 20, 48, 183, 198, 200, 202; proclaims the Moment, 183, 190–91; and reason, 195

Climacus, Johannes. *See Philosophical Fragments*

Coming-into-existence, 124–26, 128–30; and belief, 143–45; Faith and the God's, 126; and freedom, 132; and history, 185–86; and necessity, 131–33; of the self, 135–39; uncertainty of, 141

Concluding Unscientific Postscript (Kierkegaard), 1, 32, 54, 109, 111, 135

Condition, the, 116–17, 146, 161, 171, 181; definition of, 172. *See also* Faith

Conversion (the granting of the Condition), 7, 112, 114

Creation, 12, 134

Critique of Pure Reason (Kant), 127–28

Disciples (discipleship), 7
—contemporary (first generation), 101–4, 109, 123, 148, 161, 171,